CW00798177

WHAT WE DO WITH ALL THIS MONEY?

INSPIRING PERSPECTIVES ON WEALTH

love you A beans :)

JAYESH A PAREKH

CO-FOUNDER,
SONY ENTERTAINMENT TELEVISION

PopulaR
prakashan

www.popularprakashan.com

Published by
Harsha Bhatkal for
POPULAR PRAKASHAN PVT. LTD.
301, Mahalaxmi Chambers
22, Bhulabhai Desai Road
Mumbai - 400 026

© 2019 Jayesh A Parekh
First Published 2019
First Reprint December 2019

(4527)
ISBN: 978-81-7991-979-8

WORLD RIGHTS RESERVED. The contents are original and copyrighted. No portion of this book shall be reproduced, stored in a retrieval system or transmitted by any means, electronic, mechanical, photocopying, recording or otherwise, without the written permission of the author and the publisher.

Disclaimer: The views and opinions expressed in this book are the author's and the interviewee's own and the facts are as reported by them, and Popular Prakashan Pvt. Ltd is in no way liable for the same.

Cover Design: Anil Shah
Layout: Anjali Sawant

PRINTED IN INDIA
by Rashmi Graphics
#3, Amrutwel CHS Ltd.
Ganesh Galli, Lalbaug
Mumbai - 400 012

To my parents
Suvarna *and* **Arvind Parekh**
who gave me the unfair advantage
of middle-class values

Contents

Early Thoughts

There is a ton of money out there to go around. At last count, there are 2,150 billionaires and 46 million millionaires in the world, and these numbers are growing. Broad money in the world is estimated in excess of $90 trillion. Broad money includes coins, banknotes, money markets, savings, checking accounts, and time deposits. The market capitalisation of all the world's stock markets is about $75 trillion, whereas the estimated value of all developed real estate in the world is a staggering $200 trillion. And the worth of the world's 50 richest people? Upwards of $2 trillion! That's a lot of money.

While I do not have these numbers for the Indian diaspora, there are over 750,000 US dollar millionaires in India. The Indian millennials will be inheriting tens of billions of dollars in the next few decades. This book is exclusively focussed on the Indian diaspora.

Wealth is a de facto measure of success all over the world. People treat wealthy folks like celebrities and are in awe of them. They look up to them and are likely to listen to their point of view more keenly. In most cases, they don't pause to consider if the money was earned or acquired. Most youngsters have tall ambitions—they all want to become wealthy. They are attracted by the lifestyles of the rich and famous. Each strata of society is hoping and working hard to climb the ladder of wealth. This is not limited to the middle-class. High net worth individuals are striving to become very high net worth, and the very high net worth want to become ultra high net worth. Even the mega rich billionaires want to climb up higher in the rank of billionaires.

There are many wealthy individuals whose single-minded love in life is to make, accumulate, and manage their wealth. They spend most of their waking hours intensely planning, ideating, hedging, calculating, and spending inordinate amounts of time on how to invest their money, and they do this because they really enjoy it. There is a lot of intellectual stimulation in strategising asset allocation and sifting through financial deals and instruments. The wealthier clients usually have better access to lucrative investment ideas from their private bankers, wealth managers, investment bankers, and especially from their wealthy friends with whom they may co-invest. The choices are made based on the amount of investment, the risk profile, the potential returns, and the duration of time. It results in adrenaline flow like none other—maybe except romance.

Many businessmen have been successful in building their companies. They take pride in what they have built and enjoy operating and growing their businesses. As a result, their wealth also continues to increase. While there are some who never retire, many make that transition by becoming a non-executive chairman and passing the baton onto the next generation. That is, of course, if the next generation wants to run the family business. If not, at some point, the family will usually decide to sell the business and achieve financial independence. In both cases, whether the family continues to operate the business or sell it off, they have to manage their wealth and decide what to do with all that money.

How much is enough?

Since we do not know how long we're going to live, the first natural dilemma is how much money is enough? Each stratum of society is struggling with this question. Those who are High Net Worth Individuals (HNI), with wealth in the tens of millions of dollars, are pushing to become Very High Net Worth Individuals (VHNI), with wealth in the $25 million–$50 million bracket. Ultra-High Net Worth Individuals (UHNI), who have assets in the hundreds of millions of dollars, do know that they have enough, and yet they are pushing to become billionaires.

There are financial planners who can help you figure out how much money you need and how you should invest in order to continue the same quality of lifestyle until the end of life. However, as the human life span is getting longer, it is difficult to decide on this most important parameter—the number of remaining years. As a result, many people avoid insecurity by continuing to hold on to their wealth during their life. For most HNIs, it's usually not so much about the insecurity of running out of money as it is about their status in society and feeling good about how much money they have in their bank accounts. It is about reaching the next higher level of net worth, which in many cases takes a lifetime. For many fortunate HNIs 'how much is enough' is decided by their choice of a balanced lifestyle, and they deliberately pull out of the web of insecurity and status symbols in favour of spending quality time with themselves and their family and friends.

Lifestyle

The wealthy can indulge in luxury by spending large chunks of money on material or experiential things. They can acquire a private jet, a few vacation homes, a big yacht, a Lamborghini sports car, rare art, collectible gems, high-end custom jewellery, Swiss watches, fancy designer dresses, upscale hi-fi entertainment systems; or go on a Silversea Galapagos expedition cruise, get exotic massages at the Ananda spa, stay at the St. Regis hotel with butler service, drink vintage Bordeaux wines or 25-year-old single malts, watch Broadway plays from the front row, party in the VIP section of Marquee night club, enjoy at exclusive country clubs, play golf on the best courses, watch IPL cricket or Wimbledon from the VIP box, and travel in style by First Class on Singapore Airlines. This requires setting aside a portion of wealth for capital purchases and for generating on-going income to continue such a charmed lifestyle. Consumption has a propensity to expand. As their lifestyle continues to grow — condominium to house, house to villa, villa to private island — the need to service this lifestyle continues to grow with it. Every high net worth individual carves out a portion of their wealth for their personal lifestyle, though not everyone in the Indian diaspora live an extravagant lifestyle.

Charity

Almost all wealthy families strongly believe that giving large amounts of money for community and social development is the right thing to do, as it will make the world a better place. The percentage of charitable giving depends on the culture and disposable wealth available for giving. The resources are utilised on effective social development in important sectors like healthcare, education, sanitation, water, environment, waste management, women empowerment, and low-income housing. Some do it themselves — self-directed philanthropy — and others give grants to effective non-profit organisations serving the under-privileged population. There is no right or wrong way to give. The world needs all the help it can get; poverty is far from being eradicated.

Religious giving is still by far the largest percentage of philanthropic giving in the world. Many religious sects have causes like education and healthcare that they support mainly in their local region. The wealthy members of such religious sects feel motivated as their donation is being used for both religious and social causes. However, giving is declining among most religions. This is either because people cannot relate to their religion as much as their parents and grandparents, or because they feel their money is better spent on humanitarian well-being. Also, youngsters want to change the way they give. They do not want to follow the traditional way of giving to religious organisations as they are seeking purpose in their life. They try to pursue a differentiated philosophy of giving and towards making a difference.

Succession

As mentioned earlier, millennials are going to be the biggest beneficiary of succession.

Millennials are youngsters between the ages of 22–37, born between 1981–1996. Millennials and post-millennials are going to inherit trillions of dollars worldwide. Millennials of Indian origin will come into hundreds of billions of dollars over the next few decades. They will be confronted by an abundance of wealth. They will have to figure out how to manage, enjoy, and utilise their inherited wealth.

Giving money away to the next generation is tricky. What percentage of their wealth do they give to their children? Do they give them the money while they are alive, or as part of the estate after they pass away? How is this decision of passing wealth to the next generation made? Do millennials lose their ambition and motivation to succeed in life once they inherit massive amounts of wealth? Does their lifestyle get brash and exuberant, not leaving them time and mind space to work hard towards gainful output for society? The answers to these questions are very personal, and the decisions are based partly on the family's value system and partly influenced by hearsay. At the end, no matter how much money they have, they will be confronted with this dilemma, and will decide what to do based on their bias and accumulated experiences in their life. It is also heavily influenced by where they live and where their children live. Wealthy Indians certainly get influenced by others, including American, Nordic, and other cultures. In addition, no one really likes to pay the taxman when the wealth passes from one generation to the next. There are financial and estate planners who provide convoluted structures to make this tax efficient—one of which involves wealthy Indians to move overseas and become NRIs (Non-resident Indians). However, their life and travel becomes complicated and restrictive in many cases.

In the Indian diaspora, a majority of the wealth is passed to the next generation; what else is there to do with all this money?

Introduction

What do wealthy folks do with their money? What are the choices confronting them? While it may not seem like a big deal to have a lot of money, each one of us will have different ideas on what to do with a lot of money. Won't it be fascinating to find out how wealthy individuals think and what they do with their money?

This book is not about telling you how to live your life. This book is not an investment guide for your personal monetary wealth. It will not advise you on how to become rich or how to manage your money. There are many books and experts, including private banks and wealth managers that provide good guidance on wealth management, in most cases. This book is specifically about what to do with all this money. Whether you are affluent or trying to be, my hope is to inspire you to think a bit more about what to do with all this money, especially since none of us are taking it along with us.

Interviews

This book is a compilation of interviews with a diverse group of individuals. The interviews begin with their life journey. I have also asked them to share their perspective on money. These individuals are of Indian diaspora who live or have lived in India, Singapore, Malaysia, Africa, Australia, Japan, UAE (Dubai), Bahrain, Great Britain, and the United States. They are successful chairmen, senior executives, businessmen, entrepreneurs, lawyers, private bankers, professors, futurists, impact investors, social impactors, millennials, intuitives, and gurus.

I have tried to establish the background of the person I am interviewing to provide the reader with perspective on them and their views—where they're coming from and how they grew up, followed by a brief conversation on their monetary belief system. These conversations are quite casual. Instead of having few deep and long-drawn-out discussions, I have briefly interviewed many successful individuals and tried to capture their most important insights and ideas on the utilisation of their wealth. The thought process behind this structure was to provide the reader with a wide variety of views. I have tried to account for diversity based on experience, geography, and gender, hoping that it will give a well-rounded perspective on money and its utility. The interviews were conducted over a period of one year and have been edited and condensed for easier reading.

I hope you enjoy these fascinating conversations.

Chairmen
and
Senior Executives

Ratan Tata
Chairman Emeritus, Tata Sons

Neeraj Arora
Former Chief Business Officer, WhatsApp

T V Mohandas Pai
Former Member of the Board, Infosys

Amit Chandra
Chairman, Bain Capital India Office

Vipul Shah
Chief Operating Officer, Reliance Petrochemical

Naveen Bhat, PhD
Managing Director APAC, ISG Keysight

Ratan Tata
Chairman Emeritus, Tata Sons

JP: Mr Tata, thank you for taking the time. The Tata group has been one of the most successful business groups in India. Can you please give us your perspective on the wealth of the Tata family?

RNT: Contrary to popular belief, the family has not been the gainer. If you look at the past 100 years, other families might have had a brother or a cousin or a son being a dealer of motor cars or trucks when they were a monopoly or a particular transactor of steel business who become a contractor to progress the steel business or in one of the Tata businesses in any particular field. That has never happened.

The main wealth of the Tata group has been in the form of the philanthropic Trust that was set up at the turn of the century. Those funds and that wealth, which is the wealth of operating companies, has been used to propagate the enhancement of the quality of life of rural people or establish research in the area of medicine or education or things of this nature. This is directed by the Trustees of the Trust, who are not all family members. The wealth of the Trusts has grown over the years, but it is not being controlled by, or driven by wealth gains to the family or any individual in the family. As Mr JRD Tata put it, "You make wealth to redistribute it." The view that he took was that we are Trustees of the people of India, and whatever we have made in the industrial context we will give away in terms of improving the quality of life of our people.

There again there has been a change. The Trust hitherto for many years dealt with personal hardship. For example, if you lost your leg in an accident, or if you were unable to pay for an artificial limb, the Trust would give you or loan you the money because you could not afford it. Over the years as the quantum of funds accumulated, we were unable to disburse loans or donations on such a basis. We started looking at large scale projects. The Tata Memorial Hospital in Bombay, National Centre for the Performing Arts (NCPA), and Tata Institute of Fundamental Research (TIFR), which was taken over by the government, were further transformed into actual participation projects rather than giving donor funds to NGOs. We have been disbursing about a $100 million every year in the philanthropic endeavours of the Trust. About 40 per cent of that

15

over the last four or five years has gone in combating malnutrition, providing iron fortification in food, looking at safe drinking water, looking at primary health care. These are the kinds of endeavours we are actually undertaking, rather than giving donations to various NGOs. The quantum of funds is large and we have to, by law, spend 85 per cent of what we get each year. It was impossible to spend 85 per cent of that on artificial limbs and personal hardship. Therefore, we have transformed ourselves to look at bigger causes like climate change or reducing tobacco usage.

It has been a series of bigger causes rather than what we used to do, and that will now be shifting to the young entrepreneur. We have had this money for 100 years, but the entrepreneur has this money for the last five or ten years. It's his money, his idea, his handling of that business and he guards it ferociously. He is not yet in a position to give this out in philanthropy.

At the same time young companies, like Facebook could make a very generous donation to some cause or to a series of causes. Google might do the same and certain institutes like Microsoft have done a lot in putting money out to try to combat HIV or to remove diarrhoea or blood related diseases from parts of India. Bill Gates doesn't need to do this but it's his personal desire to contribute and make a difference in India. That's not the case with many of the young Indian millionaires who are still going through the "I didn't have it yesterday, and I have it today" phase, they have different aspirations. I am not criticising their aspirations because none of them have crooked aspirations, but their aspirations relate to how to make their personal net worth bigger.

We distribute a $100 million a year and then if we could distribute $200 million in the next, it's no great achievement from our side other than that we become more visible. We are not very different from Microsoft, Gates Foundation, Rockefeller Foundation or Ford Foundation in terms of what we do, subject to differences in the law. They can increase their holding by trading under the stock market, but we cannot. Bill Gates has made it his personal endeavour to go around the world trying to emphasise on wealthy people that they should commit X per cent of their net worth to charitable causes. I think in India he has not been that successful in making that happen, I think the time will come, maybe in another five years or seven years, when this will start to happen with entrepreneurs.

You have people like Kiran Mazumdar, who is, in a smaller way, giving money to various medical research projects and there may be various Indian-origin people who have also given part of their wealth to make something happen. I am quite confident that this will happen. Right now, it's very early days and yet if we go back in time you had a series of entrepreneurs who are US based Indians who have been quite wealthy and have sold their businesses for considerable amount of money and are comfortably well off. They may not be doing philanthropy but they are enjoying life, which they are entitled to, as they have used their ingenuity and their creativity to produce a business that has been successful. So, I don't quite know how to respond to what you asked.

JP: Can you please tell us about your early days and give us your perspective on money as you were growing up?

RNT: I went to a normal school in Bombay and then went to the US and graduated from Cornell as an architect. I worked in Los Angeles in an architect's firm for a couple of years. I was very happy and probably would never have returned to India but my grandmother fell ill and called for me and I went back to India to see her one last time. To my happiness, she did not pass away. She lived for about four or five years and I stayed back to be with her before she passed away. I was asked to enter the family business and shifted to Jamshedpur where I worked on the shop floor for three years. Then I was shifted from company to company, which I hated, but looking back, I can see that it gave me tremendous perspective, which I could not have gained in any other way. Eventually, I found myself being drawn into the apex of Tata Industries and then Tata Sons, and then in 1991, Mr JRD Tata called me and said he was going to step down and that I was going to be named successor. That's how it happened.

JP: While growing up did you have a wealthy family? Did you treat money with a different perspective than how you do today?

RNT: Yes, we were a wealthy family, but we were not an absurdly wealthy family. We borrowed more of an aura from the philanthropy that was done and from the image of the steel company, of the truck company, of the chemicals rather than our personal glitter or wealth. When I was growing up there was no such feeling that we were being deprived of having a life that reflected the wealth we have. Looking back on it now, I think it was the greatest thing that happened to us.

17

There was a great push from my parents to make sure that we didn't feel that we were insanely wealthy. Looking back, we did not suffer from anything, but I never had a Ferrari when I was a teenager, I never had my own house or anything of this nature. We lived as a well-to-do family might, and we were always somewhat understated in terms of what we did. I am personally very grateful for being brought up that way rather than in a wealthy image household.

JP: Did your perspective on money change after you took over the Tata enterprise?

RNT: I came at a time when India opened up economically. The opportunity to diversify, the opportunity to participate in the growth of India was enormous, which Mr JRD Tata did not have because India was a commanded and controlled environment for most of the years when he was chairman. I was very lucky in terms of timing and I took whatever opportunities that were given and to a great extent that helped when I stepped in as chairman in 1991 when the total revenues of the group were about $5 billion. When I retired in 2013, the revenue was about $110 billion. I was pleased that we were able to undertake that, partly organically and partly inorganically. Today, the group continues to be on that same growth path on which they were before.

JP: Did you get the Tata Trust chairmanship along with the enterprise?

RNT: The reason I am mulling over what answer to give you is that there are seven Trusts. I was the chairman of all the Trusts before I retired. But after I retired, I created a virtually single Trust by assigning all the people in the Trust to work on the entire Trust and not to be segregated into each of the Trusts. We had situations where Trust A would give a donation somewhere but Trust B would say we don't give a donation because you have been inappropriate in the way you run your NGO. Now, we deal with it in a rather consolidated basis and we internally divide the capital allocations.

JP: The Tata Trust—do you see any change coming?

RNT: I don't think that there will be any change or there needs to be any change. I think the Trust would be looking for opportunities that are in their defined quarters. As far as the company is concerned, they will have more cash available to them to look at growth on the one hand, or diversification. The only thing that the Tatas have always been to some extent accused of and in some cases applauded for is that we have not been brutal to get rid of 6,000 people or close down an issue by putting people out of work. We have been much more guarded and moderated about our actions in that sense.

JP: Do you have any advice for the millennials, in terms of what to do with all this money, as they are going to inherit such huge amounts of money.

RNT: I don't know what advice I could give. I think there's still a very, very small percentage of the people of India that have wealth that they have worked hard to get. I hope that this group of people does consider that there is a huge section of people out there that doesn't have the benefit of wealth. The wealthy could share a small part of their wealth, to help educate people and could consider the fact that they need to help people gain position, gain education, and gain the basic comforts of life while encouraging them to be enterprising, to work hard and climb the social ladder. For example, the Koreans that migrate to the United States are a great example of this spirit. Everybody in the family works, whether it's in a fruit stall or whether it's in a little convenience store or whatever it is. They work hard and they send their children to good schools. They demand their children study well and are achievers in school. So, you find many Koreans in the United States coming up the hard way. They bring their children up in that way, but they make contributions to other Koreans and contributions to society. Some of them become very wealthy but deep down inside, they are still the same thoughtful and sensitive people. I think the only advice I would give to every one of these people who have high net worth is that they should consider themselves to be very lucky and to make their own contribution to society, not to gain great vision or visibility for themselves but to know that they made a difference in a particular geography or a particular segment of industry or even a particular life.

JP: Apart from Tata Trust, do you have a personal philosophy of giving?

RNT: Yes, the money that I give isn't the same personal hardship money that the Trust used to give before. Somebody comes and says he can't afford this, or his wife has cancer and I might refer him to the Trust, or I might give it myself.

Neeraj Arora

Former Chief Business Officer, WhatsApp

JP: It's such a pleasure to reconnect with you again.

Neeraj: Absolutely, I feel the same way. It's been many years. I still remember the last we met in person was when I was still at Google. Maybe around 10 years back. Is that right?

JP: That's correct; we were taking a walk through Google's Mountain View campus.

Neeraj: That's correct. I think it was just before I was thinking of leaving Google to join WhatsApp and I told you about it— I remember.

JP: Yes, and I was quite concerned for you at that point in time.

Neeraj: You were not the only one. In fact, everybody around me was concerned, my family, my friends. I think I was the only crazy one who really wanted to do it. I think I got lucky in a way that I was not concerned as much as my friends and family.

JP: May I request you to introduce yourself.

Neeraj: I was born in Jammu, India. My dad used to work for the government of India, so, we were transferred to a different part of India every few years. Then I moved to Delhi and lived there for almost the next 20 years. I am practically a Delhi boy, I grew up there, went to school there. I completed my under-graduation from IIT Delhi, and it just so happened that my first job was in Singapore. It was at a start-up, but this was in 2000 when start-ups were not really the best thing you could do or work for, but I just didn't want to take up a regular job at Infosys or TCS, which were great companies back then and now. I didn't want to work in a company that had 10,000–20,000 employees; I'd get lost, so I joined a very small start-up in Singapore and spent five years there, mostly as a software engineer building stuff. I think they were a great few years to learn how to build Internet products very early in 2000, when the internet was still coming out of the first bust.

After that, I was very keen on exploring India because 2005–2006 was when a lot of Internet companies like Yahoo, Amazon, and Google had set-up shop in India and India was going through a lot of change in terms of people getting online, and a little bit of e-commerce had begun as well. I wanted to come back to India and see what was going on. I came back to India to attend Indian School of Business (ISB), graduated, and ended up working at the biggest media company in India, The Times of India group. My role was to help the corporate strategy team with the internet site called Times Internet back then. I think I spent 18 months there and that was probably the best learning I could have gotten on how to build products for India because The Times used to do everything, from commerce to advertising to e-mail, as well as a lot of different kind of Internet products, and they were super early back then.

After 18 months, I found a job at Google to help corporate development in the Asia region, mostly Asia, and a little bit of Australia and New Zealand. I did that for a few years and ended up helping seed a few early stage funds in India—Erasmic, Seed Fund and a couple more, which became the defining early stage funds in India. Google expanded just to be part of that ecosystem in India. I was then called to Mountain View in 2009 and spent the next two-and-half-years doing a lot of M&A (Mergers & Acquisitions) for Google. Google is a very acquisitive company; they buy a lot of companies. I remember in 2010 we were a team of five and ended up buying close to 70–80 companies in a year. I had a great experience there but was getting a little bored doing similar deals. I started thinking, "What is next?" Should I be a corporate development M&A guy all my life or is there more to what I could potentially do and make an impact?

I think the Bay Area helped me start thinking that a job is only a means to an end and I think what you should really think about is what drives you, what keeps you awake, what makes you stretch the boundary and then take a leap of faith. I was really trying to figure out if there was any early stage company that I could join and WhatsApp came along, super early at the time. There were five engineers and there was no business guy and I pitched to Jan and Brian, the founders of WhatsApp, that I wanted to leave Google to do a smaller thing and I would love to come help them with anything that was not product and engineering. It took me a year to convince them, and I'm really thankful that they finally agreed to hire me.

21

JP: What was your perspective on money while you were growing up?

Neeraj: I think money was not something that we had too much of. It was not something we thought too much about; the focus was just to get the best education we could. Moreover, as a lower-middle-class family in India, it was very simple living, just focus on studies and a little bit of sports and then the focus was to start working, start earning, and go from there. It was a very simple, lower-middle-class kind of thing.

JP: Let's fast forward to the day you joined WhatsApp and continue from there.

Neeraj: I think the first few years were, as you know, like any start-up, really unpredictable. There was a lot of competition. WhatsApp was not the first and only messaging company in the world. There was a lot of competition from smaller and bigger companies. A lot of money was being invested in this space. The first few years were to make sure we win, and that we were the fastest growing and the biggest messaging player in the world. It really was about how you take a few, less than 50 employees, to build the biggest Internet messaging company in the world. A lot of different things came together for us to be able to separate ourselves from a lot of other players in the market. I think the single biggest thing was focus. We just wanted to come to work and build something that everybody in the world would want to use, be it India, Brazil, Indonesia, Middle East, any part of the world and on any kind of phone. We were trying to build a mission-driven utility. I think that focus for the first five years, is what set WhatsApp on the path to getting 1 billion users and eventually, 1.5 billion users. Then, in the middle, we ended up deciding to sell the company to Facebook, which was in 2014.

JP: I'd love to hear how that happened because you played a key role.

Neeraj: It's an interesting story. It started with us becoming quite prevalent in some parts of the world like Western Europe, India, Brazil, and Indonesia—where a lot of companies want to have a good user base—and we were growing quite rapidly. Facebook, Google, and Silicon Valley are all about "If you cannot build you buy." I used to do that at Google. We were getting a lot of interest from some bigger players from China and U.S. to sell our company, or merge with them, and we didn't want to do it for the longest time because we thought we were too early—we were still on a path to become really big. It just so happened that Mark, who is the CEO and co-founder of Facebook, was very persistent. I think he tried for almost two years before we made the decision, and he was just trying to help. He was trying to get to know us and tell us what he wanted to do with Facebook and WhatsApp coming together. Mark was never pushy and I think we built a relationship over the years, and then eventually in 2014, he said, "Look, we are really serious, and we want to do whatever it takes to merge the two and it will look like a partnership more than an acquisition." That's where I think we really gave it a very hard look and we thought it was the best for our users and for the long-term of the company, to be a part of Facebook, and I ended up leading the deal. Having done M&A before, I think it was quite a thrill to be able to do the biggest deal of my life.

JP: The billion-dollar question is how do you get $19 billion in valuation?

Neeraj: A lot of different things. As you know Jayesh, valuation is what any company wants to make it look like—for the same asset. For Facebook, it was about anything that has a potential to touch a billion users—I think even Mark talked about it after the acquisition. Any product or utility in the world that has the potential to touch a billion users is very valuable—that was the first principle—it wasn't about revenue, or how we monetise this. It was more long-term thinking, where, if there are only a handful of services that would become really big in the world—Mark was very confident that WhatsApp would be one of them. We had, I think 450 million users back then. We were very confident about the pace at which we were growing, how prevalent the product was, how much people used it every day, and that we had a very good shot at becoming a billion-user company. That's where I think the valuation came from. Any service that has that many users should eventually be able to monetise really well. It was more a forward looking, potential-based valuation rather than cash flow or revenue-driven valuation.

JP: Congratulations! It's not only a spectacular deal for you, but worldwide I think you basically shook up the entire tech mobile world. Coming back to the present, I want to know your perspective on money, now that you have come into significant affluence. How do you spend your money?

Neeraj: Given that I had a very modest upbringing where we were very conscious about how we would spend money and what the focus of spending money would be, I think I just carried on with it. I think it gave us a huge cushion in life that we can go and do whatever we want. We don't have to work for money anymore— that is the only financial independence I think we have at the back of our mind now. We should be able to do whatever makes us happy, and what impact we would want to make in life is a question I asked myself going forward. As for spending money, I don't think anything changed too dramatically. I still do pretty much the same thing I was doing before. I have a little more help at home. We have a family and all that. Beyond that, it's quite similar. I do have the same set of friends, so not too much has changed. I'm not living in a castle or spending too much money on material things.

JP: Are you worried about your children and their ambition going forward because they have all this family inheritance?

Neeraj: We have two kids, and this was the biggest question I asked myself when the deal happened. When I was growing up—I had to struggle, and I think that pretty much defined what I was and what I became. And if you have resources to begin with, how do you push yourself? That's the fundamental question I think about all the time and I think there are many different ways to think about it. I think the Bay Area is probably one of the best places to understand how that could possibly work because it has a lot of affluent people, people who have done really well in their career and they're still able to raise their kids in a very normal environment, where they're not exposed to a lot of materialist things very early in life. But the focus is still on getting the best education, sports, art, and music. I think being in the Bay Area helps because a lot of friends and families around you go to the same school and colleges. It's people who just focus on getting their kids to work on the hardest problems or whatever they feel like doing in terms of making an impact in their lives. If you hold on to that and ground your kids around that, I think they also kind of realise that money is not something that defines anybody. It's more about what you achieve in life, what you want to do, how you want to impact society and the world in general.

JP: What is your philosophy on philanthropy?

Neeraj: I will be very honest; I didn't have too much time to think about it. When you're working really hard, you are consumed by what you are working on. That and family are all-consuming. You don't have too much time and resources to contribute back, I mean you would do your own thing in terms of your associations with your colleges and your alumni and try to help whenever you can, but not in a very focussed way. I'm still learning the ropes; there are a lot of great examples in the Bay Area. For me, right now I think what I'm trying to do is to spend my time understanding what drives me, what are the areas, that are not work related but are more philanthropic, where I would want to make an impact.

Sports in India is one such area, and India in general is a big area for me, I feel very passionately about India. Not a lot of people growing up in India get the kind of opportunities I got that defined my career. My goal is to help people who are super talented, whether they are in sports or any other field in India, to be able to realise their potential. I think, I chose sports first because I used to play a lot of sports myself. I support an organisation called OGQ (Olympic Gold Quest). They are trying to mentor very young kids to be able to have a chance at winning Olympic golds, and that organisation has been doing really well. They have been producing very good athletes. That's the first organisation I'm really focussing on, and focus is something I apply to everything I do. I don't want to spread myself too thin because then I won't be able to have any impact.

JP: When we met, I remember that you were interested in SONG, an impact fund by Soros, Omidyar Network, and Google. You took interest in it and you participated in our investment committee calls. I remember back then you were interested in impact investing.

Neeraj: I was lucky that I got the platform with Google and I was interested in what they were trying to do. What they were trying to do was at the intersection of India and investing with a social mission. For me, investing is something very close to my heart. I support a variety of funds in India that are trying to create the next set of companies and if you're able to invest in a company that has social impact, there's nothing like it. I think that was a great experience for me and I was thrilled to be part of that experience with you, Jayesh.

JP: Thank you. Final question—many millennials are going to inherit billions of dollars in the next few decades, is there any advice you would like to give them?

Neeraj: The biggest thing I worry about, for the younger generations including my kids, in today's world is that they are exposed to too many things very early on in life, which distracts them or has a higher probability of distracting them. Our focus on doing things, especially harder things, is going down as humanity, even though we're making really good progress; we're trying to work on solving very, very difficult problems. We have so many things happening all the time, there's too much noise coming at us, whether it is the internet, TV, or other kinds of mediums. These things are great—I mean the Internet is probably the biggest boon to development today and will continue to be. But how do you keep it positive? How do you maintain a balance? How do we use technology and still be very responsible but at the same time have a huge impact on society? That's something that even millennials will struggle with, and having that kind of awareness and understanding would really help them ensure that they're able to cut the noise or minimise it at least, and then focus their energies on trying to do things that really drives them and would eventually have a huge impact on the world.

JP: Neeraj, I want to congratulate you on behalf of the entire Indian diaspora. You've done a terrific job and we're looking forward to your next chapter.

T V Mohandas Pai

Former Member of the Board, Infosys

JP: May I request you to introduce yourself.

Mohandas: I was born in Bangalore, India. I have a degree in Commerce, a degree in Law, and I am a fellow Chartered Accountant. I started in 1982 by practicing as a chartered accountant and in 1986, I became an executive director of a leasing company called Prakash Leasing Limited. In 1994, I joined Infosys as a consultant and then as a full time CFO. I worked in Infosys since 1994 and left Infosys in 2011. When I joined INFY they were around $5 million, and when I left INFY, they were at $6.5 billion in revenue. They have more than 135,000 employees and $45 billion of market value now. I joined just one year after the IPO (June 1993) and it was a much smaller company then—I think it was valued at around $100 million at that time.

After leaving INFY, I joined with Ranjan Pai to form a partnership called Aarin Capital, where we put in money to invest in start-ups. We co-founded and have invested in 10 funds, and together between Aarin and all these funds, we have more than 280 companies. We are a large part of the ecosystem in India. I worked on governmental policy with both, the state and central government for the last 30 years. I am on the board of the National Stock Exchange and Havells India and I also helped found the Akshaya Patra Foundation in the year 2000. It is the world's largest midday meal program. We feed 1.7 million children unlimited midday meals every day. From the year 2000 until now, we have served around 3 billion meals. We are celebrating 3 billion meals, that is 300 crore meals, in Mathura, where we have a large kitchen and Prime Minister Modi has promised to come.

JP: Where did you grow up and what was your perspective on money growing up?

Mohandas: I grew up in Bangalore. I am from a middle-class family. My father came up the hard way; he lost his father when he was young. He got educated, went to Mumbai, worked around, and got a job in Bangalore. My mother was a school teacher. She was born near Coorg. They were very poor people. She stood first in the district in twelfth standard and she became a school teacher. Then they were married, and my father worked very hard. My mother as a school teacher, walked to school every day for 30 years to save on bus fare for our education, even though we did not need it, because they were different people—they were born in a time when India was very poor. There were not many opportunities; they struggled to have a decent life. They educated their children and my mother made sure that we were all well-educated and we were told, very clearly, that we had to be first in class—nothing else was acceptable. I have one sister and one brother. We grew up as a middle-class family, with middle-class living standards. We didn't have too much money but we had enough—our financial aspirations were less.

When I started my practice, people never paid much so we couldn't get much money. Then as an executive director of the leasing company, I made a decent amount of money, but not enough to save. At Infosys, when I joined, they paid decently, but nothing much until we got the stock option. For us, money was always in short supply. We respect money and the value of money. We like to live frugally, we are not ostentatious and if we get some money, the first thing to do is to ensure security for ourselves, to make sure the family is secure, you have a house, you have some decent money to live on, you help other family members and then you also go out and help people.

From the year 2000, I have been giving money to the Akshaya Patra Foundation and for all other people who need help. I want to help the most vulnerable part of society. I do it quietly, out of my own compulsion not because I want name or anything but, it's just that I think that I have an obligation to help people. I work for public causes. Our philosophy has been that money is important, it gives you security, but money is also a means to help make the world a better place. It means you help a lot of people, which you have to do because unless the world is a better place you will not be able to live in it.

JP: Would you say that your perspective on money, now that you are a billionaire, has changed?

Mohandas: I don't think I am a billionaire. I don't think my perspective has changed—I still live with little money, I still value money. I don't like to spend massively on my family or myself. Sometimes they complain but I feel that right now I am investing into the start-up ecosystem because I am a techie, and I understand technology and it is the most exciting sector to invest in. It is a very fast-growing sector that will give good returns. I am also spending part of my money for public welfare, helping many NGOs and others expand their programs, give scholarship to young people and doing many other things. My attitude towards money is to invest in entrepreneurs, invest in making bigger enterprisers, get other people together to invest also and overall, if tomorrow I get a lot of money, I will make sure that my share of it will be given away for public progress.

I have a philosophy that whatever I have, I have to divide it between my two boys and myself—each one gets an equal share. I want to do it while I am around, not after I am gone because I believe that if you have money and you want to help them then you must give it to your heirs when you are around so that they learn how to use money. My two boys have started to maintain their capital funds. They are investing what they are supposed to get from me, as their capital. They are also very careful with money. In fact, their attitude towards money is the same as mine—be frugal, invest wisely, and make sure that you take care of people.

JP: Do you have any words of wisdom for the affluent, especially for the millennials, who are going to inherit billions of dollars in the next decade or two?

Mohandas: My advice to everybody is to first take care of yourself and make yourself strong, decide whatever minimum you need to live comfortably, make sure that you invest in safe instruments that give regular returns. That may sound very odd, but it is important to have security. Second, I suggest investing a part of your money in future enterprises like start-ups and technology, which are creating wealth because of the great disruption that is going on. Invest a part of your wealth in the public market because it gives you more substantial returns, for a long period of time. In a country like India, which is a growth market where GDP is growing, it assures you of decent returns in the future.

Every year give a part of your earnings to public causes because you have to impact society around you. You have to be a good human being, you have to help society. And over a period of time give part of the assets you have to public causes. If you have children, when they grow older, and you are still in good shape to give your children what they will inherit, give them advice to invest wisely and not lose money, and not to live an ostentatious life.

Now, what is considered a normal life or an ostentatious life depends on where you are and what you are—what your attitudes are. We can't make judgment on what is required by a human being. But my only advice is, whatever you do, make sure you don't become an annoyance, and other people don't turn around and say that these are influential people who show off their wealth, because in society, in many parts of the world, people expect certain kind of behaviour from you. They don't expect arrogance, and they don't expect an ostentatious show of wealth because the norms of behaviour have changed.

Amit Chandra
Chairman, Bain Capital India Office

JP: May I request you to introduce yourself.

Amit: I am chairman of Bain Capital's India Office. I was born in Pimpri, Pune and after a few years, I moved to Mumbai, which is where I grew up. After my engineering at VJTI, I spent a couple of years at Larsen & Toubro and then went overseas, to Boston College for my MBA. I came back and soon thereafter became a banker. I spent a very large part of my career in investment banking at DSP Merrill Lynch, where I pretty much made my first inning as a professional. I retired there in 2007, as its managing director and board member, and left to start my second innings as a private equity professional. Soon thereafter, I joined Bain Capital as founder of its India Office and have now spent 11 years at the firm as a part of its Asia leadership team. While it is somewhat unusual, I now spend half my team at Bain Capital and the other half with my interests in the social sector.

JP: What was your perspective on money while you were growing up?

Amit: I grew up in a middle-class family and obviously, deep values for money were inculcated in us siblings, by my parents. During my engineering and my MBA, I was very fortunate to have had scholarships and was someone who deeply valued being at the receiving end of other people's generosity, and so I always valued money. Even when I started my career, money was obviously relatively scarce. When I got married, I remember our early years, my wife Archana and I, used to live as paying guests because we couldn't afford a rented house close to our place of work. Yet even in those days, we were clear about donating a part of our income. Therefore, we both have had that deep appreciation for relatively simple living and giving from early days.

JP: You have done extremely well in your career. Has your perspective on money changed since?

Amit: By God's grace, I have gone through my career and been able to exceed financial goals that I set for myself when I started my career. But somewhere along our journey, Archana and I decided that money needed to have purpose, so once the quality of life that we wanted was achieved, we decided the excess needed to serve a different purpose.

JP: How do you divide your time between Bain Capital and philanthropy?

Amit: Both Archana and I are very interested in the social sector. She gives 100 per cent of her time in the social sector, running an organisation, which serves the intellectually disabled. Since, I have been very interested in the social sector for over two decades, I have gradually been increasing the time that I have spent in it, more so over the past 10 years. I felt that at some point of time I wanted to take a material step up and spend more time in a much more meaningful way. A few years ago, I approached my partners with a request that I be able to spend at least half my time on philanthropy, and fortunately, my organisation was in a position where the next line of leadership was able to step up and be able to take up the responsibility. My partners were also supportive of that decision. Therefore, I now spend about half my time with Bain Capital and other half working with my foundation and other commitments in the social sector.

JP: Please give us a better understanding of your foundation. What is your philosophy on giving and philanthropy?

Amit: The foundation is called ATE Chandra Foundation. It has actually two core verticals. The first is rural transformation, wherein we work actively with farmers across Maharashtra on drought alleviation, which is a big problem in Maharashtra. There are a couple of techniques that we work on with farmers. Desilting of dams is the predominant technique. The other area of interest we are actively involved in is propagation of natural farming because we believe that it is very important for climate resilient farming as well as for improving the income of farmers. We are also involved in the transformation of villages on a holistic basis in partnership with the government of Maharashtra. We have also adopted eight villages in the district of Beed.

The second vertical that we have is capacity building for the social sector and building of the eco system for philanthropy as a whole in India. There are a number of initiatives that we have in that vertical.

We invest very heavily in leadership development in the sector as a whole, through training program that we run in partnership with organisations like Dasra, Harvard Business School, Ashoka University, ISDM, ILSS, and others. Through these programs, we are training about 500 leaders every year in upgrading their own skills because we believe it's highly impactful to empower the leadership to be able to achieve their goals. We also work with around 15 NGOs in capacity building so that they are able to be more effective writing non-program grants, so that they can go to the next level. Then third, we are making ecosystem investments in institutions or movements that are key to philanthropy like Indian Development Review (IDR), Give India, Bridgespan, Daan Utsav, and others.

Those are the two core verticals, and then there are other things that we have been involved in and supporting over the years. Our biggest commitments, historically, have been Ashoka University, of which I am one of the founders and governing board member and SRCC Children's Hospital, but we are now focussing on the core verticals. Of course, Archana spends most of her time running Jai Vakeel, which is the largest foundation for the intellectually disabled in the country.

JP: You have given us your perspective of spending 50 per cent of your time doing all this amazing work. Can you also share with us your perspective on money?

Amit: Archana and I have largely kept the quality of our life the same over time, and decided at some point that we would not spend more to buy a bigger or more houses, or very high end cars, and limit our indulgences to minimal; instead, we would use income that would keep coming in towards social causes that we are passionate about. We therefore have only bought one house in my life and since have stayed in that house. It's not a large house by many people's standards, but we are very comfortable in it. We are very happy with our quality of life and vast majority of what we have generated over a long time has gone to what she and I are very passionate about.

JP: Aren't you grappling with this question of how much is enough?

Amit: We grappled with that issue many years ago, mid way through our journey. We went through a structured exercise where we decided what was enough to sustain the lifestyle that we had at that point of time. Having defined it broadly, we kept that amount aside and beyond that, we decided that whatever cash flow we had on the incremental basis could largely be used for social causes.

JP: Millennials are going to inherit billions of dollars in the next few years. Is there any advice you would like to give them?

Amit: I am careful about dishing out advice on these kinds of issues because at the end of the day, I think each person's wealth is their own business and I think it is for them to decide. Personally, I feel I have a responsibility to think holistically about the sustainability of society around us. I am very clear that this is the way in which my life is more wholesome, and this is what gives me joy—and that's what I solve for. I am also very clear that at the end of the day, this is the most sustainable way in which I can lead my life. Others may not agree with me. There are some of us who do this in partnership. There are many who like to save their wealth and pass it on from generation to generation, and there are others who would like to simply spend it. I think that each person will discover their own journey.

Vipul Shah

Chief Operating Officer, Reliance Petrochemical

JP: May I request you to introduce yourself.

Vipul: I am 59 years old. I practically grew up in Mumbai. I am pretty much a Bombayite. I studied in Manipal, and I studied in Austin. Working life, I lived across Hong Kong, Singapore, Switzerland, US, and India, of course, and that's my home base.

JP: Give us a little background on your career path.

Vipul: I went to the US to do my Bachelor's and Master's. I came back to India in 1986. I started working for a very small company at that time called Reliance. After working for Reliance for a year and a half, I wanted to do my own business. I worked in our family business for a year. Then Dow Chemical, the number one chemical company in the US, came head hunting for me in India. I thought, let me work for two or three years in the field of my liking, which is polymer science and let's see what happens and the rest as they say is history. I spent over 27 years at Dow. Dow moved me around the globe, which was the most exciting part of my career. By the time I moved back to India, my parents were aging, and Reliance came head hunting for me again. I did not want to leave the country, so I left Dow. I actually retired from Dow and joined Reliance four years ago.

JP: What was your last position at Dow?

Vipul: I was running Dow's entire India operations. Before that, I was running Southeast Asia and India out of Singapore.

JP: What is your title, role, and responsibilities at Reliance?

Vipul: I run the petrochemical division of Reliance Industries. My title is Chief Operating Officer, and I am essentially responsible for about $23-24 billion of revenue.

JP: What is the business?

Vipul: It's the entire polymers, elastomers, polyesters—the full gambit of the entire petrochemical field. Reliance, in a way, is a very unique company, which has got both sides of the portfolio. Most company, either do polyester or do the petrochemical side of polymers and elastomers. They do both.

JP: What was your perspective on money growing up?

Vipul: I won't say that we have come from a very affluent family, but we were reasonably comfortable family. When we moved to Mumbai, I grew up with a chauffeur driven car. But we were an average middle-class family, where you are not counting money every day, but you have to budget everything in terms of your life. That changed somewhere in the mid-90s when I became the country manager for Dow in India. My salary started jumping leaps and bounds, by then I was about 33 or 34 years old. But before that, in the US, we literally lived pay-check to pay-check for five years.

JP: Fast forward to the second part of your life, from 35 to now, can you describe what money means to you and how you use it?

Vipul: I think money was never a primary driver as I was more interested in my career, working in the field of my interest. You know, when you work in the field of your interest money follows you, and that happened when I moved to Hong Kong. Suddenly, I was living an expatriate life, when I was about 39 years old. When we moved to Hong Kong, within a few months I realised that after going to international school, the kids cannot go back to do their Bachelor's in India. You only plan to fund both your kid's USA Master's degree which is a two years program, and now suddenly you have to also fund for four years of Bachelor's degree for both in USA. The first couple of years in Hong Kong went in building up savings for their education. In 2003, when I moved to Switzerland, we built capital that was required to keep the family afloat, and for making sure that if anything happened to me, my kids' education does not suffer. Then the fund accumulation became a lot quicker.

JP: Your money management was more to do with preservation—looking after the family. As a CXO, what is your perspective on money?

Vipul: Your salary can change dramatically, which happened to me when I moved to Hong Kong—for two or three years we did not change our lifestyles but instead built up our savings. Then, you change your lifestyle based on the earnings of your savings. This means that the savings rate goes up dramatically and that, I think, has made an incredible difference in my life.

JP: Today, you are reasonably affluent, and you have a good lifestyle. What are your thoughts about your current lifestyle, compared to your previous one?

Vipul: From a lifestyle perspective, I don't think our lifestyle has changed. I think we remain what we are. I have been an expat in Dow for 15 years before I retired. We never lived the typical so-called expat lives. I think that makes a big difference. When your needs are less, your risk-taking ability is very high. That's what made a huge difference in my life, in my professional career I have always taken risks and the rewards followed—and touchwood, I am lucky to not have much failure in my career.

JP: If I can ask you, what are you doing with all your money?

Vipul: In the last few years, in a very small way, we as a family have decided that a certain amount of money will be donated every year. A large part of our donation is made in two fields: one is education, especially for the deprived; and the second part is health care for the deprived. These are the two areas where every year, very diligently on a need basis, whoever requests help, we send it through the system. We ensure that the funds are going through to the right channel and are not going to be misused by anybody and that a large portion of the funds goes to the people versus administration of the NGOs.

JP: Are you currently supporting religious charities as well?

Vipul: No, there are no religious charities as such but more of a spiritual charity, and then there is also an institute where my father was educated.

JP: Going forward, with all of this affluence that you created, you will set aside some amount of money for your family's welfare and I am assuming that then you will set aside some amount of money for your next generation. Can you describe that process?

Vipul: I think fortunately, by working for an American multinational in a senior executive position for a while, I have enough pension for me and my wife to survive without touching any of our savings, including our health care, everything is taken care of for life. There is enough money for us, and part of the reason is because we don't have an expensive lifestyle.

Now, it's just a question of making sure that the children are able to do what they want to do, and they follow their passion. In following their passion, obviously, they are not going to make enough money, but you want to make sure that they have a decent lifestyle. You put aside a certain amount every year—you're going to support the kids for at least the next 10 years, while they find their passion, which will match their lifestyle earnings. My daughter is more than happy to go and live as a paying guest, which you would never want them to do. I think that is something you set aside money for, over a period of time. Then you give on an annual basis rather than giving it at one time.

I do prefer to give money and support to charity every year and over a period of time when I ultimately hang up my boots, I want to contribute with sweat equity as well, both physical as well as mental.

JP: Do you prefer to spend your money on branded, material things or would you rather spend it on experiences?

Vipul: I don't think I have ever been on the branded side of the equation. In fact, in the last four-five years, I have actually moved away, even in terms of food. For example, if there is a little less salt or whatever, I never complain and eat whatever is on my plate and that's something that is ingrained in me. Having said that, once or twice in a year, we take some exotic vacation and enjoy ourselves, because that helps me recharge my batteries, and chill out.

JP: You are going to leave behind a certain amount of wealth for your children. Do you worry about how this affluence may affect them?

Vipul: No, I'm not worried, because the kids have been raised that way. I think, until my son did his summer internship in 2010 at Dow, he did not know how senior his dad really was—he had no clue.

JP: Today both your children are aware of the affluence you possess. Don't you fear they might while away that money when they receive it?

Vipul: No. Even today they don't. In fact, we have to push our daughter, Khevna, to stop wearing torn jeans or t-shirt.

JP: By the way, torn jeans are more expensive these days.

Vipul: No, no—this torn is not the fashion torn—this is a rugged torn. I think, Harshil, has a little bit of an expensive taste, but nothing extravagant. They are very conscious about the money they spend.

Naveen Bhat, PhD
Managing Director APAC, ISG Keysight

JP: May I request you to introduce yourself.

Naveen: My name is Naveen Bhat, and I am working as the MD APAC for a global telecommunication company. I'm a 54-year-old global citizen, having spent equal amount of time in Singapore, US, and India.

JP: What subject do you have a PhD in?

Naveen: I have a PhD in Artificial Intelligence and Neural Networks applied to the fields of chemical engineering, so we did a lot of cognition, cognitive learning, how the brain works and then applied it to machine knowledge.

JP: What was your standard of living, and your perspective on money while you were growing up in Bangalore, and then in the US?

Naveen: We came from a lower-middle-class family. My parents struggled to make ends meet. My dad couldn't afford to pay fees, which was about ₹50 per month, which in today's currency is $1 per month. My mother had to start working just to be able to put a little bit more money in our bank and food on the table. I worked through a fairly modest childhood and then a simple college life.

After graduating from engineering college, I left India with $250 in my pocket. When I went to the US, I built my career and assets. During this phase, our perspective on money was that it was our safety net. We did not have anything to fall back on in India. I took a very conservative approach to building up my finances.

JP: How did you end up in Singapore and what is your perspective on money?

Naveen: We had spent about 15 years in the US, lived the American dream, had homes, kids, dogs, and the urban lifestyle. We travelled the world and then at a point asked, "What's next?" We were leading a good lifestyle, but we realised we were far away from our culture. We wanted to spend more time with the kids, we felt that being in some other place, where we could share some of the workload would be easier as both my wife and I work. I came to Singapore on work and realised this was an awesome place. I also realised that we could have a domestic helper here and be closer to our parents back in Bangalore. So, we moved to Singapore.

JP: What is your perspective on money and what do you spend it on?

Naveen: Our perspective on money has changed over time and so have our expenses. Earlier we pursued our careers with a passion, with a goal to earn more. Over time, we have ceased to chase money. From an income standpoint, we fall in a high-income category because both of us are working in lucrative jobs. However, we now lead a low overhead lifestyle and most of our expenses are around life experiences. We have chosen not to acquire material goods, and decided that we were going to do everything that we wanted to do in life. No pending bucket lists. Whether it's sky diving or scuba diving or just experiencing things in a rain forest or safaris, we have done most of them. We still continue to do all of those things, but around 10 years ago when I was 42–43, we felt that we had done a lot of things for ourselves, so we started thinking about what else we could do with our money for others.

JP: In terms of spending on experiences, what are the key experiences that both, you and Mousumi have gone through?

Naveen: First of all, we decided we set a goal to climb Mount Everest. That was an extremely ambitious goal. People said we were nuts. We thought, if everybody thinks we are nuts, then that's more reason for us to do it. It was a 10-year plan. Each year we wanted to experience different mountains and honestly, it's not really the climbing of Everest, but the journey towards climbing Everest that matters. As part of the journey, we have gone to Malaysia, New Zealand, Mont Blanc, Longs Peak in Colorado, Mount Fuji in Japan, and Mount Kilimanjaro in Africa. We have been to Nepal many times, and we are still on that Mount Everest quest. We have delayed our 10 year journey to a 15 year journey because we realised that Mount Everest was going to be a dangerous adventure, and thought it more prudent to complete our remaining obligations to our kids.

We also thought, "If we can climb high, we can go low too." We started diving, and now we are advanced certified divers who have been to great depths in the ocean, in different parts of the world. We also began running and we did multiple marathons. We included our kids in all that we did be it golf, or diving or climbing. This whole experiential lifestyle brought us very close together as a family.

JP: And have you conquered the Base Camp?

Naveen: Yes, we have been to Everest Base Camp. A highly recommended trek for anybody who has not been there.

JP: What else are you doing with your money?

Naveen: About 10 years ago, we decided we wanted to give back to society and you were the one who told us that there are four ways to do it—you could either give money, or you could give time, or you could make use of your profession, or you could bring about systematic changes through government policy and organisations. We decided that we were going to use our profession; use our contacts. We work with groups in Ahmedabad and now we have started expanding that role to other places. We realised one important lesson on that journey—compassion for others brings happiness to our own. The fact that we opened our hearts and released the compassion that we have, just made our life a lot more joyful. When we are joyful ourselves, we are able to spread that joy to other people and not just for ourselves, but for our kids as well.

So, that took us on another journey where we asked ourselves, "What do we need to do for our kids?" We had already given our kids the best education, experiences, and our ethics. We decided that our kids no longer needed our money. We told our kids that they would not get any inheritance.

The next question we asked ourselves was, "What do we want to do with the money that we have?" Four years ago, we decided to put this money back into something that we would find meaningful and our channel was kids' education. We wanted to be part of some kids' life and their future. We put together a unique program. We decided to take on a kid a year and take them through their complete education for at least eight to nine years. We pick kids about 11 or 12 years of age and then we would educate them until they finish college, so their education was our responsibility. But that was not it. We wanted to make sure it was not just signing a cheque, but it was a life changing experience for them and us. We go to their homes and stay with them. But more importantly we bring them over to Singapore and they stay with us for a week every year. The kids love the experience of staying in Singapore with us. It opens their eyes to new dreams and possibilities. We have started a 16-year program and we are in year five. I think the financial outlay of this is probably over $1 million. We began this journey with two boys in Ahmedabad and two girls in Delhi. Now, we have two more kids in Bangalore. We have just added two more kids in Ahmedabad.

JP: Besides the 16-year programme, is there anything else you both are planning to do with your money?

Naveen: We don't plan to save more money for a lifestyle that we desire. Instead, we plan to lead a lifestyle with the money that's remaining. Some people start 'giving back' very late in life. We started at the age of 50, which is roughly the halfway point of our lifespans. We have the rest of our lives to return to society what we obtained. We have started diminishing our assets and simplifying our lives. We have all we need. We do not want to pander to our greed.

JP: Does it give you incentive to keep working and continue to accumulate wealth so that you can give more?

Naveen: No, absolutely not. My wife and I both work because we are extremely passionate about what we do. If that brings us money, that's great. We will work as long as the passion is alive and we enjoy what we do, and then if we need to switch and start our own company, we are happy to go that way as well, but we are not earning money to accumulate.

JP: If people are inspired by what you are doing, but don't know how to go about it themselves, would you and your wife, Mousumi, be interested in forming an organisation and going about it systematically?

Naveen: Absolutely, yes. If this idea inspires other people then that in itself is a reward. It's something that we just started and if enough people come and say, "Let's do it together!" and that can multiply the positive effect to more people, then we would love to do it.

What we are doing with 8 kids, if 10 families do this, now you've got 80. If a 100 families do this, now we have 800. It could be 800 lives that could be significantly enhanced.

JP: Any parting words of wisdom?

Naveen: Wisdom comes from wise men. I'm not there yet. For now, I will continue to 'give back'.

Businessmen

Manubhai Chandaria, OBE CBS EBS
Chairman, Chandaria Foundation

Vijay Goradia
Founder and Chairman, Vinmar International

Raman Maroo
Managing Director, Shemaroo Entertainment

Raghuvinder Kataria
Chairman, Kataria Holdings

Rakesh Malhotra
Founder, Luminous Power Technologies and SAR Group

Satish Gupta
Founder, Excel Cabinets and Interiors

Suketu Shah
Managing Director, Novotech

Manubhai Chandaria, OBE CBS EBS
Chairman, Chandaria Foundation

JP: May I request you to introduce yourself.

Manubhai: I am one of the senior-most member of the Chandaria family. We have a joint family; there are about 50 members, they live in London, Geneva, Nairobi, Toronto, and Singapore. They have to be in one of the offices and three or four families will remain in that area so that we can continue to remain as a family.

I was born in Nairobi. I am 90 years old. I won't say I was from a very poor background—people ask me whether I was born with silver spoon and I say, "No, but we had spoons in our home."

I have a Master's degree in Engineering from the United States. My brother has a second degree from Berkeley in Food Technology and my eldest cousin had a Civil Engineering degree and my younger cousin has a Commerce degree, both from Bombay University.

During the Quit India Movement, Gandhi and Gandhi's philosophy were at the centre of things. Sacrifice was the first principle that we began to understand, that to get anything, one has got to give, and it's not possible to get anything without giving.

I started looking after the major businesses in Kenya, Africa together with my family. We were advised that since Kenya had independence, other countries would start getting independence too. Tanzania was the first, Kenya was second, Uganda was third, like that, every other country was going to get independence, and they're not going to remain the market for our goods, as they would ultimately like investments. In five years, we sent our family members to Tanzania, Ethiopia, Uganda, Zambia, and then Burundi. It was very difficult, but we not only survived but we prospered and that gave us the confidence to repeat what we were doing in one country, in other countries as well. Subsequently, we sent our family members to London, some to Toronto, some to Singapore and as such, the whole family was spread out. The essence of the whole thing is that collectively we can survive in any conditions that come along and I think it worked out well.

After three or four years, all of us younger people went to our father and said, "Let's create a foundation; the Chandaria Foundation."

And he looked at us and said, "Is something wrong with you guys? You know we have 36 people at home, there is a big hole over here— fill it up. Forget about creating a foundation!" But when we had about 300–400 people working, he came back and said, "I liked your idea of the foundation." Our idea was based on a very simple principal that if we had a Foundation, it would be a focal point to draw our attention that we have a responsibility towards the society that we work and live in. That gave birth to the Chandaria Foundation in Kenya, in 1956.

The Chandaria Foundation started with one scholarship and from one scholarship to 10 scholarships; now for the last 30 years we have given 100 scholarships to 30 university graduates. Chandaria Foundation started endowing various institutions which always carried the name of Chandaria i.e. Chandaria School of Business at United States International University, and Chandaria Centre for Performing Arts at University of Nairobi, as we felt that it was the only way we could express the family's intent to serve the community in Kenya. It means we prosper in our businesses but at the same time we do not forget the welfare of our people.

JP: From humble beginnings, the Chandaria family has grown dramatically. Can you share with us the scope and size of the Chandaria Group as well as the Chandaria Foundation?

Manubhai: We employ approximately 40,000 people throughout the world and operate in 40 countries. We can't say that we are extremely rich, but we are quite okay. At the same time, we keep on making sure that our children participate in social work and do not walk above the ground, their feet must always be on the ground to understand the reality.

The Chandaria Foundation is a great vehicle for us to be closer to society, be more considerate towards people rather than towards our own selves and that is why our institution has grown so well. Now we are in 40 countries manufacturing a number of products. What we were manufacturing in Africa were considered sunset industries in the east and west. We had to pick up newer products, but we had the attitude, ideas, and resources—everything required to grow, and to be counted. At the end of the day, we used part of that funding for social work, not just by writing cheques, but by getting involved and as such I became a trustee and chairman of many trusts, as well as created a number of organisations. The point was how could we, as individuals, try to help in as many ways in as many areas as possible? And there are no limits. But at the end of the day, what shows is (i) the family, which is united, (ii) it shows the business successes, (iii) the social impact that we have been able to create.

JP: You have kept the family well knit together through all these years. Isn't it true that the Chandaria Trust is a case study?

Manubhai: Well it is a case study; I think it has been written by Harvard and they have printed a book. And it is also presented at Wharton. The point is to make the younger generation understand that life is not only about earning and living lavishly. It has responsibilities, and those responsibilities are sometimes against one's wishes. Unless and until one has a heart to do it, is prepared to do it, which does not come automatically; it has to be taught, nurtured. As such, you will find most of the Chandaria family members have their feet on the ground. It is not just, "Oh my God, he is a Chandaria!" No, that is one thing that we have been able to do. We get together every 6 months, sometimes every 12 months, and sit together discussing different views, arguing over them, but fundamentally, the aim is to remain together, to do good, and to grow. Having 40,000 people working for us means their families depend on us. There are huge responsibilities that go with it. To keep the fourth and fifth generation going on the same path one has to be very, very sure and plant the seed in a way that it grows into a tree and blooms.

JP: Give us your perspective on the future, as you see it, especially your message and wisdom to millennials about what to do with all this money?

Manubhai: When we were living in one house, there was always some issue with one another, but we were still together under one roof. All of us were born in the same environment, the same thinking and the same values, but today the next generation is born in Singapore, Toronto, London, and Geneva. These are very different environments. To keep them together and interested in a joint family is an issue on its own, it's not an easy job. But we try placing them on a better platform of thinking that they have the capacity and that capacity must be utilised for the best of the family and the society they live in.

My grandchildren were born in Singapore and presently studying at Stanford, US. Some other members of the family are born in Toronto and studying in UK. My worry is that because they are so diverse, that managing their mental attitude will be most difficult. It's their time, their intelligence, and with their education, the support they have, and everything that's been laid out for them—we would like to see the best that they can do.

God has been good to you and you are doing well, and he will help you, but at the same time, if you're not doing good for others then that goodness and greatness of yours will stop where you are. You have to involve yourself in more and more social work. Only when tears roll down one's cheeks on seeing someone else's pain and suffering, will you realise that there is something fundamental for you to do—whether it's your pain or somebody else's pain doesn't make a difference. You have got to cultivate that attitude. That is why we make sure that our children begin social work, we get them involved. Millennials require more and more examples of good people, why they are known, why people talk about them, because they are always there to extend help.

JP: Are there any specific projects or vertical sectors that the Chandaria Foundation will be working on?

Manubhai: We work on three areas—education, health, and disability. There's so much pain in the world today. We cannot just ignore that. The examples are already set for our younger generation to follow. Either they learn to follow the examples of doing good, not only living good, extending good work and support to society, or they end up becoming people who just enjoy partying and don't care for the rest.

Let's hope that the future generation is groomed to give rather than take. To give from one's pocket is very difficult. I think it depends on the generation. Here in Kenya, we have already celebrated 100 years, but we see that there are very few prominent families left—they drop out because the third and fourth generation's ideology is to enjoy themselves and that's it.

Vijay Goradia
Founder and Chairman, Vinmar International

JP: May I request you to introduce yourself.

Vijay: I am currently living in Houston and have been for about 35 years. I used to live in New York City before that. I grew up in a large family in a suburb of Mumbai called Matunga. We were 10 siblings and we grew up in a very modest family. My father was a businessman. He was an orphan, who came to Mumbai at the age of 13, worked for his uncle and started his own company, went through lots of ups and downs. But we grew up in a happy family, where we learnt to be tolerant of each other and education was always very important.

I went to the Jesuit school in Matunga called Don Bosco, and it was a very good school for me as it was not just good from the perspective of education, but also inculcating good moral values. I can't say that I grew up religious. My parents didn't go to temple every day, but they put a lot of value on being a good human being. I didn't have any major creature comforts. We didn't have a refrigerator, or a phone, or a car growing up, but we certainly looked up to our three square meals a day and a pretty good education.

JP: Where did you go to college and how did you get to the United States?

Vijay: I went to Poddar College to study Commerce and then at the age of 17, I started my own company along with my brother, who joined me later. I used to go to the gym at four in the morning, from six to nine, I would attend college and then from nine in the morning to nine in the night, or however long it took, I would work in a little plastics factory that my brother and I setup when I was only 17 years old. We did reasonably well, built another factory and then another one.

When I was in my mid-twenties, I decided I was caught in a rut and that's not what I wanted to do. I persuaded a friend of mine and together we took a backpack and started hitch-hiking, beginning from India. We flew from Amritsar to Kabul because we couldn't go to Pakistan, then from Afghanistan we started hitch-hiking by road, with just about $70 in our pockets. We hitch-hiked through Afghanistan, Iran, Turkey, Greece into Eastern Europe and then on to Western Europe. I did that for little over 10 months, and then came back to India. My siblings had already migrated to the US and I decided to join them. I landed at my friend's apartment in New York City with the goal of getting a job and then may be studying music. But this was recession time in the 70s and I couldn't get a job. I started my own company brokering in plastic raw materials, from my friend's one-room apartment. And that was 40 years ago. We have been lucky of course, but I had to work very hard.

The hard work and the experiences that I had in India growing up and running my business there, as well as the hitch-hiking experience taught me many lessons that stood me in good stead while I was building up my business in the US.

JP: What was your perspective on money growing up in India, and then in the United States?

Vijay: Growing up we didn't have a lot but whatever we had, I learnt early on that there are many people who have even less than us. So, (a) I had to be very thankful for what we have, and (b) to try to help whomever we could. Even though we didn't have a lot, we could still afford helpers, usually young kids from a poor family from the mountains near Mumbai. My father always made it a point to put them in night school and made them learn, if nothing else, at least the basics of reading, writing, and arithmetic. I learnt early on to share whatever we had but at the same time there was a desire to make more money, to be able to afford some creature comforts, maybe a little bigger place to live, to be able to travel and then to help others.

JP: Tell us more about the successful business that you have setup.

Vijay: From the business of brokering in plastic raw materials, we got into trading, from trading to distribution, from one country, which was India, we have now grown to doing business in over 110 countries. Our revenues are about $4 billion a year and there is a certain satisfaction of having provided employment to a lot of people around the world, not only that, but also paving the way in the US for Indians that came after me.

JP: What line of business are you in?

Vijay: We are still in the polymers and chemicals business, but now over the years, we also own manufacturing plants, so besides distribution we now have manufacturing assets.

50

JP: You're incredibly successful, very well-known and have won many awards. What is your perspective on money today?

Vijay: I mentor college kids or young people who are getting into business. One of the things I always tell them is, never ever pursue anything just to make money. Money is an outcome. It should not be the be all and end all, instead pursue something to make lives better. Do it because you are passionate about it and money will follow, and that success will never be measured in terms of the amount of money you make. Then the other side is when you do make a comfortable living, always lookout to help others, whether its people working for you or people within your circle of relatives or friends, your society, and do what you can to help, but do it with a purpose.

For a number of years, we would just write cheques for lot of different causes. People would come, ask for help and over the years, I have realised that while you have to do some of that and it's good to do some of that, it's even better if you develop a mission on what it is you would like to do most, the most impact you can make with the money you have. Stay focussed on that and as far as possible, do it to make a difference in the lives of others and try to do it as anonymously, as possible.

For example, I founded Pratham USA 20 years ago. At that time, it was a very small program in the slums of Mumbai. I saw that the model was very scalable, very replicable and was very low-cost, and the need in India was so great. There was no way I could write a cheque to cover the potential that this program offered. I came back to the US, from that trip to India, and I rallied some of my friends to contribute money along with my contribution and now this NGO impacts as many as 8 million children a year, and over the last 20 plus years, it has impacted 60 million children in India.

JP: Can you describe the thesis of Pratham?

Vijay: Pratham was originally started for pre-school education in the slums of Mumbai. But in a very joyful manner, we trained people from within those slums with just tenth grade or SSC education, to round up a few children in the neighbourhood and teach them basic reading, writing, and math skills, in those four major years between the age of three and seven. We found that if they learnt well during those years, then the chances of them continuing to go to municipal schools and not dropping out increase dramatically. The program then grew to many slums in different cities in India. Then we realised that there was a need to deal with kids who are going to school but not learning well, either because the teachers didn't teach properly or didn't show up at school. We developed programs to teach these children by putting our own people in the schools and helping them. Then we developed a methodology for accelerated reading, writing, and math where we would take these kids that did go to school but were lagging behind, for example, fifth grade children only had second grade capabilities, we would have an immersive learning program for 45–90 days for them, and then get them up to speed. The amazing thing was to track the progress that all these kids were making.

JP: How old are you? Going forward, what's your plan with all this money?

Vijay: I am 68 years old. I am still busy; I am active in my business as well as in philanthropy. Our foundation has supported other programs like Pratham, both in education and health in India and to some extent in the US. But the other programs we have not come out and put our name to it because I realised the danger of getting on an ego trip and I don't want to fall into that trap. This goes back to what I alluded earlier about trying to give money quietly and anonymously, to the extent possible.

In terms of our goals, we have provided sufficiently for our children but not so much that they can afford to be spendthrifts and luckily, they are not. They are both very careful with the money they spend because they know that the money is of much more value to those that are in need. Beyond that, my wife and I have decided that we will give away our wealth while we are alive, not leave it for posterity. So much of the wealth that we have we will give away during our lifetime.

JP: Have you put a process in place for that? What is the plan going forward?

Vijay: We have a family foundation, my daughter runs that foundation full time with help, and we have put a plan in place to accelerate the giving. Many people may not realise but to give in the right way, to make the right impact, it's not easy. It takes a lot of work and it takes a lot of deliberation. We are going about it as methodically as we possibly can. We are learning along the way and hopefully we will accomplish what we set out to do.

JP: Can I ask you about the importance of impact and outcome versus the journey, for you, for your daughter, and the family?

Vijay: My daughter, who worked for NGOs and has a Master's degree in Public Health, is much, much more focussed on measurable impact. She is very numbers driven, metrics driven and for the most part, she is right but at the same time my wife and I believe that there are some things that you cannot measure in very concrete terms. You just know that it's the right thing to do and you just have to take your chances and do it. For the most part, these NGOs are run very professionally, but then we also have side buckets where each of us have the freedom to write cheques for things that we feel good about, even though the impact may not be immediate and measurable.

JP: Based on the amazing experiences you've had in life, what advice would you give millennials who will inherit great wealth and affluence?

Vijay: I don't know if I am qualified to give advice to anybody. I look back to the old days in India—everybody gave but differently. They would take care of their immediate family members, and make sure that the family members were well taken care of before they went out to help others in society. That's certainly a form of giving so obviously everybody—millennials or otherwise—the first thing they should be doing is take care of the needy within the immediate family and the extended family, before they go out to help others. Then, the other part that is very common is to build a school or a hospital or some such thing in the name of your parents or grandparents, and then insist on being involved in operating and running it. That model I think has limitations in this modern day. My recommendation would be to not try to reinvent something but instead go look for NGOs that are already doing good work and contribute to those in terms of money and time, as you can afford both.

Raman Maroo

Managing Director, Shemaroo Entertainment

JP: May I request you to introduce yourself.

Raman: I am your partner in co-founding Sony Entertainment Television. I run my own company called Shemaroo. I am 67 and live in Mumbai and I have Kutchi roots. I also spent time farming in Kutch.

JP: Tell us a little bit about your background—where you grew up and how you ended up in Bombay.

Raman: My father was a farmer from Kutch. My elder brother came to Bombay for his education and I came in 1963–1964 for my higher education since Kutch has limitation. My brother had a humble beginning, a very unique business space where he was renting fiction books, comics, and periodicals.

JP: At what age did you come to Bombay?

Raman: I came to Bombay when I was 13 years old, which was in 1964, and completed my SSC at that time; then I finished my BSc and my brother asked me to join and assist in the business.

JP: What is the background of the business?

Raman: The business was a very unique business at that time. When I joined Shemaroo after I finished my studies in 1970, it was a book circulating library. I saw the opportunity in 1975, when VHS was invented, to do something similar and go beyond just renting out books, to renting out VHS cassettes. That led me to assembling blank video cassettes for industrial purpose, for mass use, and that gave me the chance to start my own VHS video label named Shemaroo in 1986.

Since I was in that business and interacting with all the prominent film production houses and all the big creative people, I also started getting some cable rights and some paid television rights. The story is very interesting after that, it took a turn in December 1993 when I met you. It was an interesting journey being in the promoter group for Sony Entertainment Television, with some very important partners like you, Sudesh, and Shergill. It was a fascinating journey.

JP: Beside Sony Entertainment Television, you continued to grow Shemaroo very actively.

Raman: Yes, Shemaroo is my first love and is very special. When I started a video label, my idea was to make Shemaroo a complete content house, or in US terms—a studio, in which you produce, you aggregate, and you own content—and I am happy to tell you that today Shemaroo is a mini Bollywood studio which owns the perpetual rights of over a 1,000 movies—we own those movies. The second thing, my vision was for Shemaroo to grow especially by exploiting the rights, whether in home video which is DVD or Blue Ray or licensing to movie channels or Doordarshan. It gave me tremendous growth since I had perpetual rights, it also gave me the power to be in the digital world. And the next story is going to be in the digital world.

JP: Shemaroo is listed on the public stock exchange. Tell us about that journey.

Raman: We had a small offering to the general public; the IPO was done three and half years ago. I am happy to tell you that we are the third biggest content partner for Google out of India on revenue terms. We are also the content partner and have a good relationship with all prime digital platforms like Netflix and Amazon Prime. We are among the must-carry content for all the networks, including the prominent four networks. We have a licensing relationship and business with each of them and a considerable business with Doordarshan, which is still mainstream, and their reach is unimaginable, it's a local traditional network.

JP: You started from very humble beginning and have successfully achieved wealth and affluence. What is your perspective on money?

Raman: I am a little philosophical in that sense. Money did not matter to me when I had none, and I don't give importance to money even today. My life philosophy is that we create money, money doesn't create us and that humbles me. I am a farmer's son and we have gone through life—I would not say hardship—but I would say I really loved those kind of lessons that life taught us. I don't give too much importance to money.

JP: Have you thought about what you will do with all this money?

Raman: I personally always believed that I owe it to society, and we must give back. Different people give in different ways, I do my own thing. My elder brother, who founded Shemaroo and who is still our chairman, has a philosophy for his philanthropy work. He believes in giving back to society. I did not understand it in the beginning, but I never questioned his intention. Our roots and connection are very different as it is a backward district in Gujarat; and we thought about what we could do there. Since we have 22 acres of our ancestral land, I started thinking about how do I do modern farming, how do I generate employment, how do I show the kids and other people how to do modern farming?

So, I invested in (a) infrastructure, to show people how you can make a difference, (b) attract experts, as it is almost a desert where water is scarce, rainfall is irregular or negligible, and the water quality is medium. In these circumstances, I have taken up the challenge to farm in a different way by hiring an acclaimed Israeli consultant firm to guide me and advise me, (c) generate local employment. I am very satisfied with what I have been doing in the last four years.

JP: Tell us more about this experiential life that you are living, because you live in Mumbai and the 22 acres are in Kutch.

Raman: I was in Kutch six years ago for my spiritual journey and it allowed me to introspect on what else I could do. Being a farmer's son, I thought I should be setting an example, attracting youth and other people to make similar investment or effort. A lot of people come to see my agricultural method, my dripping system, the making of my composite fertiliser, and then sending the liquid form through to the plant. There is a precision water system requirement for each plant, which I have developed with Jain Irrigation. I don't know yet whether I will generate any profits or not, but I want to make it self-sustained; I want it to generate employment, I want to show people the way to get inspired to have similar infrastructure. Whether you want to do cash crops or other crops, at least you can get some advice based on my effort and research to find out what is the optimum possibility on your land.

JP: We all worked through the days of building the business at Sony Entertainment Television and you took Shemaroo to the public market; and then along the way you discovered spiritualism. Please tell us about your spiritual journey.

Raman: I was a complete non-believer or whatever term you would use. But as it happened, in the formative years of my life I had a friend from 1964–1969; we were together in school, the same batch and somehow, he became a Jain monk and achieved such brilliance in 43 years. I met him periodically, but I was in my own 'dhunki' and running my own rat race. Each time I met him, he would say one thing, "You lost out." The question in my mind was, "Why did such a brilliant person chose the path of renouncing the world?"

It so happened, seven years ago Jain Muni Mohodey Sagar, my childhood friend, had a chaturmas in our village, and I met him again a year ago to pay my respects. During that meeting, he said, "I am going to spend chaturmas in your village, so can you attend one chaturmas, since you are my childhood friend?" I thought that this is an opportunity to learn about my religion, and why is he on this path. This is about six years ago. I promised him that for 163 days I would be in his command, I would not do anything without his command. I had almost virtually cut off my relationship with the world and the business world, except I had told him to allow me one hour of communication in the afternoon, in case my office had a question. That completely changed my life. In my spiritual journey the net net thing that I learnt and should be practicing is how to know your inner self. Basically, the four principles are the 4Ss—Shradha meaning implicit faith, Sweekar meaning complete acceptance, Samarparn meaning total dedication, and Sambhav meaning that in any condition you must not yo-yo between a state of unhappiness and happiness. It takes a long time to realise, but I am just trying to practice these four basic pillars.

As you go deeper in each of them, the two important things— Shradha, which is implicit faith, and faith you cannot question, it is paramount and the foundation of the spiritual journey. And the second is Sweekar, which is acceptance of any condition we are put in—be it economical, physical or relationship-wise. In any condition we cannot get bogged down with the thought "Why me?" You have to follow these four principles completely. I think it helps.

I don't want to be intelligent. Instead, I want to be the most non-complicated, non-manipulative person. Can I achieve that? That's my motto. I have a long way to go and I am just at the beginning. Jayesh, I would also like to say that you are a very spiritually blessed person who has corrected me on a few things in my life in the last 19–20 years of our friendship.

Raghuvinder Kataria

Chairman, Kataria Holdings

JP: May I request you to introduce yourself.

Raghuvinder: I am approaching 70, now settled in Dubai and basically retired. I grew up in Uganda. I went there when I was five years old and did all my primary and secondary education there. Then I moved to London for further education. I became a chartered accountant and then treasury management. Then I took up a job with a computer/telecom company and I was there for 17 years.

JP: All in London?

Raghuvinder: All in London. Then I moved to Bangkok to start a telecom company there, which was highly successful and from Bangkok, I sold it and moved to India to start yet another telecom company.

JP: And where was this?

Raghuvinder: In India, we had bid for mobile licenses, one in Karnataka, one in Andhra Pradesh, and one in Punjab—we won all three. Then I set up a consortium with Telia from Sweden and my Thai company Jasmine from Thailand. We had local sponsors as well—United Telecom, India Cements. But then there was this Asian crisis and the Thai telco could not honour their commitments, so, we had to buy them out and bring in another investor. We brought in Sunil Mittal who was running a telecom company in Delhi. The name of the game was footprint. We got started from connectivity and it had to be seamless. That was our first step to building connectivity and later on, because of our size and being a dominant player in the Indian market, we started picking up all the small operators who were struggling. They were struggling for finance because government policies were not clear. That's how we built Bharti Telecom as India's largest telecom company.

JP: Which year was that?

Raghuvinder: That was 1998–2001, and in 2002 I handed over the reins of the company to Sunil Mittal, and I took a backseat. He is much younger than I am, and with much more energy to fight the Indian bureaucracy. I moved to Dubai.

JP: What was your perspective on money as you were growing up in various countries like Uganda, London, and India?

Raghuvinder: Money was always a scarce commodity. I came from a lower-middle-class family and until my student days, I was depending on my father's remittances of £50 a month, which was not great, but was enough for me to survive.

JP: And where was your father living?

Raghuvinder: He was working in Uganda. Then Idi Amin kicked him out, so he became a refugee. He came back to India and then I was on my own, I had no money. Then I was offered an opportunity in India to drill borewells for irrigation purposes in Andhra Pradesh. All the wealthy people were investing in vineyards because it was a way to gets tax-free income, but it's a semi-arid region, water was scarce, and so everybody needed a borewell. The water level had fallen so low, that normal local machines could not drill down to that. These people persuaded me to buy the latest equipment from America, which could drill through the rocks. After some research, I took up that challenge; went to India and I was offered equity participation—which was driving me. But life was rough and this equipment from America was too sophisticated for the working conditions in India. It kept breaking. The breakdown time was more than the time it was working, like an aircraft when these rigs are not working they're eating money, and after about two and a half years, the business packed up. I was penniless. I borrowed some money from somebody to buy my ticket back to London, and from then on it was a struggle, until I got a job. I did all sorts of things, I did paper rounds, I did driving, and I washed cars.

JP: What was the inflection point, when from being a salaried employee, you decided to become a businessman?

Raghuvinder: The inflection point came when after 17 years of working, constantly learning, and contributing to the company, they were not able to reward me in a commensurate manner. Also, I was the first Indian to hold the position of a treasurer at that time, and I was paid half the salary of other treasures in the same position. I decided that it was not working for me, that I needed to do something for myself, and then I went to Thailand.

JP: But you had the ability to take risk?

Raghuvinder: I had nothing to lose.

JP: Fast forward to today, you are here in Dubai and you have done extremely well. Share with us the journey of how you got here, your perspective on money, and how it's changed.

Raghuvinder: Well, from the days of hardship when you were able to take risks because you had nothing to lose, the coin has turned upside down. Today there's plenty of money for our every want and need, but we have become risk averse in the fear of losing this wealth through stupid mistakes, and are trying to avoid these mistakes all the time, and they are happening everywhere, every day, whether by governments or central bankers or bankers or whoever. I learnt that you should not get bogged down in any investment in which you have to spend your personal time and effort to make the show happen. Today, you want your money to work for you, not you working for money. In that process a lot has changed but my value for money has not changed, and I still like to tell everybody — don't waste money, use it for a good cause. When you have plenty, then you automatically feel socially responsible for your surroundings, friends and relatives, whoever, to make sure that they're comfortable in their own life.

We run a philanthropic trust, primarily to finance medical treatment and education because with education you can change the lives of people. Then they can stand on their own feet and be more successful, and then they will take care of their surroundings. There is so much poverty that people are not able to afford medical treatment, and every now and then, we come across a case that needs to be handled. About five years ago, we started Heart Care Foundation in India, where our aim was to carry out one heart procedure every day. We try to save one life every day. That's working now, hundreds of people have benefitted from it and it's not just doing procedure or heart bypass or stent or valve replacement, it is the cost of medication post-surgery which these people cannot afford. We have also committed to giving them free medicine for the rest of their lives. I have a dear friend, who is a consultant cardiologist, he was also head of the Medical Society of India, he is also been honoured by the government.

He was the president of the Medical Association, and he is in charge of running this foundation. Today a lot of hospitals have come forward to contribute what they have, either make available the operation theatre, doctors come and perform surgeries for free, we supply all that's required and after-care, so the machinery is working. We've been in the northern part of India, and we are gradually spreading all over India and to other countries.

JP: A lot of millennials are going to come into a lot wealth. Do you have a view in terms of how wealth should be passed to the next generation, and do you have any worry in terms of how that wealth will be utilised by the next generation?

Raghuvinder: Yes, what I observed is that millennials do not know the value of money. It's just been easy for them to have access to whatever money they require. They only know how to spend it. They have no real appreciation for the value of money because they have never been starved. The second thing, the attitude of the millennials is such that they only want to enjoy the moment, to do what they think they want to do instantly, without considering the wider impact in the community, society, family, friends, whatever— that's not on their agenda at all. As long as their needs are being met, they don't care about where the money is coming from. If you let them, or if you believe that they will be able to look after this money, I think you will be highly mistaken.

JP: The big question is, what shall we do with all this money?

Raghuvinder: Well, money on its own is not everything. It's a means to an end; it's not an end in itself. But it's better to have the money than not have it, because then at least you're in a position to be able to do something that you want to do, to improve lives of people or your own family or friends, so that you are in a socially responsible position to be able to do it. Now to sustain that you need a well-managed team, who will professionally manage this money to make sure that it grows consistently, to be able to meet all your philanthropic activities and the family's requirements. You're not depending on any one person, it's a professional body; we call it a Family Office. People will come and go, but the structure is such that guidelines have been laid down, and we have to follow it.

JP: Would you like to share any wisdom or give any advice to the millennials?

Raghuvinder: According to millennials, we don't know anything. They are the people of the twenty-first century, and we don't understand what this life is all about, we are old-fashioned. We are not dynamic enough according to their perspective of life, and something needs to be done to change that. You have to be able to size yourself up in comparison to this big world, be it the media, the hype, Bollywood, Hollywood or large philanthropic trusts, and you'll understand that you are only a small operator, and so be responsible in whatever you do. You can't change the world, but you can contribute towards the change.

Rakesh Malhotra
Founder, Luminous Power Technologies and SAR Group

JP: May I request you to introduce yourself.

Rakesh: I was born and raised in Delhi. My father was a civil servant and my mother a homemaker. We had a comfortable life but disciplined to the core. An upright bureaucrat, my father wanted at least one of his children to become an IAS officer—but both my sister and I chose a different career path. I passed out from Jadavpur University, Calcutta, my engineering school in 1983. About a year and a half and four jobs later, a restless soul, I wanted to do something on my own. By March 1985, I was already on my way to starting my first business.

JP: What was that first business?

Rakesh: I started off designing a power backup system for PCs. The first DOS PCs with monochrome monitors were just being introduced. I got hold of two experienced engineers who used to work for C-Dot (Centre for Development of Telematics), who helped me with the design of our first product. We started out of a room in the apartment we were living in and business actually went off pretty well in the beginning. However, the products were not fully tested for reliability and after selling a lot of them, they started to fail at customer premises all over the country. The next year and a half were spent trying to fix these problems unsuccessfully. We chose to refund the money to our customers and take back the defective products. All the money that came from friends, family, and my father's provident fund was wiped out.

JP: Growing up, what was your perspective on money?

Rakesh: Growing up in a middle-class home with strong values, you are conditioned to not be too materialistic. I don't remember any time that I felt that I needed a lot of money. It was never in my DNA because we never felt that any other way of life would be much better than the way of life we grew up with. Our perspective on money was that it's good to have but it's not what it takes to be happy.

JP: Where did the ambition to become an entrepreneur come from?

Rakesh: I think it was the desire to create something meaningful. I am not even sure if I had an ambition to create a large business. It just happened.

JP: At the end of that first business, did you shut it down and start the second one?

Rakesh: Yes, I did shut it down with a significant debt on my head. The second business started in 1988, this time at the other side of the pendulum—over-conservative, never take on debt, never introduce the product before you are ready with service, and it has been tested for reliability.

From 1988–2006, we built Luminous Power Technologies one brick at a time, with zero debt and zero outside equity. The business grew from scratch to about 100 odd crore in revenue by 2006. A successful brand, reasonably well recognised, well reputed for quality—Luminous became a branded consumer durables business but by that time competition had caught up. In fact, by 2007, two of our closest competitors who started after us were about twice our size because they took all the risk, expand quickly, moved in to new geographic areas and introduced products faster. I guess we stuck to our guns and that became a part of our value system—to do it right, not necessarily be the first. That eventually paid off.

By 2006, we realised that we had to be cautious and prudent but not necessarily completely risk averse. In 2007, we raised our first round of private equity from CLSA Capital Partners, late stage private equity infusion 19 years after starting the business. Of course, the strong foundation paid off very well. That was also the time when India was recovering from the aftermath of the 2008 financial crisis, and as a country we weren't doing as badly as the rest of the world. We experienced exponential growth as the economy recovered, our revenues went from ₹100 crore to ₹1,200 crore in just five years' time by 2011. That was a rapid rise and all our competition was left behind in those four-five years. Our foundation was extremely strong and then once we decided to loosen the limitation, it just took off. Luminous Power Technologies was a company that was involved in power back-up solutions and home electricals like fans and lighting.

In 1991, one of my cousins joined me as a partner. Navneet and I have travelled our entrepreneurial journey from 1991 till date. We grew the Luminous business together and both of us had no personal assets outside of this business—zero personal capital. I used to joke that we are both poor founders of a rich company. The company was making ₹150 crore profit every year and both of us were still drawing our middle-class salary of ₹50 lakh a year, happily living our life.

In 2010, I got a bit of a health scare (which turned out to be false). I was diagnosed with liver infection, my doctor told me it was really serious. I thought myself, "This is not really good."

This sudden health scare was like a wake-up call for me and I realised that I had to concentrate on my health, devote time to my family and follow a more balanced lifestyle.

I felt that this concentration risk was not worthwhile for the family and the other stakeholders. We decided that we should diversify ourselves and get some liquidity by monetising our shareholding in Luminous. At that stage, we looked at partially selling off the equity that we had built in the company. We owned pretty much all of the business. The private equity partner had just 10 per cent and we owned 90 per cent of the company. We could afford to sell a fair bit without losing control.

JP: What was the transaction?

Rakesh: You asked me what money meant to me—money meant freedom to me at that point in time. No matter how much money we had in my company, I had no time to devote to my family. Both my children had grown up without my having spent much time with them.

Although Yash was still in school, Kamakshi was ready to leave for college in the US that year. I went to their first parent teacher meeting when they were in kindergarten and then the next time was when she was passing out of school, nothing in between. My wife, Nirupama, had to take care of the children pretty much on her own. There was a certain amount of regret I had about not being able to give time to people who mattered the most to me.

I realised that if I sold the company then I could do a lot of things as I was still young at 49. I could do things that excited me, whether it is creating new businesses or working on social impact, and do so at my time and pace. That got me hooked. I said, "Ab to ye poori hi bechhenge."

Schneider Electric came along and made us an offer very, very quickly. I think I met their country head on a Monday and by the end of that week, one of their ExCom members was in our office and the week after their CEO was there. We agreed on the transaction and shook hands in two and half or three weeks' time. Of course, it took six months to close the deal thereafter. We agreed and said, "You buy 74 per cent of the stake and we will keep 26 per cent. We will still run it like a joint venture." Navneet and I, both, continued on the board and I took on the role of the chairman of the company. We grew the company together pretty well. It actually turned out to be a very successful acquisition for Schneider.

JP: Please tell us more about the transaction?

Rakesh: We sold 74 per cent for something close to ₹1,400 crore and out of which our charitable trust held a little bit of the equity, our employees had a little bit and the investors had about 10 per cent of the equity.

JP: What about the remaining 26 per cent equity?

Rakesh: It was between Navneet and me. We retained that.

JP: And you still have it today?

Rakesh: We sold all of that in January 2017, finally. We are completely divested out of that business.

JP: At that point in time, when you came into money, what were the thoughts that went through your mind?

Rakesh: Frankly, it was relief at having monetised something that was a super growth business. We knew that it had a lot of potential ahead of it and that's why we insisted on keeping 26 per cent and it turns out that was the best thing to happen to that business. When we sold it was ₹1,250 crore top line and about ₹130 crore of EBIDTA, and in 2014, by the time we were actually supposed to exit completely, it had already become a ₹2,300 crore business. It turned out to be a successful relationship eventually and worked well for everyone.

JP: At that point in time, after the multiple exits that you had, did you know what you wanted to do with the money?

Rakesh: We set up a family office structure with a dedicated team and conservatively started investing the corpus that we had created. We also started a company called LivPure, which is a brand for purity, health, and wellness related appliances in India. It's already the third largest player in the country. Navneet is the chairman and there is a professional team managing it. There are about 1,800 people in that company, it is already quite a sizeable business, two private equity investors are invested and the business is going full steam ahead.

JP: Is that the only business?

Rakesh: That was the first one. Then in 2014, we were supposed to get out of the Luminous shareholding, when they wanted us to stay back, we negotiated to buy out the automotive battery business out of Luminous. It was a tiny ₹30 crore business and they were not focussed on it, as they wanted to focus on the electrical segment. We said, "We will buy this out from you, and you clear our non-compete clause in automotive and electric vehicle segment." We created that business, which is now at a substantial stage—2,000 employees and ₹1,600 crore of revenue this year.

JP: What is your perspective on money today?

Rakesh: It's no different. It's given me freedom. I can travel and spend time with my family. I can invest with confidence and help create start-ups and I can enable social impact at scale through our foundation and its partners.

We moved to Singapore in 2015. Kamakshi had started working here, so that was a good reason to come to Singapore. We have setup a platform called Ncubate Capital for making investments in early stage start-ups. Even entrepreneurs who are at a stage where they are not very clear about their model, we can partner with them, guide them through that process, provide them with seed capital, and may be even handhold management for a while and then leave it to the founders. This is what I spend some of my time doing now. I am having fun doing this.

JP: What is your philosophy on utilisation of wealth?

Rakesh: The philosophy is that one is not going to give more than X amount of money to their kids—enough to give them a head start but not enough to spoil them. They should find their own way. You have given them good education and values along with a bit of capital, enough to allow them to build their own life. That is my philosophy and its returns are infinite, because it prepares them to take on the world. I think this is working well.

We have been putting a part of our equity of any company that we start into our charitable trust. We started this trust in 2008 and its objective is to focus on primary health, primary education, and employment generation at the very bottom of society. There is an organisation of 14 highly committed people who are running the activities of this trust along with other partner organisations. These are folks that are personal friends, they are done with their careers, and want to do something good. We have set up a rigorous filtration and funnel management process for various special impact projects that come to us. We have also established a robust partner evaluation process using which we choose partner organisations for implementing our various projects.

In the early years, from 2008–2011, we tried implementing projects directly. We realised that you can only do so much execution yourself and while it may make you feel emotionally good because you are connected to the actual action on the ground, it does not leave the impact that is required. From 2012, we created a partnership model for implementation and over the years we have developed close working relationships with nine high quality partners. We are scaling up every year with these partners and also adding new relationships that come up through the collection process. In India, we are currently present in West Bengal, Maharashtra, Punjab, Haryana, Himachal, and UP. Last year our projects impacted about half a million people.

JP: What do you plan to do with all this money, in terms of the future?

Rakesh: I think institutionalising the process is the most critical issue. What we have found very clearly is that you don't need more than what is necessary for the family's requirements—that's figured out. We still have to figure out a complete alignment even within the family; I might have one view and my wife might have another view. Mothers would generally want to be more protective of the kids, none the less that is only a matter of percentage of so much allocation, X or Y, which still won't be a major part. Thus, you have funds available to give to the other two causes—supporting entrepreneurship is one area that I am pursuing, and the other one is the social impact at grassroots level.

JP: Do you still have companies that you are invested in which are doing extremely well?

Rakesh: Yes, hopefully they will create more value that leaves the trust with some capital in perpetuity to work with. It can't flow to individual family members any which way, beyond a point.

JP: Any words of wisdom for the affluent and wealthy in terms of what to do with their money?

Rakesh: To each his own. Everyone will have a different view of what they want to do with their wealth. There is so much to be done, you pick your little piece and work on it. I think with everyone doing his or her bit the sum total will work out well. There are plenty of resources and there is plenty of intent—I see it all around. All these people that we partner with have started these initiatives after having been successful elsewhere in terms of business or careers. Clearly, the intent to make an impact with the wealth that you create is quite widespread now. People are still struggling though to figure out what is the right way to do it. I think that is where the real challenge lies. I think that's the discovery process all of us have to go through.

Satish Gupta
Founder, Excel Cabinets and Interiors

JP: May I request you to introduce yourself.

Satish: I live in Gig Harbor, Washington; it's a small fishing town. Basically, retirees live here. It's right on the ocean. It's a little bay and people come here to retire, and especially if they are into fishing or boating. It's about an hour and fifteen minutes southwest of Seattle and I moved here in 2001, from Nebraska.

I used to own a factory, manufacturing cabinets, and custom cabinets. Then I sold that company and moved over here to retire. For eight years, I was a bum; I didn't do anything, and I enjoyed it. I wanted to pursue my hobbies, which are several. I was only 44 when I retired. My wife said to me that I was too young, and I needed to be more productive. I was only 44 when I retired. I am on my second career now. I am a part time professor at a college, a local college, teaching micro and macroeconomics.

JP: Where did you grow up and what brought you to the United States?

Satish: I was raised in New Delhi. I have done my BA Honours in Economics from Delhi University. I wanted to pursue my Master's in Economics and become a professor, but my parents did not approve because my father was in business and he said there is no money in being a professor. He sent me off to Bombay, where my brother had a big business. He wanted me to learn business, help them, and be a part of the family's business. My brother knew that I wanted to study; he said that in India the law is always changing. He told me that he would teach me all about the business, but he wanted me to go to school again, but this time he wanted me to study law. In the morning, I would go to law school and in the evening, I would help him with his business. I did that for two years. I finished the two years of law, but I did not finish the third year. Then, I got a chance to come to USA.

I decided that I am going to do what I really like, which is economics; I went back to school and earned a Master's degree in Economics from the University of Nebraska. Unfortunately, I graduated in 1981, and there was a big recession, and there were no jobs. I went back to school, learnt a little bit of computer science and got a job as a programmer, but I did not have a background in programming, just enough to write simple programs. I was then hired by a company to run their purchasing and personnel department. It was the biggest in that area, manufacturing custom cabinets. They liked my work and I became a general manager there; I did that for four years.

The owner and I had some conflict about the direction the company should take—we disagreed and then I started my own business. In 1987, I started my own custom cabinet business with a local partner, an American from the neighbouring state of Iowa. I was in Nebraska and from 1987–2000, I ran this company and became very successful; and then somebody made me a good offer to buy the company. I thought it was a good opportunity to sell the company and pursue my hobbies—so I sold the company in December 2000 and moved to Seattle in 2001.

JP: Why did you move to Seattle?

Satish: I knew that business was not my passion. I was good at business, may be because my family background is business. But at the back of my mind, I really wanted to pursue my hobbies— reading, travelling, gardening, watching documentaries, and listening to music. I have several hobbies. I knew at the back of my mind that I am going to sell this company at some point, so I bought a couple of books on the best places to retire in America and during the time I was running my company, I would go and visit those places. I picked seven places out of those two books. One was in Florida, one was in Texas, one was in Arizona, a couple of places in North Carolina and one was in Washington and when I came over here, as I am very much into nature I was really overwhelmed by the beauty of this area. Another beauty of this area is that it's so close to British Columbia, which is very beautiful. It is very close to Idaho or Montana, and to the south is Oregon, which is very beautiful and then you go further south, it's California. To me this was just the perfect place to retire and the icing on cake was that there is no state income tax in Washington State. My economic interest and my natural interest converged, and I decided to move to Seattle. I did not know anybody here when I moved, but to me it was a good choice to move to Gig Harbor.

JP: Most people engage themselves in managing their money—how about you?

Satish: I have a background in economics, and I read The Wall Street Journal every day, cover to cover. They have a lot of articles about how to invest money. They also review a lot of books. Since I know economics and I have an accounting background, it is very easy to follow financial books. I managed to find some friends here. There are five or six of us and they all are retired, they all are Americans and we get together every other month at somebody's house and for three hours we just discuss different ideas, somebody has read another book, or somebody has a better idea about investing money. Between reading Wall Street, financial books, and having friends that are in a similar boat—retired well off and they also want to get a good return on their investment—all this combined allows me to stay retired and not have to worry about money.

JP: Tell us about your travels.

Satish: I am into train travel. Sometimes, I will just take a train trip across Europe or take the train trip across South America, whenever I go to California, I take a train rather than the plane. I am also into drives. I have three friends that are also into drives, so what we do is we just take our car and drive—not just any drive, we read books which shows you which are the most beautiful drives. Once, we drove to Alaska for 10 days. Another time, we flew to Florida and rented a car and for 10 days we covered all the scenic highways in Florida. Last September, we took a train across Canada. I don't like cities, I like nature. For example, my friend is visiting so we will go to Montana and Idaho for a week and then we are going to drive along the coast from Washington all the way to LA, along the coast on Highway 1 and 101.

I support some schools in the foothills of Himalayas, so I go to India every year, and I supervise my schools for poor people. They are up to fifth grade. Every year, I go to some new part of India that I have not seen, whether it is Sikkim, Ladakh, Kerala, or Karnataka. This year, when we go to India, we are going to cover some parts of Rajasthan we have not seen.

JP: What is the longest train journey you have taken?

Satish: The longest train trip I have done is from Vancouver to Nova Scotia, which takes five nights by train.

JP: It sounds like you have discovered what to do with your time. My next question is, what shall we do with all this money?

Satish: I strongly believe that we should donate it. I have told my wife and kids and they agreed. I am going to divide my money into three parts. I have two daughters. I am going to give one-third to each daughter, and one-third I am going to donate.

JP: Are your daughters going to inherit this money while you are alive?

Satish: No, the reason they will not inherit the money while I am alive is because if I give it to them now, they will not have any sense of self-accomplishment. They will get this money only when they don't need it. I want them to be completely self-sufficient and not rely on this money. This money will be like icing on the cake. They know that this money is not for them until we leave this place. They also know that if they do not care for us in our old age, then they will not be inheriting any money. It depends upon their behaviour towards us when we get old.

JP: And do they know this?

Satish: Yes, they know this.

JP: Do they know what they want to do with that money when they get it?

Satish: Well, my younger daughter wants to retire like me, at 45. She says, "Dad, I want to retire young." She wants to pursue her hobbies, like me. My older daughter, she has not decided what she is going to do, she does not even know what she is going to get. She is not a money-minded person, so she doesn't care. They know that if they never come to visit us or take care of us when we are old, then we will just donate the rest of the money.

Actually, my daughters are doing really well. They are too young — they are only 22 and 24. If they do very well, they don't need my money, and then my goal will be to donate all of it.

JP: Can you tell us a little bit about your philanthropy?

Satish: In India, there is an organisation call Ekal Vidyalaya and they run schools for poor people in the remote areas of India, I am supporting them. If I find somebody, for example, I was in Calcutta once and I found a driver who was very nice, and he was poor. He was working in Calcutta and his family was in UP. I send him money every month to supplement his income. My goal is to find more people like that, people that have worked all their life, but in India, there is no social security system. I want to be their social security system for people who have worked all their lives, and are now in their old age, but they are not able to support themselves. In terms of charity, there are so many alternatives in India that you can pretty well decide what area you want to focus on.

Suketu Shah
Managing Director, Novotech

JP: May I request you to introduce yourself.

Suketu: I was born and brought up in Mumbai till the second standard, and then I shifted to Tokyo. My father was a director in a Japanese company and I finished my schooling in Tokyo, where I attended an American school. I had a choice either to go to the US or to India for my Bachelor's degree—I chose to go to India. I got into IIT but did not enjoy it as much and decided to follow a regular Bachelor's degree in Science at St. Xavier's, Mumbai. After that, I moved to the US to do my MBA and for the last 25 years, I have been spending most of my time in Singapore and in the last 10–12 years, commuting back and forth between Mumbai and here (Singapore). The primary reason for staying in India was that my parents and my wife's parents lived in India, and I wanted our son to experience Indian culture, which I had missed out on.

JP: Tell us about your standard of living while you were growing up. What was your perspective on money then?

Suketu: While we were growing up, my father was employed by a Japanese company. It was quite tough for him because he had two children to take care of and he refused to put us in a local school. He wanted us to go to an international school and this is in the 60s and 70s, when there were very few foreigners in Japan, in Tokyo. Most of the people were employed either with a large multinational company or the embassies. It was a challenge for him, and my mother sacrificed a lot to ensure that we at least have good education. That's what my dad said, "Look, I can't give you all the fancy things in life but in your education there is going to be no compromise." He never drove a car in Tokyo, so we used public transport. We used to go to India once in two years; we couldn't afford to go every year. No real perspective on money then as my parents gave me a weekly allowance for school and snacks, while they took care of everything else. I will always remain grateful to my parents for having the guts to settle in Japan, for securing our future.

JP: And you read and write Japanese?

Suketu: Yes, to a certain extent. Japanese has several different ways of writing: hiragana, katakana, and kanji. I am quite okay with hiragana and katakana.

JP: What is your perspective on money today?

Suketu: God has been extremely kind, and I have been extremely lucky being at the right place, at the right time, doing the right things. I was fortunate enough to do a dual MBA in Finance and Marketing and straight out of college, after finishing the MBA, I had a job waiting for me. I was able to move into the work stream very quickly without any financial pressure or burden. We got married within three months of starting my job. We were going around for four years prior to getting married in the US and life was fine between the nice pay that I had with my company and whatever my wife wanted to do. We didn't really feel the need for money. Then after working there for two and a half years, we were asked to move to Singapore. We were on an expatriate package where housing was paid, car was given, education was supposed to be covered. Thus, the lifestyle growing up, and then during the young starting-off phase where a lot of people had to go through tough situation, didn't really have any detrimental effect on us. When we were assigned back to the US, we had enough savings where at a very young age I was able to afford our own home. We got cars, homes; all those were fairly easy to come by.

JP: And then you switched from being an executive to an entrepreneur?

Suketu: I was at a crossroads because when I turned 30 and it came down to—do I want to continue with the corporate world, or do I want to do something on my own? As far as the corporate world was concerned, I was extremely happy. There was no issue of not really being able to do what I really wanted or being unhappy from the job perspective. I knew that if I chose to stay in the company, I would have continued with that same company and probably retired at that company.

The only thing that drove me was the fact that I came from a business background from my father's side. After working in a Japanese company, my father started his own business and even before he went to Japan, while he was employed in a mill, he was always doing something on the side and earning income from a business perspective. I said to myself, "I really want to do this!" Then I got out of the corporate world.

JP: Describe your business journey then.

Suketu: Basically, we decided with my wife Ami's full support that we are going to get out—so, first things first—we sold our house; we sold our cars, and only after those things were done, did we put in the resignation.

At that time I had come into contact with an individual whom I called Kaka, a person with spiritual powers graced by Mother Goddess; he told me that I would flourish in the far-east. That made my decision a lot easier; and we narrowed it down to Singapore because we had already spent a couple of years here. Our son was gifted to us and we went through the simultaneous journey of a new born, new business life, and new friends in Singapore. I did reach a stage where I had exhausted all our funds. With no income in sight the only option was to go back to a job. I appealed to Kaka and he assured me that he would take care of it. Within a short time, an MNC agreed for me to distribute their products and our financial struggles soon became history. Whatever I have become today, regardless of my efforts, it is only because of the blessings and grace of Kaka, who we consider our Guruji, and Mother Goddess.

JP: What is your perspective on money in the current times?

Suketu: To be frank, we have been extremely blessed, so we never felt the desperation or the difficulties that can come with not having sufficient money. As far as money is concerned because of being in a fortunate position and as my experience in the business world grew, different sorts of investments were considered and suggested, and I got involved in all kinds of things—whether it's a start-up, whether it was mezzanine project, whether it was funds, whether it was property investments. Slowly, over the years I built up various assets in different geographical territories and it has been a good journey. By and large, I feel very comfortable that there is nothing that I really need to be worried about. Money is not a concern.

JP: Besides family welfare and of course the next generation that we all want to look after, but beyond that, what shall we do with all this money?

Suketu: I am under the umbrella of my Guruji, due to which, about 20 years ago, I realised my life's mission, and I spoke to him about donating and he said, "Yes, you must." I started going down that path anonymously wherever possible, and we have been doing that for the last 20 years. We started saying, "X percentage of whatever I earn I need to donate." And that has been consistent—nothing other than pure donations to different causes. My wife Ami has wholeheartedly supported me throughout all these years. Over the years, we have always worked and strived to keep increasing that percentage. We are at the stage where, in rough terms, whatever I spend on my family, and myself, I should be able to spend the same to help and serve others as well. There has to be a certain amount of passion and joy in doing that. I started identifying a lot of different causes in a lot of different ways and I have started working more at a grassroots level, which is appealing to me rather than going to massive organisations and fundraisers.

JP: Please share a little bit more about the philanthropy you are doing. Are you giving to individuals or to non-profits?

Suketu: Both. Having spent the last 10 plus years in India, we have found a huge need in India, which is unbelievable, and what is surprising is how a small amount of money can impact in such a huge way, especially in India as compared to other countries. Being of Indian origin India is close to my heart and to our family, and we stay there a lot of the times. We do a lot of the work in Mumbai, the surrounding cities and villages, and of course we have branched out a little bit into neighbouring states and other places as and when we get a request.

On an individual level, where anything and anybody via the media or through our contacts, whosoever comes to us, no questions asked—simple, basic information just about the individual, no evidence, nothing—we simply try to help that person. Now that can be in different forms. It could be in the form of medicines and medical treatment; it could be educational support, books, and things like that; there are no specific guidelines that limit us. The whole idea is that we want to make it a very, very simple process for anybody who needs help to feel very comfortable to ask because it's not an easy thing to give or to ask.

Of course, we cannot reach out and do all the things that we need to do. We have to work with excellent organisations that exist and are doing a huge amount of work, but my focus has always been more of the grassroots levels. For example, where these institution are directly running a school or running a hospital or doing things that I can visit, I can see, and if asked, I help in whatever way I can—that is fun and a pleasure.

Ami and I are extremely grateful to everyone and God for even being given such opportunities to help and most of all, to our Guruji, for enabling us.

JP: Please describe the institutional giving.

Suketu: Institutional giving consists of two segments—(i) educational institutes, and (ii) medical institutes. We had an opportunity to tie up with several educational institutes, orphanages, as well as hospitals. That consists of helping with infrastructure facilities, planning, development of the institution, as well as doing whatever it takes on the site.

JP: I want you to have the final word in terms of what shall we do with all this money?

Suketu: Based upon my own Indian value system, I would be remiss to say that everything is just to be given away. I am sure that a certain percentage will be given to my family and for their needs, my son and hopefully his family should not have a lack of anything, I have ensured that.

Other than that, we have enough of a cushion where we can do whatever it takes and not say no to anyone who is in need. I should not have to calculate and wonder if I can do it. The answer should be yes, when, and how.

JP: Do you have any words of wisdom to share with us?

Suketu: I think everybody is giving back to the best of their capabilities. I think the whole generation is evolving. I think we have all gone through different phases in our life, where we used to basically look at doing things for our parents when we were very young, then our teachers, and then probably our girlfriends or spouses, and then our children. Now it's time to just do it for others—that's it and I think everybody is doing it.

Entrepreneurs

Syed Ali
Founder, CEO, and Chairman, Cavium

Sanjeev Bikhchandani
Founder, naukri.com

Kunal Shah
Founder, FreeCharge and CRED

Pranoti Nagarkar
Founder, Rotimatic

Venky Iyer
Founder, Goli Vada Pav

Syed Ali
Founder, CEO, and Chairman, Cavium

JP: May I request you to introduce yourself.

Syed: My career has been pretty much in semiconductors, building microchips since 1981. That's a long career in semiconductor. I was born in Hyderabad, India and spent a few of my early years in Bombay, did my middle school and high school in Hyderabad at Hyderabad Public School. I then attended Osmania University, Hyderabad for my undergraduate studies in Engineering. In 1980, I moved to the US for my Master's in Electrical Engineering at the University of Michigan, Ann Arbor. I graduated in 1981 and I was recruited to move to Silicon Valley, which was at the very early stages of becoming the high-tech mecca of the world. I have been in the Silicon Valley from 1981–2018, except for four years, from 1994–1998 when I lived Seoul Korea.

JP: What were you doing in Seoul?

Syed: In Seoul, I was working with Samsung Electronics in their semiconductor division and I was pretty much the only foreigner in the management team there. That was a very interesting experience, learning and living in an Asian culture. It taught me a lot; it give me an inside look into how large and very aggressive Korean businesses think about strategy, products and how they execute that strategy to become major players in the end-markets that they target. It was a very interesting learning experience. Obviously, Silicon Valley is kind of what honed me, but this was a really interesting, different look, if you will, at technology and how companies in Asia operate versus those in the US.

JP: Growing up, what was your standard of living and your perspective on money?

Syed: I came from a very typical middle-class background. My father was an engineer who worked for the central government. He worked in the department of atomic energy. He was the team recruited by Homi Bhabha to build the first nuclear reactor in Trombay. That's why we were in Bombay for my early primary school. Then he got

83

transferred to build ECIL, Electronics Corporation of India Limited — he was the chief engineer there. After that was done, he was moved over to Nuclear Fuel Complex, which is where they built nuclear fuel rods, so, pretty much a very standard middle-class background. My father was also born in Hyderabad. He also attended Osmania University for under graduate engineering.

JP: What was your standard of living and affluence once you started working in Silicon Valley?

Syed: I was hand to mouth. I came to the US with probably a total of $5,000 in my pocket and I had to pay my fees, and my living expenses so I did a teaching assistantship to supplement my income, but I was always broke, always. I still remember my total budget for the month, including my rent and food was $300 — half was for rent, as I shared a small place with four guys and the other half was for food. Essentially, my budget was $5 a day.

JP: Please tell us about your crossover from a senior executive to an entrepreneur.

Syed: I have been involved with start-ups since 1984. The first start-up I joined, I was one of the first 10 employees, and it was a company called WSI, Wafer Scale Integration. I was there for about eight to ten years after which I went to Korea; and then I came back from Korea and I co-founded a company called Malleable Technologies in 1998. The company was acquired in June 2000, right before the mid-market crashed. It was a great exit. There were only 30 people in the company, and we exited for like $180 million. We couldn't complain because we raised only $5 million in funding, there was a great return for everyone. After the acquisition I left and started a company called Cavium, founded that and got my first round of funding in June 2001; and we went public in 2007. Cavium was acquired by Marvell Technologies in 2018 for roughly $6.5 billion. The acquisition closed in July 2018. It was a good exit.

JP: What was the total amount of investment?

Syed: Roughly, around $45–50 million was the total funding, in four rounds of funding. The first round we did was $8 million.

JP: Congratulations! What is your perspective on money today?

Syed: One of the toughest things that both my wife and I find is that since we grew up in a middle-class environment, we can't spend money. It is very difficult for us to spend money. For example, even now, obviously we spend more than we did, but if I tell my wife, "Why don't you buy this $10,000 bag?" She replies, "I'd rather take that money and donate it than take it for myself." She spends almost nothing on herself. She says, "Okay, give me the money; I will do something rather than get these things." Obviously, your standard of living goes up, but we are still careful about trivial expenses and spending money on ourselves because you are what you grew up with in the first 20 years of your life, which pretty much defines who you are. It's not like an athlete or someone who wants to get money to go and buy yachts, private jets and then go broke at the end of the day. Essentially, we lead a very comfortable life but there is absolutely no way that we can spend even 10 per cent of the money, even if we did crazy stuff, and that's one of the challenges.

JP: You will set aside some money for your family welfare and then you will pass some money to the next generation. Beyond that, what will you do with all this money?

Syed: Actually, I think from an overall viewpoint, you have to give back. You have to give back to what made you or who made you or the region that made you. We do some stuff in the US. My wife has a non-profit in India that does a lot of work there. It's called We Are One, where she adopts villages, one village a year. If there is a borewell needed in the area because people have to walk a long distance to get water we pay for the borewell. We also pay for school supplies, scholarships, streetlights, and things like that. She is increasingly doing that sort of work. On my end, what I plan to do quite aggressively is help the industry in India, the technology industry in particular. I am just starting to get involved with state governments and I intend on getting involved with small start-ups as a mentor or investor or as a guide. The way I look at it—India is probably one of the most under-utilised resources of the world, very inefficient and most of the people think small and they are left small. I'm interested in mentoring companies to really think of a bigger stage, think about becoming global companies. I think this is going to be a very good and an extremely interesting endeavour for me.

JP: You want to spend more time nurturing these companies, but are you are also looking at making investments, either in the social development sector or in the technology sector?

Syed: Absolutely. I am just kind of spreading my wings, if you will— doing it on a global level and a local level. Silicon Valley, India, and Southeast Asia will be my primary focus.

JP: Have you also thought about the next generation? Do you want to hand over some of your wealth to the next generation now or in the future?

Syed: The way you do it is you set up a trust, which gives some access, say on a regular annual basis or something like that. Overall, there will also be charitable contributions allocated from that trust. I am in the process of putting the whole structure together; I had no time to do it before. When you are running a 100 miles an hour, these are not the kind of thoughts you have. You need to get some free time to just kick back and relax.

JP: Are you concerned at all that your kids know what you did?

Syed: They do, because my son is a venture capitalist.

JP: Are you concerned at all about the next generation because of this windfall that you just received?

Syed: No, I'm not. My son, Arman, says something very interesting. He makes a reasonable amount of money, but he also has difficulty spending it. I say, "Arman, why don't you buy these designer jackets or whatever it is?" He says, "You know what dad, we grew up middle-class." When they were growing up, we were kind of middle-class, even during Silicon Valley. Essentially, they really can't change their patterns dramatically. Obviously, the standard of living is higher than ours was, when we were growing up in India. Nevertheless, as we move forward those values that were engrained in them, they may change a little, but they are not going to flip completely to the other side.

JP: If I ask them what shall we do with all this money, what do you think their view will be?

Syed: Actually, it's very interesting, millennials are more socially conscious than people of our generation are, and they start from a very early age. They have very clear understanding of right and wrong, good and bad. I think they will actually be able to take it to the next level.

JP: Any words of wisdom for our readers?

Syed: Whenever University of Michigan has asked me to talk to their students, I say, "At the end of the day I was an average guy and kind of middle of the class, not a topper by any stretch of the imagination." The key advice I am giving to pretty much everybody is, "If I can do it anybody can."

JP: That's very humble of you. Congratulations, you have done an excellent job. One last thing, you are now in the transition of moving from Silicon Valley to Singapore. Tell us a little bit about that.

Syed: It's a very interesting transition. I lived in Silicon Valley forever and I wanted to move to Asia, obviously closer to India. Also, just spreading our roots in India in terms of mentorship, in terms of investment—that's going to be one of the things we will be focussing on, and who knows I might start another company. When you get two or three months to think fresh without any day to day pressures of running a company, you start to think of many interesting things and your thinking has no bounds. I think this is going to be a very interesting next phase of my career. I should be sitting on a beach somewhere, kind of kicking back—but I just can't do it.

Sanjeev Bikhchandani

Founder, naukri.com

JP: May I request you to introduce yourself.

Sanjeev: I am 55 years old. I've been an entrepreneur for the last 29 years. Among the companies and the brands that I have co-founded are Naukri, 99Acres, Jeevansathi, and Shiksha. In addition, we invested in start-ups like Zomato, Policy Bazaar, Meritnation, and a bunch of others, maybe 20 start-ups. Apart from that, I am the co-founder of Ashoka University. I grew up in Delhi and spent most of my life here. I studied at St Columba's School in Delhi, then St. Stephens College and finally I went to IIM Ahmedabad. I have worked as an executive in companies like Lintas and GlaxoSmithKline. I was in advertising, then marketing and then finally I became an entrepreneur.

JP: What was your standard of living growing up? Did you grow up in an affluent family?

Sanjeev: I wouldn't call it affluent. My father was in government and you know the way it was in India, at least in the 60s or 70s, if you were an honest government officer there wasn't a lot of money. There was no family money either because my parents had been refugees who had come over from Pakistan. We weren't affluent, but we had access to education, and I think that meant a lot.

JP: What was your perspective on money as you were growing up?

Sanjeev: Well, growing up there was never enough money because, as I said, my father was a government officer, and my mother was a homemaker. Therefore, there were always constraints for money at home, but you accept that, live within your means, and you get by.

JP: You have an illustrious entrepreneurial life. Take us through your journey from a career professional, to becoming an entrepreneur.

Sanjeev: I joined advertising straight after college, at Lintas. I worked in client servicing. Then I did my MBA from IIM Ahmedabad and post that I worked at GlaxoSmithKline in marketing. I was managing the brand Horlicks for a couple of years. Then I quit and became an entrepreneur. There was no venture capital then. You had to bootstrap and for seven years, I drifted into a whole lot of small stuff, running out of the servant's quarter above the garage in my father's house. Finally, after doing 50 small things we launched Naukri as one more small thing, and that kind of thing was very new in India. There were just 14,000 Internet accounts in the country. I thought it was a nifty small idea. I had no idea where Naukri would go. As I said, there was no venture capital in those days. We just did it because it looked like a good idea. We had to bootstrap for three years and then finally we raised venture capital, which I think was a turning point because we were able to invest in product, technology, and people and grow the business. In the year 2000, we raised venture capital and in 2006, we went public. Along the way, we diversified into matrimony, real estate, and education classifieds, and began to invest in other start-ups as well.

The company is now listed. We employ over 4,000 people. Our existing investee companies have over 10,000 people. It's become a fairly decent sized enterprise.

JP: What was the inflection point in your ongoing journey as an entrepreneur?

Sanjeev: There's never an inflection point, it's all a continuum. You sort of keep working every day, it's a daily fight. The challenges continue. It's not as if after we raised venture capital it's all okay, or after we went public it's all okay—there are new challenges all the time. Entrepreneurship is a continuous challenge.

JP: How did naukri.com suddenly become a huge enterprise?

Sanjeev: Well, it didn't suddenly become a huge enterprise. Like I said, for three years we bootstrapped. Then we raised venture capital, and then we had a challenge for another four years as we tried to scale the company and there was a meltdown at that time. There were always challenges. It took about 10 years to scale up.

JP: But somewhere down the line that idea must have been growing in your mind that this is a fantastic thing to do?

Sanjeev: Well, it was a good idea. I always felt it, but I never knew how large it would become, until maybe three or four years into the business, when we discovered that this could in fact be a large business.

JP: How has your perspective on money changed today?

Sanjeev: My perspective on money changed long back, even before we launched Naukri. I figured two or three years after being an entrepreneur that I was not chasing money. I was just chasing good work, excellence, innovation, and impacting people. Money is the happy incidental outcome of doing something you love.

JP: Today your family is affluent—is there a philosophy, a thesis on money in terms of how to use it. What shall we do with all this money?

Sanjeev: First, there is an institutional commitment. It basically means that a lot of the so-called affluence is tied into the shares of Info Edge, and if you want the institution to be stable and steady shape, you've got to be there, and you've got to have a stable ownership. It's not as if I'm here to sell the company and then have a lot of money in the bank. I think we are trying to build an institution that outlives the founders. You know successful companies really last 100 years, 150 years. We aspire to be that kind of an institution.

Having said that, I do a fair bit of philanthropy. There are at least 10 or 15 philanthropic causes that I back and as and when I get liquidity, I support those causes and the biggest one is Ashoka University.

JP: Can you please tell us a little bit about Ashoka University?

Sanjeev: It was conceived around 12 years ago. We felt there was possibly a need for a new kind of university in India which is focussed on liberal arts and sciences, which is what we went on to build. And it has taken a decade to bring it here.

JP: Can you also expand on some of the other philanthropies and your philosophy on giving?

Sanjeev: A lot of it is focussed on education, naturally. I have given to my school, college, and business school; to the institutions that shaped me. Other than that, we do look at doing stuff around healthcare, rural India, rural income, and around education for the underprivileged.

JP: What is your philosophy on the next generation? You have children—what is your take on upbringing vis a vis money?

Sanjeev: That's not a specific conversation we have had, but it is implicit that they would always have enough, but they have to work. It's not that they will be able to live off the family wealth. They all want to do something independent; none of them want to join the business.

JP: What is your perspective on life and money going forward?

Sanjeev: I haven't thought about it deeply because I'm always working, every day. However, I do think the first task of capital or wealth is (a) to preserve itself, (b) to grow and (c) to put it to good use so that you can make an impact on other people and all three are important.

JP: As we are aware, the millennials are going to inherit billions of dollars going forward. What advice or wisdom would you like to give them?

Sanjeev: I think it's really important that you work for any wealth that you have or want to earn. However, if you are fortunate enough to inherit it, work hard to preserve it, grow it, and put it to good use.

Kunal Shah

Founder, FreeCharge and CRED

JP: May I request you to introduce yourself.

Kunal: I'm the founder of FreeCharge and have been involved with multiple start-ups before that as well. I have also been doing a short stint in Y-Combinator and Sequoia Capital, and I am now involved in a start-up again. I grew up in Bombay; spent most of my life there; recently I moved to Bangalore.

JP: At what point in your life did you become an entrepreneur?

Kunal: I think it was probably sometime in 2008. What I realised was, even when I had a job, I was pretty much behaving like an entrepreneur. I became the CEO of a company at an early age of 23, because of my initiative and trying to do something of my own within the company. What I realised was that what I was doing is just being an entrepreneur but doing it for someone else—I had to do something for myself. In 2008, I decided to take the plunge—I asked myself, "Should I buy a bigger house or bigger car, or should I risk it out?" That's when I decided to do it.

JP: Did you grow up in a wealthy family?

Kunal: I was born in an upper-middle-class family. My family went through a financial crisis by the time I was a teenager and we were absolutely and completely bankrupt. I had to start working from the age of 16, to take care of the family. I've done all sorts of odd jobs at odd places to pay for my school, college, higher education, and many other things.

JP: And then you got into the entrepreneurial world? Describe your journey as an entrepreneur.

Kunal: I actually started dabbling in multiple things. I did FreeCharge and I was also working on three or four other ideas. I was doing an e-commerce thing where I was importing laptops from the US and selling them on Indian e-commerce platforms. I was playing some arbitrage game over there. Then I was doing a little bit of marketing promotions for PaisaBack, a mail-in rebate company for India.

Then, through that, I had the insight that it made sense to build a platform where people can actually recharge their phones and the idea was to make that free by giving equal value coupons. It automatically created a strong pull and I started getting involved doing that.

JP: Fast forward to your exit from the company, can you just tell us a little bit about that and how well you did?

Kunal: We started the company in August 2010, sold it in March 2015. It was approximately a $450 million exit.

JP: That was a fairly successful exit for you as well, right?

Kunal: Yeah, I barely made enough money even when I was doing my own start-up—my compensation was extremely low. In fact, I remember when I got my exit; I had a loan from three employees of the team to pay off.

JP: Now that you are a part of the affluent class, how are you enjoying your wealth? What are you currently doing?

Kunal: I don't think I have changed much; I think the only thing I have done is probably push myself to travel a lot more which I did not do earlier. During my start-up, I'd say between 2008–2016, I didn't take a vacation. I could not get myself to take a break. I did a bit of that. I am not very keen on buying expensive cars or getting things. I definitely went ahead and got a good apartment for my family in Walkeshwar. It was a form of emotional closure for me because when my family was in a massive financial crisis, they had to move into a very small 100 square feet apartment, and it was a massive struggle thereafter. It felt like closure to at least the struggles we faced then. I don't live there—I've never lived there; but it definitely felt like that was a great way to bring closure to that life.

JP: Why the transition to Bangalore?

Kunal: It's very hard to find the quality of technical talent you find here—it's extremely strong in Bangalore, and that's crucial, if you want to build a tech company. Even at FreeCharge, we had moved the team to Bangalore in 2013—I was flying back and forth. Now I have moved here instead of going back and forth.

JP: What are the things you would like to do with your wealth, besides ensuring that your family is well taken care of in the future?

Kunal: I am mostly an angel investor. We have probably done 50 odd investments. In addition, I would say that most of them were not necessarily of the mindset that I would be making more money out of them. I have a mindset of helping entrepreneurs in different shapes and forms. Often, I even write on social media, with the intent to pay it forward and at least share my life and thoughts so that more people can learn from it, and kind of use that in their journey. I think people just assume founders gain massive joy after getting an exit or making a lot of money. I think what I have found is that people go through massive crisis after an exit because what they realise is that the purpose is bigger than money and once you don't have purpose, I don't think money feels good.

JP: You are still very young. How old are you?

Kunal: I'm 39 years old.

JP: You have not even hit 40, and you've come into affluence and you have changed your lifestyle from Bombay to Bangalore. You are continuing to invest as an angel investor—going forward, what are you going to do with your affluence?

Kunal: I think the only good use of affluence is access. You have access to better people; you have access to knowledge, which is not possible without affluence. You have the access and the ability to make a change and to make an impact. That I think is the only good use of affluence.

JP: Do elaborate on why you feel that the access is better?

Kunal: Well, I think a lot of people don't understand that every human system is designed based on signalling. If you are meeting an entrepreneur, you are likely to wonder if he or she is from IIT, or Stanford or Harvard; that is the signalling value. If you meet a founder who has sold his company for $500 million, it's also the same signalling. And one of those days, you meet a Philosophy major—I had dropped out of the science stream and pursued my degree in Philosophy. I had no signalling value in my degree. When you say you have sold off your company for half a billion, it acts as a signal for the opposite person, and therefore, you are likely to get any meeting you request.

JP: What are the things that you want to do with your life and money?

Kunal: I thought I would do some investment but then I realised that I was not enjoying it too much. Also, I realised that the world has too much capital, so it is probably not a wise idea to be an investor. I'd like to be in areas where they compete less, so, I decided to be an entrepreneur again.

JP: What is your philosophy on giving?

Kunal: I guess people have misunderstood giving as philanthropy. I think if you feel empowered and enable 100 or 1,000 people to be able to make an impact and create wealth, I think that would create a lot bigger impact than trying to do philanthropy and kind of making an impact on may be 10 or 100 people. What I've realised, that at least from my journey, is I did not talk about extreme lack of finances until I got my exit because I did not want sympathy from anybody. I don't believe that people need to help you because you are not financially stable. In this world, in today's time we have enough opportunities to make an impact if you really want to. My fundamental belief is that one needs to move forward by enabling people—I tell people it's much easier to get my money versus my time. If people understood this concept well, they could do the same thing in their life as well.

JP: Did you ever think of starting your own venture capital fund?

Kunal: Multiple local VCs have offered $50 million to $100 million to start a fund, but I've decided that in a time when there's way too much capital, I don't think it's wise to be a VC investor.

JP: What do you think will happen to your wealth, after you?

Kunal: I guess, I will be saving it and it will be used to propagate it forward. I do not believe in holding on to wealth. I've not thought what the answer to that is, but I definitely believe that it will be used to propagate some system. I don't know what it is. I haven't thought about it, but I guess there'll be many interesting ways that can help make society move forward in some manner.

JP: Do you have any other favourite sweet spot beyond supporting entrepreneurs?

Kunal: Actually, it's a good question. I don't think I have another sweet spot. I definitely see there's an impact that needs to be made on education. But what I have realised is that instead of trying to make an impact on education, I think you can have this tall ambition and figure out the education required for that.

Pranoti Nagarkar

Founder, Rotimatic

JP: May I request you to introduce yourself.

Pranoti: I am a mission driven entrepreneur and a fun-loving mother of two little boys. I currently serve as the Co-CEO of Zimplistic Inventions, a company I co-founded with my husband Rishi. We both are deeply passionate about technology and health, so we founded Zimplistic to make it easier for busy families to eat fresh homemade food.

Our flagship product is a kitchen robot called Rotimatic, which simplifies the complicated task of making flatbreads, such as rotis, tortillas, and wraps. Launched in 2016, it is now in over 60,000 homes and our community continues to grow.

JP: Tell us a little bit about where you grew up.

Pranoti: I had a very cozy middle-class upbringing in Pune, a city near Mumbai. My parents are grounded yet growth-minded individuals who raised my younger brother and I to always be curious. They entertained our questions, they humoured us, and they never discouraged our inquisitiveness. We also benefited immensely from our parents being deep-thinkers. They both provided a balanced influence—my dad being a very logical engineer, while my mom being an artist at heart with a strong passion for design.

JP: Where did you go to college?

Pranoti: I went to college in Singapore. But there is a bit of a story there. My dad, at the age of 45, decided to start his own company. A major financial undertaking, which made me feel that I should not put any further burden on him. I was in the middle school at that point and figured that I should proactively apply for scholarships, which can help me take care of my own education. I was aware of a scholarship by Singapore government, which covered high school studies as well as college. I patiently waited till I could apply and gave it my best shot. I was fortunate to make the list, which resulted in me coming to Singapore right after tenth standard on a full-ride scholarship for junior college as well as university. I majored in Mechanical Engineering from National University of Singapore.

During my time at NUS, I also spent a year abroad at University of California, Berkeley, which became a defining experience in many ways.

JP: What did you do after engineering?

Pranoti: During my engineering studies, I got very interested in doing product design and opted for a bunch of design modules. Designing was always my passion—but those modules helped me refine my interest further towards designing product solutions. I undertook a year-long design project, which involved building an automatic iron for shirts. It was exciting and satisfying, but in college you don't learn the full set of skills needed to actually take the product all the way through manufacturing and get it to market. So, I decided to take up a job after graduation which would give me that exposure. I joined a design consultancy in Singapore and my first assignment was a job with Phillips to design an automatic vacuum cleaner (unlike the ones we have now, it had a power cord). A big robust vacuum cleaner meant for carpeted homes, it had camera vision to guide its movement and a cord winder that winded or unwinded based on its location in the room. Handling the cord right was super important so things in the room aren't toppled, and the vacuum itself doesn't get entangled. I was in-charge of designing the cord winder. It's a sub-assembly within the vacuum cleaner and it turned out to be a great experience. I worked there for about three years and I saw it from concept on paper all the way through to manufacturing. I was able to build the right contacts, pick up the right knowledge, and gain valuable perspective.

JP: When did the epiphany happen?

Pranoti: When I was working at the design consultancy, I always knew that this is not a long-term thing for me. I wanted to do something on my own, work on fixing a big problem. Around that time, Rishi and I had just gotten married. Thanks to my conditioning, I grew up with these old school thoughts that the woman of the family has to be the person taking care of the nourishment of the family and nourishment can come only through homemade food. For me, it was a very straightforward thing—I had to make sure I cook food at home, especially after we got married. I tried doing that along with the job that I had and the daily commute. It was a big challenge and a daily chore. Every day you come home; you have to make fresh food. Roti making especially would always be a big bottleneck because you have got the dal, the sabji and the salad sorted, but when it comes to roti, I couldn't for one, guarantee that I'll make a perfect roti every time. I just couldn't. You need to master many skills, and it takes about almost half an hour of your time, end to end. And there it was, right there, a big glaring gap in the kitchen, a giant problem faced by almost every Indian. There are washing machines, dishwashers, rice cookers but there was nothing for rotis. There were roti makers like those hand-press ones. We experimented with those to see if they do the job, but they are really a poor and incomplete solution. So, we decided to embark on this adventure which became Rotimatic.

JP: You went through multiple iterations of it over the last few years.

Pranoti: When I started, I wasn't sure if it was possible to invent such a thing. Initial couple of years I invested all my savings, $20,000 to $30,000—to buy equipment, materials, and worked out of a small office space in the NUS incubator proving the concept. Building a new product from the ground up is a very iterative design process. I knew all along that I can't have a full solution in one go, so I went prototype by prototype. The goal was that the end product had to be a 'one click operation' while being compact and versatile. We wanted to give our users the full freedom to choose any flour they want. Achieving that is a very hard technical problem, which needs various disciplines from food science to ML (machine language) working together seamlessly. We had to go through numerous prototypes to refine the user experience plus product performance.

JP: How has your perspective on money changed, from growing up to where you are at today?

Pranoti: When I think about money, the first memory I have is very distinct. I remember as a kid, I must have been seven or eight years old, I became very conscious of what money could do. I grew up around both sets of grandparents—mom's side and dad's side. My mom's parents, and my mom, have a very strong sense of social responsibility and have focus on money. For them, it was more about money as a means to get to something and I distinctly remember both, my maternal grandparents and my mom have a social service mindset.

On the other side, my father's family was extremely focussed on making sure that we saved enough money because with that base you can build anything on top. A practical mindset with money as a core is an enabler for pursuing bigger things.

So overall, I grew up with that concept that money is just a means to get you to the greater good. When I think of money now, for me it remains as a stepping-stone to make some kind of big social impact. The power and voice that money gives you is very important to make those changes.

JP: Now that you are a very successful entrepreneur, my question is, are you going to be a Unicorn—a billion dollar, maybe multiple billions of dollar enterprise? Once you do have that amount of money, what shall we do with all this money?

Pranoti: My upbringing is so simple and grounded that my needs are not that many. Luckily for us, what happened is that Rishi got an exit in his first company, after that point we never financially struggled. Until that happened, we were enjoying the start-up struggle too. We lived with our friends even after getting married, because we couldn't afford to have the whole place to ourselves. We got motorbikes to save money; we didn't want to sink time waiting for buses or MRT. We always had a different outlook towards life, and we enjoyed with whatever we had. Money was never a bottleneck, but when it comes to building a company, definitely the capital is very important. Fundraising becomes such a crucial part.

If I am fortunate to have resources to invest freely, I want to invest in orphanages. I've always felt that the system of orphanages in India—or anywhere in the world—is something that needs to go through an overhaul. That's one cause, I would love to pick up and get my hands dirty with. I want to get to understand the process, why things are the way they are and then get the right people in to find better solutions. Of course, it will become so much easier once you have easy access to resources.

JP: Besides philanthropy, is there anything specific you would like to spend the money on, on a personal level?

Pranoti: Our needs are very simple and minimal. It's not as if we want a big car or lots of diamonds and great clothes—nothing of that sort. We are simple. We love to travel light. I think travelling light through life is also something that we love to do. It's a simpler life, and then you set aside your energy to take on complex problems to improve the world, leveraging our skills as entrepreneurs and utilising the entrepreneurship toolkit.

JP: What advice would you like to give to the millennials, in terms of what to do with large sums of money?

Pranoti: I think it's a huge power to have access to money. Please make sure that you utilise it for the right cause, whatever you're drawn to. Pick up a cause that can have a sizeable impact. It's a great opportunity and privilege to have resources, so it will be such a shame if you don't capitalise on it. Because if you think about it, what do we actually need to be happy in life? It is very simple—have our loved ones be happy and healthy. What else does one need? I think the comforts of life are there but you don't want anything beyond a certain threshold. So, one can only get real bliss and happiness by picking up meaningful causes to elevate one's life purpose.

Venky Iyer
Founder, Goli Vada Pav

JP: May I request you to introduce yourself.

Venky: I am the founder and CEO of Goli Vada Pav. I am in my early 50s. For the last 14 years, I have been running a company called Goli Vada Pav. I was born and brought up in a suburb of Mumbai called Dombivli. I come from a middle-class family. My father was in a very senior position at Colgate Palmolive. We had most of the comforts but no luxury, that's how we were brought up—no telephone, no car, no holiday and lot of books, lot of festival celebrations at home. We were always happy, and we were taught in our childhood to look after people who don't have a house, who don't have food to eat, who don't have clothes to wear. Can you do something for them? Can you help them? That was the background—a little bit of a socialistic background. That was my upbringing.

JP: Where did you study?

Venky: My schooling happened at S K Patil English Medium School in Dombivli, but we all spoke in Marathi only. Then I attended Mulund College, and afterwards I got into the financial services in the early 90s.

JP: What were you doing then? What about your career?

Venky: My first job was with a manufacturing company, which was into contract manufacturing for Unilever and Colgate. The second job was an internship, which I did for a year and a half. Then I joined a financial service company called the 20th Century Finance Corporation. It was an NBFC, run by ex-Citibank people. Then I joined Apple Industries, Atul Nishar's company, and Aptech. Then I started my own financial service company in 1992–1993.

JP: Can you give us your perspective on money growing up?

Venky: Those days, even though my dad was working at Colgate, the money was limited—no telephone, no car, no holiday. We never felt the paucity of money as we always celebrated festivals like Diwali, Ganpati, and Dussehra, as a joint family. We felt that we had everything, and we never felt the need for big thing like "Gaadi chahiye, holiday chahiye." We thanked God for whatever we had. We had a lot of happiness.

JP: As you began progressing in your career, accumulated some money, and so on, did your perspective on money change?

Venky: No, my strong childhood values were more socialistic, it was more about helping society—we produce, now how do we distribute it? Money was there as a means to help others. It's not about accumulating wealth for oneself. Sone ka chapati thodi na kha sakte hain. If at all you create wealth, it's for all your stakeholders, for example, your employees, your investors, your dealers. When the ship goes down, the captain of the ship is the last person to leave the ship, in the same way; you are the last person to take from the wealth that comes in.

JP: How did Goli Vada Pav happen?

Venky: After spending 14–15 years in financial services, I think I must have met most of the small-time corporates who had dreams. Kishore Biyani and Big Bazaar were struggling those days with hardly ₹30–40 crore of turnover revenue top-line and from there it became ₹10,000 crore business. That really motivated and inspired me. I said to myself, after spending 14 years could I do something, which can contribute to India, because the stock market had started booming, India's GDP had started growing. Can I start a business, which will help society and the country? Being born and brought up in Mumbai, I thought vada pav was a good idea. I wanted to set up a business that would create education, employment, and entrepreneurship for the underprivileged. Typically, all the store boys in our business had not even passed eight grade or some were school dropouts. If they can be given a Goli academy certificate and education, they can be given jobs and a bit of handholding, and tomorrow, they can become entrepreneurs who are individually running stores. And what if we get listed and wealth was created? Like when Infosys created wealth, middle-class engineers became rich, they got a huge amount of money—if we get listed then all these boys will have stock option, they will suddenly see ₹25 lakh or ₹50 lakh which they would have never seen at one-time in their life.

So, Goli began in 2004 in a place called Kalyan and from there we ended up building over 300 stores across India, in 100 cities and 20 states—we have stores in Punjab, we have 60 stores in

UP, 60 stores in Bangalore, in Chennai, Coimbatore, Kerala, from Porbandar to Kolkata, and from Chandigarh to Calicut we have stores.

JP: What is your business model?

Venky: Ours was more of a franchisee model. We had vada pav as a concept and we outsourced everything to a third party. Our backend partners are the people who make burger patties for McDonalds worldwide. Coming from corporate finance, I thought about what I could add to vada pav on a handcart. We brought in franchisees, supply chain, branding, and funding. The same handcart, which was on the footpath of Mumbai, the moment a corporate or a branded person comes, and he brings in whatever he has learnt in 14–15 years, things change. We supply the vada, chutney, pav; everything to our franchisees across India and then we also supply the fryers and refrigerators. They remove the product from fridge and fry it in our temperature-controlled electrical fryer, and they push the vada inside the pav and give it to the customer. It's as simple as that. The entire supply chain and franchisee runs the business. It's a completely outsourced business model. We only own the brand and that's how we built the business, so far.

JP: How big is Goli Vada Pav now in terms of the number of vada pavs served?

Venky: We serve around a minimum 100,000 vada pavs per day, across India. We don't do that much business in Mumbai, Delhi or cities where the rentals are very high, the Maharashtra business comes from Nasik, Aurangabad, Nagpur, Amravati, Akola; the small tier two and tier three cities like Basti, Gonda, Allahabad, Banaras, Lucknow, Kanpur in UP, same in Ludhiana, Amritsar, Chandigarh and Coimbatore—the rentals of these small cities are very low, ₹20,000–25,000. Mumbai rental is ₹1–1.5 lakh. In the first stage of business, we are focussed on tier two and tier three cities.

Our price points differ from place to place; Maharashtra will have a low price point, Karnataka will be a slightly higher price point, Punjab is as good as the Karnataka price points. We have products starting at ₹15 and going up to ₹50 as well.

JP: What is your equity structure now?

Venky: There is a venture capital firm that has invested money and there are some HNIs who have put in money. We raised money in 2011 and we again raised money in 2017, but not very big. We tried to raise a 20–25 crore loan because it's a bricks and mortar business.

JP: How has your perspective on money changed now that you're running such a fascinating business?

Venky: I still live in the same 2BHK flat, I drive a Maruti Ignis, and I still feel kya karenge paise ka. I have a wife and a daughter whose perspective will be different because the society is different. Somehow, despite all this, for so many years the perspective is that you have to create wealth and distribute wealth. The whole idea is if you become too much of a consumer yourself, your energy gets wasted in consumption, rather than that, you should focus on production. My perspective is that after a limit sone ka chapatti thodi kha sakta hain, so the money has to be ploughed back into the business, in people, in your own employees, to your distributors, to your vendors.

JP: Do you have expansion plans and how do you see your prospects in the future?

Venky: The franchisee that has got capital is not willing to stand in the store and the guy who is ready to stand in the store doesn't have the capital. The truth of the brand is when the under tenth-standard pass boy hands over the vada pav—that is the truth of the brand. Going ahead it will be more franchisee invested company operators. We will raise about ₹10 crore and will put up our stores and we will get these boys as operators. The whole idea is to focus on the boys because they are the one who are building the brand, if he is taken care of, then the brand and the company become successful, that's the thing I am trying to tell my investors and franchisees.

JP: That is a very noble philosophy. The business is growing, and one day when there is a massive windfall and you get hundreds of crores of rupees by divesting, the question is, what shall we do with all this money?

Venky: I feel the same way as the Tatas and Infosys—I think we should become trustees after some time. If you leave too much money to your kids and the family, they will become materialistic. I think each young person of the next generation should have hunger. Hunger for success, hunger to do something on their own. Zero is a great place to start from. I have seen many examples, where a huge amount of money has been handed over to the next generation, and that spoils them, they don't want to take risk because they feel that their father has created the business and wealth and that they shouldn't end up losing it. I think we should leave a decent amount of money for our next generation to have a good education and to start something on their own. If you leave too much on the table for them, they will be spoilt and end up doing nothing in life.

JP: Have you thought of what you will do with all your money?

Venky: The whole idea is to take Goli academy, entrepreneurship, employment, and education for the underprivileged as the mission, the cause. The whole idea is to focus on the boys because they need a lot of support. Most probably, they will need some kind of accommodation in Mumbai and Delhi where the rentals are high. They will need education, training beyond Goli Vada Pav. We can help and support them in becoming entrepreneur. The whole thought processes is when you create 5,000 Goli Vada Pav stores, there are 10 boys per store, 50,000 boys will be coming from UP, Bihar, interior Maharashtra or somewhere else, with no background; can you help them? The whole objective, later on, would be to be associated with them beyond Goli. Goli is a business, a strong foundation, but afterwards to take care of the academy, getting more boys into the system and making them entrepreneurs, that's our goal and that's the area we would like to focus on.

JP: Along the way, you wrote a book. Please tell us about it.

Venky: When the Goli Vada Pav story became big and Harvard, IMD and ISB came and did the case study—it became even bigger. Then Harvard started teaching it as a case study, so I ended up becoming a speaker. I have done more than 300 talks in various business schools from SP Jain, Welingkar, IMD Switzerland, ISB, Harvard, and IIM Bangalore and then the media started writing about it. CNBC came to us and said that this is a beautiful story and we want to do a book on it, so *My Journey with Vada Pav* came into being. It's become quite popular across India. This book shares the journey that we went through. We went bankrupt three times while building this business. There was a mission, there was a purpose, like Mahatma Gandhi said, "Find purpose, the means will follow." We kept on going even though we fell down, we picked ourselves up from wherever we were, and Goli went to the next level.

Somewhere, there has been the unseen hand of God in Goli. I think if you have a selfless motive then the universe conspires to help you achieve it. *My Journey with Vada Pav* and the talks have helped me connect with people across India and the globe.

Lawyers

Navneet Chugh
Managing Partner, Chugh LLP

Suril Desai
International Lawyer, Nishith Desai Associates

Navneet Chugh

Managing Partner, Chugh LLP

JP: May I request you to introduce yourself.

Navneet: I was born and raised in Nagpur 56 years ago, lived in Nagpur for 20 years, did my BCom there and came to California in 1981, did another Bachelor's degree, did my MBA and CPA, and started a CPA practice 33 years ago. I went to law school part time for four and a half years, passed the bar and have been doing legal work since 1992, for 26 years now.

Today we have 500 people in 12 offices. Seven in India, five in US, Atlanta, D.C, New Jersey, LA, and San Francisco Bay Area. We do full-service legal, full-service accounting, tax, financial, corporate work, immigration, and litigation. We have a couple of hundred CPAs and lawyers. Of the top 100 Indian companies doing business in the United States, we work with over 50 of them; all the big names that you've heard of, especially in the technology area.

Fifty per cent of our work is Indian companies, and the other 50 per cent is local, domestic US work. We do a lot of real estate and medical healthcare work. We have done 400,000 immigration petitions, 100,000 tax returns, 10,000 new corporations, and start-ups.

I am very thankful that we are involved in the non-profit world and giving back. We do a lot of pro-bono work, never say no to anybody because of money, if they don't have any, we'll do their work for free. We are involved in endless charities around the world. The most selfish thing to do is to do charity work because you get 10X back in return.

JP: Congratulations on your great success. Over this period, you have amassed a reasonable amount of wealth and you have seen other people amass a reasonable amount of wealth as well. You're involved in a lot of non-profits that you've been helping over the last few years. Can you describe a few of those and what you've been doing for them?

Navneet: At a young age, I got involved in charity and I'm very grateful for that. When I was in my early 20s, I helped set up a charity, the Nargis Dutt Memorial Foundation in 1985. We did the first fundraiser and bought equipment for hospitals in India.

I started realising that usually people will wait till they are in their 50s and 60s till they have grey hair and then they will start doing charity work. I thought to myself why not do it while you are young and alive so you can see what's happening? I started doing charity work earlier on and then helped many non-profits set up shop in the US or set up charitable organisations. Every time a client would sell a company and make a lot of money, more often than not, we would set up a charitable foundation for them.

I got involved in many other charities like Pratham. For the last 20 years, we've been helping Pratham. I got involved with setting up the American India Foundation (AIF), their Southern California chapter in 2002, I ran it and was on the board of AIF for six years and learnt a lot. I did massive fundraisers, learnt how to sell $500 per seat, learnt to beg, borrow, and steal to fulfil the quota of a million bucks. Then amazing things would happen and somehow, we would hit $1 million. For the last six years, I've been on the Pratham board and helped Pratham in Northern California, Southern California, and New Jersey, and we have set up the Pratham Atlanta chapter. The first time we got involved in Pratham 20 years ago, we raised $35,000 in California, last year we raised $4 million.

JP: And does that come from just the South Asian diaspora or from the whole of United States?

Navneet: All over the United States, we have 13 chapters. Last year we did $16.5 million in revenue, and up from $20,000 in the first year in US. New York, Houston, LA, and the Bay Area are the four big chapters for Pratham and between the four of them, we raised about $10 million. We have great donors, there is one donor in LA who has given us $10 million in the last 20 years.

JP: One of the questions that keeps coming up is that what is it about United States that makes it such a generous country because the total giving and per capita giving is probably the highest in the world—is that true?

Navneet: By far the highest. Last year, Americans gave $400 billion to the 1.5 million charities in US. I think the charity world is a big huge secret that nobody talks about and it's not disclosed, and I guess there is no vested interest for somebody to talk about it. Why is the

US what it is, why is it that 5 per cent of the world lives here and enjoys 22 per cent of the world's wealth and if you were to look at the top five reasons: probably the number one reason is the law. The law is followed, everything works, and the engineers, doctors, plumbers, accountants, lawyers, and everybody behaves because there is a legal system and there is recourse. One big reason is the non-profit world. One out of ten Americans work for a non-profit and that is shocking, but it is not shocking if you realise that 90 per cent of all hospitals and colleges and universities in US are non-profit. Stanford is non-profit, Harvard is non-profit. Massachusetts General, Johns Hopkins, the largest hospitals are non-profit. Last year Americans gave $400 billion to 1.5 million charities. The non-profit GDP of the United States is 1.1 trillion, which is 6 per cent of the total country's GDP and gives employment to 14 million people. All the arts and culture, all the literary stuff, all the scientific stuff, all the educational research, medical, healthcare, and tragedies of America are all solved by non-profits. The government in the other 196 countries in the world, besides the United States, is doing all this stuff for education, healthcare, and natural disasters. In the US, it is the non-profit that is doing this.

JP: What is the motivation for the people to give so much to the non-profits?

Navneet: I think there are a few reasons. One, it's a new country and so there are no old habits holding back the country. I mean new country in the way that in the 1850s to 1900 some of the richest people in the world were already in the United States. Andrew Carnegie for instance was the world's richest person with $100 billion in 1900. It probably started with him in 1890, when he wrote an essay called *The Gospel of Wealth*, which is still very popular today. Everything that you see Bill Gates and Warren Buffett doing, the genesis of that is in that essay. In that essay, he wrote that if you are rich and you leave money to your kids, then that's a crime. In 1890, there was no tax code, it was not like he was getting a tax deduction. He was worth a $100 billion and he had one daughter, Jennifer, I think, and he left $6 billion to her, and gave away $94 billion to charity in today's money, built 3,000 libraries around the world, established Carnegie University, which became Carnegie Mellon. The culture of giving has been there in the country.

Second, in 1916 taxation began in US and then there is tax deduction and because there is tax compliance in the US, unlike other countries, they are looking for a valid legal deduction, and so the government in its wisdom decided that charities that are doing so much good in the country, the least the government could do is help people who are helping the charities and start giving them a tax deduction. Moreover, taxes are high—in California tax is 50 per cent so if somebody gives away $1 million, they get at least $500,000 back from the government. That's the second reason.

Third is probably religious. The Bible calls for tithe of 10 per cent and every other religion that is prevalent in the US, including Hinduism, Sikhism, Judaism—all of them call for making donations, some written, some not. The Quran calls for 2.5 per cent of net worth to be given every year. I think because it's culture, that helps. Corporations are allowed tax deductions for giving to charity—up to 10 per cent of their net income. Over a period of time people give, whether it's for a selfish reason of tax deduction and/or death tax, where if you die with a $100 billion, the government is going to take away 40 per cent.

JP: What about estate tax?

Navneet: Estate tax or death tax. The rich people are like, "Wait a minute, if I just set up a charity and give away all the money to the charity and make my kids the board of directors of my charity, then they have something to do for the rest of their life, they don't need to work, and I don't have to give $40 billion or so to the government." Therefore, whether it's self-preservation, whether it's motivation to save on tax, it's become a part of the culture. Every single day in the United States, there is a charity gala happening, maybe a 100 in a day, even on weekdays. In New York, they prefer charity events on weekdays so that the CEOs don't have to come back from Greenwich, Connecticut on a Saturday or Sunday. We would do AIF charity events on Mondays every year. Then the CEOs would ask their spouses to come to the city in the evening and then they would stay at the hotel where the event was. Then the corporations want to give, the CEOs are honoured, the CEOs want to give. The going rate for a Fortune 500 CEO to be honoured by a charity in the US is somewhere between $50,000 to $250,000. If you invite them to a charity event, and if the CEO likes your charity he not only agrees to come, but you also get a call from the company saying,

"What's expected of us in return? The going rate is 50K to 250K, what do you want?"

JP: This is the opposite to a lot of other celebrities who actually ask for money to do charity events.

Navneet: Yes. Hollywood celebrities—you can Google this, won't ask for money and they all have their favourite charities, every single one is attached to something. There is a whole index of stars and the charities they support. Between the Hollywood support and the corporation support as well as the rich people wanting to give... you know it's now become a fashion statement in the United States for the rich to attend charity events and write cheques.

JP: Is it also part of the reason why university endowments are so big?

Navneet: Yes Jayesh, another secret of this country is that there are 200,000 professionals whose job-title includes the words 'Developmental Fundraising' and their average salary was $57,036 last year, and each one is expected to raise $1 million per person. You look at every big charity in the United States, they have development people who were earlier fundraising people but that became taboo so now they are called Developmental People.

Harvard, for instance, has 500 people in their fundraising department. Last year they raised $250 million. Their budget was $500 million, they charged fees at 250, and 250 came from present and past donations. Harvard has $36 billion in their savings account, which in the last 25 years has averaged 10 per cent a year in growth. All of the universities have this going based on the same principles. The beautiful thing is that one out of two people at Harvard are getting financial aid. If somebody's family income is less than $65,000, their tuition is free. Over $165,000 of family income, there is no financial aid; between $65,000 to $165,000, there is a sliding scale of financial aid. Here are the Harvard's of the world that are doing so good that they are removing a poor person out of a poor household if their grades are good and putting them in Harvard, especially the disadvantaged people and immigrants and other ethnicities that haven't done so well in their country, and paying for their food and educating them and changing that person's life forever.

JP: Is this a similar model for other big universities like Stanford and MIT?

Navneet: All of them, unless they are government affiliated, like the University of California, which are largely funded by the government, but they also do their own fundraising. All of the private universities, like the Ivy League, all the big private schools, all of them have scholarships, financial aid, grants, and you can get loans as well.

The beautiful thing is that all of the hospitals are fundraising, they have fundraising people and so in the rest of the world, fundraising is an art and a difficult thing to do, but in the US, it's a science. It's just how it's done; out of the $400 billion, one-third was given to religious institutions, one-third to educational institutions and one-third to everything else. Moreover, $135 billion went to temples, churches, and religious institutions, which is a lot of money. However, if you look deeper, the temples and churches of United States are also doing a lot of social work, and they all have adult family child services. The bigger temples, the bigger churches, anybody can walk in, if there is a teenage pregnancy or domestic violence or somebody has died and there is no money for the funeral or the kids are having problems in school or drugs, the churches and the temples will support and help. If you dig deeper, they are taking care of senior citizens, they are putting them on buses and taking them to Las Vegas. They are doing Bingo parties at the churches with wine, which would never be allowed at a Hindu temple or any Indian temple. They have legal clinics, dental clinics, medical clinics, they have seminars on how to get into Harvard, and their counsellors will come. Therefore, the temple is not just a place for religion and spirituality, it's to help everyone.

JP: Here in the Silicon Valley, you have seen a lot of these entrepreneurs succeed. Do you have some sort of general case studies in terms of what these people do with the hundreds of millions of dollars?

Navneet: The good news is that a big percentage of them are contributing and donating and setting up foundations. You probably know that the Tatas gave $50 million to Harvard; the Jindal family gave $25 million to the University of Texas Dallas (UTD). The business school at UTD is called Naveen Jindal School of Management.

Chandrika Tandon gave $100 million to NYU. Their engineering school is now called Tandon School of Engineering. Dr Kiran Patel and his wife gave $200 million to Nova Southeastern University (NSU) in Florida, that's probably the highest Indian gift in the United States.

What I am finding with rich Indians in Silicon Valley is the same issue as in India, that there is a trust deficit with Indian charities. There is no United Way, no Red Cross, no YMCA of India, no Salvation Army, and no Goodwill. There isn't a famous, successful, popular, efficient, and trustworthy Indian charity that can handle millions of dollars. Because there is no such charity, because there is a trust deficit, most of the rich in the US set up their own foundation and start programs on their own.

JP: You are also based out of LA (Los Angeles) and you come across the media and entertainment industry. Do you see any similarities or differences between the way they give in LA?

Navneet: LA is a more complex organism in that it's not tech-based, so, there is real estate and media and there is tech and there is healthcare. Generally speaking, there is not as much wealth in the Indian community in Southern California as there is in Northern California. There have not been many exits, and unless there is a big exit, people are not very motivated to give, but we have considerable donors in the LA area, from the manufacturing field, from healthcare, lots of physicians and some technology companies as well.

I think the world is going to be a fine place in the future. I think people are getting better and better and people are giving more and more. Indians in India, that were famous for not giving, well, last year 28 per cent of Indians in India gave their time or money. Last year $6 billion were given in charity to organisations in India. There are about 3 million non-profits in India, which is double of that in the US. Unfortunately, 99 per cent of them, their budget is under $100,000. Giving is increasing in India and amongst the Indians in the US. On an average, the 320 million people of the United States are giving over a $1,000 per person. If you look at the 3.6 million Indians in the US and if you apply the same average of a $1,000— that's $3.6 billion that Indians are either giving or have the capacity to give. Given that an average Indian's per capita income is double of an average non-Indian in the United States, double of the other religions and other ethnicities in the US, therefore, we should be giving $7 billion. So far, we have only been able to track about a $100 million a year to the top 20 Indian organisations that we know of, that are India-centric charities in the US. There is a giving capacity of $7 billion; we've been able to track a $100 million. Either $6.9 billion is not being given or given to non-India centric charities like the University of Florida or Indians are not yet giving as much as we can.

JP: However, there is a rule that if they set up a 501(c)(3) foundation, then they have to give a minimum amount every year, right?

Navneet: The rule is that whatever amount of money is in the non-profit 501(c)(3), 5 per cent of that they have to spend that year.

JP: There are people who are making incredible amounts of money and are incredibly affluent. They have worked extremely hard to make all this money, and then there are some who work hard to make more money on their money. Are most of them working hard to give away their money?

Navneet: That's a good question. What I have realised at one point in my life is that making $1 billion is very hard, but it is even harder to spend $1 billion in charity because I can give you $1 billion and then say, "Do some good charity work." It is very difficult. Whom would you give it to? What charity is out there that is scalable, that is transparent, and that has governance that can use your $100 million donation? If there is no charity, then you have to start one. You have $1 billion of your own money that you are trying to invest and grow; and the number of bank statements you get every month take about 3-4 hours a week. This is what rich people tell me, that they are so busy handling all the paperwork from the investments that they have done; and then you've got to live life and enjoy as well. Now you are old, obviously, you have to take care of your health and medical issues as well. It's very difficult.

I think our community has done a great job—we are struggling, learning, and giving. We could do more. Some people are passionate about children's education, so they focus on that. The Arora family—they've given Pratham about $10 million in addition to the $10 million I talked about, for vocational training in India because they feel that there are enough institutions, enough non-profits doing enough work for education but what about the kids that drop out of eighth and ninth grade, but who require some vocational training to make a living.

Some people are focussed on development of charities to help charities in India as they don't have good governance, don't know how to raise money and don't have a board of directors, are not efficient, they don't have a technology platform. Some of them have decided to help other charities scale and teach them what's going on in the rest of the world, which I think is a great idea.

There are 4,000 cities in India and 750 districts and 600,000 villages. If a group of rich people who used to live in, for example, Ranchi or were born there, got together and proposed to take Ranchi's per capita income of $2,000 per person and we would multiply it times five in the next 10 years. That's what they did with their businesses, that's how they became so successful. I think if a concerted effort goes on in one city, we can slowly transform India.

For instance, there are wonderful articles and books written on how to scale up a city — water and sanitation, roads, colleges, schools, and hospitals. Given the experience amongst this donor group of Ranchi based people, if one person took healthcare, one person took primary education, one person took sanitation or governance or whatever. I think if five billionaires went to Ranchi and said, Ranchi's per capita income today is $2,000 per year, we want it to be $10,000 in the next five or seven years and we are going to come here and invest and we are going to help, then I think the next day the per capita income of Ranchi increases by 10 per cent, by just this statement.

JP: This sounds similar to some consortiums that have been formed in the US, for example, Peggy Dulany, she has a club of affluent people called Synergos and they come together and decide on what vertical sectors to give to and decide on how much money to allocate. They have a full-time professional team and then they collectively go out and do something. Do you think that's something that's catching on? More and more people are interested in that, if someone takes leadership and leads these kinds of consortiums.

Navneet: Yeah, that would be wonderful, and I think that's badly required. I had read a study once that the 30 million Indians outside of India make as much money as the 1.3 billion Indians in India, and if you look at the amount of wealth that Indians are making outside of India, that certainly seems possible. These people are not necessarily going to go back to India, but their heart and soul is still in India, and they would help. If there was a consortium like that, that would do wonders, and I think there is some affinity people have to the place they were born in or were educated. Let them take care of their own cities.

JP: The final question is, what shall we do with all this money? One part of it is giving to the next generation and looking after family welfare, one part of it is for philanthropy, are there any other experiential causes that you have come across or you yourself are going through in terms of smelling the roses and utilising that amount of money?

Navneet: I think in the US, especially, there is a culture of giving. There are two levels of tax deduction, one when you give and the second when you die, you save on death tax, which is 50 per cent, while you are living and 40 per cent when you are dead—put together, that's a lot of tax. Whether it's tax motivated or incentivised, there is a culture of giving, and I think Indians are giving and will continue to give.

Somebody once told me that we should give as nature gives, without regard to the recipient. Nature gives oxygen to a criminal as well as a rich person and doesn't worry about who's getting it. Same with water, and if an apple falls anybody can pick it up. To some extent, I think people have to stop worrying about who's getting the money and just give. Because, yes, there's a little bit of wastage in a non-profit in India or anywhere else, but there's a little bit of wastage at IBM and AT&T as well. Thus, 10–15 per cent is wasted everywhere. Also, you just got a 50 per cent tax deduction, so the wastage can be more than 50 per cent, so even if there is 50 per cent wastage of all of your money, you're still ahead! And furthermore, if you look at the top charities in the world and even in India, the top charities in India have more than 10,000 employees, those 10,000 people got a livelihood, and becomes part of your giving even if the ultimate result is not that great.

I think at the end of the day, if people start giving and started trusting these non-profits, while not giving it blindly but doing some due diligence—so that's one. Second, they could give it to their pet causes and third, they could give it to their cities. Fourth, especially with the ultra-rich, what are their kids going to do? Their kids are studying at Stanford and Harvard, and then they'll start a business, they'll do their start-up and succeed or fail. If they fail, no big deal they've lost a few million, fine. If they succeed, now we add another $50 million to their already $500 million pot. Then what are the kids going to do afterwards? They are going to do charity work, so then, might as well hand over the kid the charity that you started to begin with and that's their livelihood.

JP: Do you meet and talk to some of these millennials and find out what they think about all these ideas including the wealth of the family, as well as giving away the wealth?

Navneet: Yes, I do. These are very interesting conversations and sometimes it takes about three or four meetings for them to see their entire world. First, we have to tell them of the secret non-profit world, of how all of the good in America is actually being done by the non-profits. By the way, the Fortune 500 companies only employ about 7 per cent of America; the small businesses employ almost 80 per cent of America. The largest employer in America is the non-profit world, it employs 10 per cent of the country and doesn't go away anywhere. The Googles of the world come and go but the non-profit world doesn't go.

My favourite moment is to sit in a room with a rich mother, father, and three kids in their 20s and the kids know their parents are worth $300 million. At some point in the meeting, I turn to the kids and say to them, "You know kiddos I have some advice for you. Let me share a national statistic with you. Most people get their parents' wealth in the United States when they are in their 50s, so please don't wait for your parents to die. You are not going to get their money for the next 30 years. Please manage to live your own life and figure out what you want to do in life. Your parents are going to live a long life. They have money now, so they are going to get surgeries and they are going to get a new heart and a new liver, and everything else. They are not going to die anytime soon. They are going to live into their 90s. They are fitter today than they were 10 years ago when they were running their business, so they are not going anywhere.

Andrew Carnegie died at age 94, 150 years ago, because of wealth."
It's interesting to see how the kids react. Some of them are very good,
very mature, and they realise all of this and say, "Yes, we want to do
charity work. We will be involved in our parents' foundation. But we
also want to prove ourselves—that we can also do what our parents
did. We also want to try to build up a business and that we'll do on
the side, but yes, we'll run the charity."

JP: In Asian culture, it is common for people to tell their kids how
much wealth they have.

Navneet: It's actually becoming more and more common, partly
because they want their kids involved in the estate planning. They
need to tell them, because now the rich mother and father are
travelling a lot. They are concerned that they might not wake up
one day. They want to tell their kids where their wealth is because
it's very spread out; it's in 50 LLPs, several real estate ventures,
in the stock market with several brokers in several countries, and
in several mutual funds, and they actually have a small army of
people just managing the wealth, 10 people at a time just overseeing
their wealth.

JP: Isn't that overwhelming for the millennials?

Navneet: It is, but I think they grew up with it. They have a different
mindset; they have travelled enough.

JP: Where do they get their motivation? Money is not a motivation
for them anymore, right? They know that there is a big bag of money
that's sitting on the side.

Navneet: You know when you get on a ladder and climb up to 20
feet; you see a different world that you and I may not see from the
ground. When you climb up to, let's say 50 feet, all of a sudden, you
see a world which includes Northern Trust which is a trust company
that manages rich people's money. It's a 130-year-old company
with several trillion dollars under management. Their offices are
built like heaven, with sofas, plants, and welcoming suites and then
they'll have seminars for rich kids. There are organisations that do a
one-week or a month-long camp for rich kids. When you climb up
another 100 feet you see another world, of YPO (Young Presidents'
Organization) doing a seminar for their rich kids and recently

I read about one of the big US banks doing a one month camp for the rich kids of their clients, where the bankers tell the kids every day about what the other rich kids are doing. Another world becomes visible to them. They swim in that aquarium, they get to know all that stuff, and that's motivating for them, that they are not alone.

JP: What about ambition? Their fathers ventured out and came to live in the United States, for example, and started a company, worked extremely hard, struggled through the ups and downs and then exited and suddenly came into money. Are they ambitious to strike out on their own?

Navneet: Some, of course, waste their parents' money, enjoy, and party—their parents have created that atmosphere for them to enjoy. But most of them are very well-educated at prestigious colleges and once you end up at Harvard or Stanford, now you have to compete with your colleagues and whether somebody is rich or not is no longer relevant. Money is actually out of the equation.

Then there's colleges like the Babson College that has a course on family wealth and family generational wealth and how to transfer wealth from one generation to another, they have an undergraduate degree in that, so some may end up there. Some of my rich clients for instance have big families—three to four brothers, sisters, their kids, and they are 60 people now living off one core business that they either sold or built. Sometimes I do these seminars with their entire family present. We can hire consultants that will show up and speak to this family of 60, once a year. Then the seniors of the family will present seminars on how the business is going and where they can invest and get the younger generation involved.

JP: What have you thought for yourself? You are still young, but in the next 10 to 20 years, you would begin to think about all the same issues with your wealth.

Navneet: I have always told my kids about our wealth—I share my tax returns with them. When my son was 10 or 11 years old, I taught him how to do my tax returns and he did my tax returns. They know everything about our financial situation. Very early on, I got them involved in the charity world. My son had an allowance of $1 per week when he was six, but I would only give him 65 cents. He said, 'What happened to a buck?" I said, "Well, 25 cents went into taxes and 10 went to charity." That's the first time we touched money. I've told them to do whatever they want; they want to get involved in a business, that's fine, if not then they can do whatever they want.

Personally, I contribute a lot to India but not enough and I want to do more. I feel that the next liberation of India will come from law. We had economic independence in 1991 and political freedom in 1947. However, the next revolution will come from law, but lawyers are treated very badly. There are 30 million cases pending. There's no justice in India. Period. Law is the grease that runs the commerce and industry of a country. There's immense amount of contractual fraud; contracts are not enforced. We have started the Indian Lawyers Association in India, finally. After 70 years, we now have 102 cities that have an Indian Lawyers Association chapter. We want to invoke the goodness of law and the importance of law. I will be dedicating a lot of my time to that.

Suril Desai
International Lawyer, Nishith Desai Associates

JP: May I request you to introduce yourself.

Suril: I am a lawyer, a documentary filmmaker, a big crypto currency block chain enthusiast, and now also an artist. I got my Bachelor of Science in International Management from Menlo College, California. I spent six years in Silicon Valley before deciding to come back to India and I pursued my degree in law from Government Law College in Mumbai, where I specialised in Criminology. Soon after, I attended a Diploma course in Advanced Legal Studies in Counter Terrorism at The Hague, Netherlands. I took this course mainly because the 26/11 terror attacks in Mumbai were very close to home and that got me thinking about this issue a lot. I was also amongst the first few people to visit the Jewish Chabad in Nariman House after the attack.

Currently, I am in the middle of completing my second documentary feature called, *The Mumbai Jews*. And more recently, I completed my documentary *Iron Khan*, which is about a former militant mujahedeen commander of Jammu & Kashmir Liberation Front (JKLF). I have also worked very closely with Nobel Laureate, Professor Muhammad Yunus and on several occasions travelled with him to Europe and Bangladesh.

JP: And you're part of Nishith Desai Associates.

Suril: It's a family law firm, which my father founded. My journey actually began in the year 2000. That's when I had just started studying in the US. My father decided that he wanted to open an office in Silicon Valley. I transferred out of my university in the Midwest to Menlo College. I got an opportunity to meet a lot of venture capitalists and new age entrepreneurs. I came back to India in 2006 and decided that I would pursue my law degree from India rather than the US, mainly because to practice Indian law, I would have to be an Indian qualified lawyer.

JP: What was your lifestyle and perspective on money growing up?

Suril: When I was born in 1980, my father had just decided that he would take a sabbatical from work and write a book called *The Non-Resident Indians*, for NRIs who wished to invest in India.

123

The first four-five years of my life were in Khira Nagar, in a small apartment, probably about 250 square feet in which all of us lived including my sister and me. As time progressed, we moved from Santacruz to a bigger apartment at Juhu beach, which was about 1,000 square feet. Growing up in the 1990s, as a kid, I had never really felt that we were falling short of anything but obviously I wouldn't get as many toys like the other kids my age, probably because we were not as affluent at that point. My father had his big break when liberalisation took place in 1991 and the Indian markets opened up.

As a kid, we didn't take too many holidays. My first international trip was at the age of seven. In those days, we would mostly spend time at my dad's friend's place in the US and in Europe. I'd never really thought too much about money because by the time I was 14, I was aware of my dad's business of international taxation.

I got my first experience of money when I turned 18, and my dad decided that I should go on a backpacking trip to Alaska for a month. I was given some $200 and I thought that would be enough. Within the first 15 days, I had already finished my money and at that point, from the middle of Alaska I called up my father. It was not easy to send money to Alaska. If it was some other part of the US at least some family friend could have sent something. At that point, I decided that I will continue to stay, and I ended up washing school buses and painting fences and in exchange for all those things I was shown Alaska by the locals. That was the first time I experienced the shortage of money in my life.

JP: Tell us about your lifestyle. Has your perspective on money changed?

Suril: For me now it's not about how much money or wealth I've accumulated but it's more important that I have access to credit, because access to credit is far more important to me than holding wealth. Being credit worthy is a very important issue for me. I've worked very closely with Professor Yunus and in microfinance, what I have realised, is that if people are given access to even a little bit of money to improve or empower themselves, it can change the world for the better.

JP: Is there anything specific you enjoy spending money on?

Suril: I do spend my money. I mean I do enjoy my luxuries, good clothes, and good brands, but I recently spent a couple of thousand rupees on helping these Dharavi rappers make a music video. I like doing those kinds of altruistic things—like if I find someone who is creative, I can choose between spending on buying a pair of shoes or spending it on improving someone's life—that's what excites me. I like to see people being empowered when I spend, more than anything else. Even when buying a luxurious item, if it's empowering the sales person, that gets me excited.

JP: What is your philosophy on giving or philanthropy? Do you have any ideas of what are you going to do with all the money that you're going to inherit?

Suril: At the moment, a lot of my money will go to things that encourage innovation and things that can inspire people. For example, my documentary film company is called Yugen Media, which is more of a passion project. There are certain issues that I want to focus on. One is cross-border terrorism, so I made *Iron Khan* for that. At the same time, I'm making another one which is called *Mumbai Jews*, with an Israeli production house. And then there's a third one in the process which is about an Iraqi refugee, who is a Sufi musician and is married to a contemporary dancer, she's from Jerusalem—so I'm trying to make interesting, inspiring documentaries showing the goodness that's there in the world, because I feel there is a lot of good in the world and many a times it's there in front of us but we don't seem to be able to focus on it. That would be one, and the other part would be sponsoring things like snowboarding in the Himalayas. One of my pet projects right now is to start this thing called Boarders Without Borders, to build a winter sports league in the Himalayan region, because I realised that it's one of the most heavily conflicted areas of the world and it's one place where winter sports can really make a world of difference.

JP: You also mentioned that you follow the FinTech industry and crypto currencies, so what do you think is the future of money?

Suril: I believe the way we look at money is going to be drastically different in the future. Crypto currency has become very exciting. I started reading up about Bitcoins in 2011. The way I see it, more crypto currencies will become the norm in the near future. For example, gaming has just become a huge industry and some of the earliest crypto usage was in the gaming sector. If someone was playing a virtual game and they wanted either a new weapon or they wanted to proceed to another level, they would need points; while they were playing these games, in the middle of the game someone from some part of the world would ask them to send a pair of head phones and in return that person would give you 1,000 points for it. I look at money as becoming more gamified and different crypto currencies are just gamification of finance, in my opinion. Once it becomes a game in which there are rules, then each currency will have its own regulations and its own way of use.

I look at crypto currency as more like gamification of finance, which has not happened in the past. Everything is becoming more interactive and finance has been the one lagging, as it has been kept as a very serious domain; but once it gets gamified it opens up for a lot more people to participate. Also, the existing financial system has not really changed much in the past 200 years. Now, when I think of Bitcoins today, I think of email sometime in 1985–1986, or the Internet at that point where everyone thought that it was just going to be about sending and receiving messages. Now, it's not just sending and receiving messages, it's about e-commerce, it's about video streaming. The same kind of wave is going to come in the financial sector of fintech and crypto currencies.

JP: Do you have any advice for the millennials who are going to inherit billions of dollars in the next decade or two.

Suril: We are in an age where there's so much fear being put into the minds of people, from climate change to wars and political unrest and things like that. I would like to tell the millennials that all these things have happened in every generation and that they should be fearless and follow their hearts. They also have to take on some kind of responsibility towards the ones who are not as fortunate as they are. For me, a successful human being is someone who makes two or more people more successful along with them. Success should not just be about how much wealth you accumulate, that's just one part of it. It should also be about how many people you are able to empower. They should not get enamoured by competition, instead they should collaborate with each other and do things that brings joy, fun, and excitement into their lives.

Private Bankers

Shiv Gupta
Founder and CEO, Sanctum Wealth Management

Nilesh Shah
Desk Head, UBS Bank

Sanjeev Sardana
Founder and CEO, BluePointe Capital

Shiv Gupta

Founder and CEO, Sanctum Wealth Management

JP: May I request you to introduce yourself.

Shiv: I am a 44-year-old wealth manager, born in Lucknow, Uttar Pradesh. My father was a civil servant and my mother was a university lecturer. We moved around a lot when I was growing up, although a lot of time was also spent in Delhi. Over the years, I went to a succession of schools, with the last five in a boarding school in the north called The Lawrence School, Sanawar. I then went to Delhi University and read economics at Hindu College. I am married to my college sweetheart, who I also knew in school, and we have two wonderful children aged 12 and 10.

My career started in Switzerland, where I worked as a trainee at the Citi private bank. This was my accidental entry into wealth management, at the time meant as a stop-gap. As things evolved, however, I kept getting drawn deeper into it through a succession of fortuitous events and here I am, 23 years later, still going strong in the same business. From Switzerland, I had moved to Singapore and after 10 years there, I moved back to India in 2009. In the course of my career, I have held several different roles within the wealth management domain, the last few being in leadership positions.

JP: Growing up, what was your perspective on money and what did money mean to you?

Shiv: First, some background along the lines I mentioned earlier. I grew up in a civil services family on my father's side. My mother, whilst erstwhile royalty, was a teacher. Five children of a distinguished police officer, who were all equally distinguished in their own rights, with four going to the civil services—three to the IAS, one to the IFS. They all studied at top institutions of their time like the Allahabad and Delhi universities, and were generally at the top of their respective classes. They could have chosen anything they wanted to do with their lives. But at the core, there was this deep, social contribution orientation that ran in the family, and this is what may have led most of them into the services. Alongside this, the idea of amassing wealth beyond that considered adequate for meeting your fundamental needs, and comfortably navigating your day-to-day life with dignity, was not considered appealing.

In the year before he joined the IAS, my father was selected for a senior management training programme at a premier private sector organisation. This was a sought-after programme where, in fact, one of his colleagues was Shiv Nadar. They remain friends to this day. And whilst my father left the programme and went on to distinguish himself in his civil services work—it gives you an idea of the kind of paths that may have been available.

We didn't grow up with a lot of money. Despite this, I don't think we ever felt deprived. We lived in large government houses and went to the best schools. Being from a middle-class family, education was a major imperative. But disposable income was limited. I do have several memories of 'living-within-our-means', such as the ones where we went shopping with my mother, in cyclerickshaws in Lucknow, looking for bargains, including at flea markets. These experiences played a huge role in shaping the way I think about money. I'm not driven by it, but I do value it and recognise the importance of having it.

JP: How did your dad do, career-wise?

Shiv: My father handled some of the most sensitive, dangerous, and difficult assignments over the years—including many law-and-order situations in riot-torn areas. He had a distinguished career and retired as a Union Home Secretary after having been Chief Secretary of Uttarakhand, and having held several very important and productive assignments over the years.

JP: You had an illustrious career in the banking sector and now you are the founder of an enterprise. Can you describe that journey?

Shiv: Thanks, Jayesh. In a 20-year career span, I had the good fortune of working with three top global private banks across Europe, the Middle East, and Asia, including holding some challenging leadership positions. Fifteen of these years were with The Royal Bank of Scotland (RBS) group, which was heavily affected by the financial crisis. In fact, it is because of this that I got an opportunity to become an entrepreneur. In one of several rounds of post-crisis reshaping and restructuring, RBS decided to sell its private banking businesses outside of the UK. This was in 2014 and was also the time when some other foreign private banks were leaving India. Having built out a successful RBS private bank here (India), we wanted to find a way of continuing it in any form that we could find.

We also felt it was a good time for India, from a structural growth opportunity perspective. Together with my management team and a bunch of illustrious and supportive mentors, partners, and investors such as yourself, we went to RBS with the proposal for a management buyout (MBO). This was a first-of-its-kind initiative, and complex at many levels, with possible failure at every turn. Despite this, through a systematic approach and the goodwill of many people within and outside RBS, we succeeded with the MBO deal. To house the new business, we set up a new firm and called it Sanctum Wealth Management. Our thinking was that if we can combine the best attributes of foreign firms with those of domestic firms, and get rid of the undesirable ones, we would have a winning combination. That meant being well-governed and well-packaged on the one hand whilst being flexible and agile on the other. This, in our view, is the essence of Sanctum Wealth Management, which was formally launched on 1 April 2016. We really like that date!

JP: Based on your personal journey, how has your perspective on money changed from the days you were growing up in Delhi, to where you are today?

Shiv: My thinking on money has evolved not just because of my own professional and financial growth, but also because being a wealth manager, these principles are at the core of what we think about and do for our clients. Based on my own experiences, and those of our clients, over the years I have come to see money as serving four functions. First and foremost is that it provides security, the presence or absence of which influences many other emotions. It provides access to opportunities, which can be manifested in a myriad different ways. It is also a means to indulge your interests and experiences, which is a source of well-being and affects the quality of your life. The final one relates to the top of Maslow's hierarchy, whether through an esteem or self-actualisation lens, and is based on the idea that if you are fortunate enough to have accumulated a certain amount of wealth, it allows you to contribute to your community or causes you to care about and this provides a form of spiritual fulfilment.

JP: As a private banker and wealth manager you have been in Switzerland, you have been in Singapore, and now you are here in India and you have a reasonably large client base. Can you share some examples of giving and community building?

131

Shiv: To begin with, let me say that there is a lot more happening in the giving space now, Jayesh, then there was before. It is encouraging to see that a lot of philanthropic activity is being led by prominent people like the Premjis, the Nadars, the Murthy family, and others who are helping to shine the right kind spotlight on the subject and creating a sense of strategic philanthropy. Further, organisations like Dasra are playing their part in trying to get the ecosystem working in ways that can be catalytic. Looking at them, many people have started setting up their own giving vehicles or identifying vehicles through which they can contribute. Traditionally, a lot of giving has happened through religious institutions or close-knit communities or networks and has been heavily skewed towards causes driven by or linked to those institutions. And even though the wider ecosystem has been getting stronger more recently, we have some way to go for the scale and scope of giving to achieve its transformational potential.

JP: As a wealth manager or personally, what advice would you give millennials who are going to come into billions of dollars in this next decade or two?

Shiv: You know how difficult this question is to answer, Jayesh, in an environment where these days we are asking millennials to tell us how to do things. Nevertheless, I'll give it a try with two pieces of advice.

The first really applies to any young investor, who should spend time focussing on learning the boring fundamentals of investing, many of which are core principles that endure over long stretches of time despite the disruption all around. This is particularly important for people with non-financial backgrounds. In today's noisy environment, it is increasingly difficult to separate the signal from the noise and the best way to do so is by applying strong fundamentals and hands-on experience.

The second is really more encouragement than advice and is driven by the social consciousness that I have observed amongst many of our millennial clients. A lot of them care about social causes and take issues such as responsible investing very seriously. I wholeheartedly support this and encourage millennials to think early on about causes they consider important, explore philanthropic activity in a strategic way, and look for ways to systematically weave their social contribution into how they construct their investment and corporate portfolios.

Nilesh Shah
Desk Head, UBS Bank

JP: May I request you to introduce yourself.

Nilesh: I am from Mumbai originally, I moved to Singapore in late 1990. In Mumbai, I've done my MBA in Finance. I come from a lower-middle-class family. To give you an idea, we were six people in a one-bedroom flat. I've seen life in a very different way when I was in Mumbai. And then I have also seen a little bit of affluence coming into the family, and how we made money. You have a very different feeling about money when you are in India; and when you migrate to Singapore, you get a very different perspective about money again. Suddenly, you realise that whatever you felt was very big over there, is very small in Singapore, but the same amount of money makes a big difference just because of the geographical change.

JP: Where did you study?

Nilesh: I studied in a simple Parsi school. I think that was one of the best things that happened to me, because Parsis have a unique way in which they bring up children. I've lived in a Parsi community, so a lot of my friends have been Parsis. The Parsis are one of the best communities to learn from how to be humble. I was in R A Podar College and I did my Commerce accounting, and then I did my MBA from N M College.

JP: What was your perspective on money growing up?

Nilesh: That's of course a relative thing, right? How much, how big, where—you take that amount of money and you move to a different location and suddenly things become very small and the reverse works too. Many times we think, if I have this pot of money, I can retire nicely in India because I can afford the so-called luxuries over there. Then as you grow older, probably your needs are lesser and then you say I can make do with that money. Perspectives do change as you grow up, you mature and you see other people, perspectives change because you see things on TV and social media because now you're looking at being them, whatever you see there. Perspective changes because your friends change. The kind of friends I had growing up are very different from the friends I have today.

JP: Tell us about your transition from Bombay to Singapore.

Nilesh: I came to Singapore; I joined the family business here. My mama (mother's brother) is from Singapore. I joined the family business and surprisingly, I transitioned into becoming a banker after 14 years in business. Since 2004, I have been a private banker, thanks to all the friends who motivated me to do that—Jayesh you are one of them. I'm a private banker; I work with a large multinational bank here. Again, the perspective is very different because now you're working with a very different group of people where the number of zeros in their bank account are much more than what you would traditionally see.

JP: How has your perspective on money changed in this transition?

Nilesh: Well, earlier, before I got into spirituality, my perspective was that every time you meet somebody who is so called 'better off' than you, you want to be that person. You would want to be saying, "Hey, can I be that? How can I get that?" You are constantly just thinking about materialism, constantly just thinking about how you can make more money. Ever since I've been a banker, and luckily, spirituality came into my life at the same time, things have begun to change slowly. I'm not saying it happens overnight, but it changes because you're open to new experiences. The important part is that you have to be open to new experiences and then you come around and say, "I think there's another way of looking at life." Suddenly a completely new world opens up and you realise that you know what—it may not be just money after all. There could be many more things.

In a simple example—suppose I give you $50 million but you have to give me something in return, and that thing I want happens to be your peace of mind on a permanent basis. Would you do it? Most of the time the answer I get is, "No way!" Moreover, 99.99 per cent of people, without the blink of an eye, have told me, "No, I need peace of mind." This clearly shows that it's not just money. There's something more to it. Just because somebody is rich or affluent in terms of wealth, it doesn't mean that he has peace of mind, doesn't mean that he's having a great family life.

JP: But since you've transitioned into relative affluence, would you not say that there is peace of mind that has come into your life, because of that affluence?

Nilesh: Definitely. You know Jayesh, I have also gone through that phase where we were struggling to pay tuition fees. I know you've been there too, that time where you come around and say, "Hey, let's just forget everything else. Let's just run the family first." That's why I'm telling you that I've been lucky that I bumped into somebody at that point of time and my perspective changed. Again, I'm not saying it happened overnight, but because of your willingness to experiment, the turbulence that you're going through changes completely, without money. Instead of having volatility, suddenly you will find that there is a little bit of peace coming in. I'm not saying that 'chinta', the part where you constantly think about money goes away, but it definitely reduces.

JP: As a private banker, you manage large sums of money for affluent clients. Please give us some ideas and examples of what affluent people are doing with their money.

Nilesh: Oh, it's very interesting Jayesh, you know, from 2004 to now I have seen a huge, huge, huge difference. One of the differences I've observed is that, the baby boomers are retiring and they're handing over their wealth to the millennials and they, surprisingly, have a very different thought process. The millennials still want the fast cars, they still want luxury watches, they want to go to the best universities, but when you talk to them about investments, they are willing to listen and implement. They are coming around and saying, "I only want to do sustainable investments. I want to do investments which mean something to this economy, there's a social impact or it means that I invest into, for example, something to do with the earth being green, alternative investments, alternative energy investments, solar energy investments." That's the reason you would have seen so many ETFs (exchange-traded funds) being launched now on sustainable investing.

JP: How is that transition working in terms of passing on the wealth and shift in the investment allocations, with respect to the senior patriarchs of the families?

Nilesh: How the patriarchs react is different from culture to culture, some of them don't want to let go. They still like the control.

That particular group, what we've observed is that they use the returns derived from the financial assets for a better cause. For example, they could be running hospitals in a third world country; they could be doing women empowerment in a third world country; they could be doing cancer palliative care in the third world countries, doing something for vision impairment. Yes, they do spend money, however they're not hands on, I would say. They believe in just giving it to somebody and running with it. However, now I do see growth where they come around and say, "Let's form our own organisation where we employ professional people." They are deploying the funds in a professional manner or they are handing over funds to other organisations that are running it in a professional manner.

JP: Do you have a personal philosophy on giving and philanthropy?

Nilesh: Yes, I do. It used to be only donations to be honest, when I first came here. You are part of a particular society, so you'll donate to the society because one of the values that were inculcated when we were young is always give back. As things have changed and as life has gotten better for me, my perspective has also changed, and now I ask myself, is giving money enough? At this point, I've come to the conclusion that it isn't. I would rather ask, when I have the luxury of time on my hands, which I do now, can I make a difference in somebody's life? You can do that in various ways, whether it is just helping that person who is ill, or it could be making an entrepreneur out of an ordinary plumber.

JP: Any words of wisdom for the millennials who are going to inherit billions of dollars in the future?

Nilesh: I'm experimenting with the question: can I make a difference in somebody's life? If they can just ask themselves the same small question every day. Try not to make a difference by just giving the $5. Try to come around and say, "I've got something nice. I've learned something from my parents, I have learned something from my teachers, and can I now share that with somebody who may not get that same opportunity?"

Sanjeev Sardana
Founder and CEO, BluePointe Capital

JP: May I request you to introduce yourself.

Sanjeev: I am a wealth manager and Founder CEO of BluePointe Capital. We manage money for tech entrepreneurs in the Bay Area.

JP: You know there is a lot of money out there. I want to get a glimpse from you, as to what all these affluent people do with their money. The first thing that most people would like to do is to take care of their next generation—is that true?

Sanjeev: That is true, and it also depends on what stage of your life you make money. As a wealth manager, having been in the business for about 20 years, what I have seen is that people who made money in their 40s and today are in their late 50s or early 60s, are closer to accomplishing their philanthropic goals. They carve out separate money and the goal is to only increase that amount of money into either a private foundation or a donor advised fund.

For people who are in their 30s, this is not something that they are focussed on, no matter how much money one has made. With very young entrepreneurs, what I am finding is that philanthropy is the first thing that they talk about. From age 20–30, they have more of an interest in doing philanthropic work or at least setting money aside for it; people in their 30s to 45, not so much. Within the Indian community, which is essentially the community that I work with, it is changing in the last 10–15 years, it was not something that was on the priority list, but now I am seeing that more and more—and I hope it continues.

JP: What about the people who made a lot of money throughout their life? Are they busy making money on their money or are they doing something different?

Sanjeev: Most are definitely busy making money on their money, and some don't really understand what they need all this money for. It is still very rare to find people who actually have thought through, what they would do beyond the money that they need for their family, how they would effectively give it to charity. There are a few people I know who are like that and I have a lot of respect for them. Still, I feel, there aren't enough people out there, thinking strategically about what to do with their money and about creating a legacy.

JP: The balance, which is for their wellbeing, what are they using it for?

Sanjeev: They are thinking about the generations ahead because as they say, you can go shirtsleeves to shirtsleeves within three generations, if you don't plan for that money properly.

JP: Can you talk about that a little bit?

Sanjeev: There is the first person who ends up making money. If they don't invest it wisely, then the second generation comes along and does not have the same appreciation for the money that was made by the parents. That money slowly starts to dwindle away. The third generation comes along and again if there is no discipline that money is gone. It is something that we talk to our clients about, they are cognizant about that and what we start to see now is that generation-skipping trust are being formed so that the next generation is taken care of.

JP: Are there any wealthy people who have figured out a life beyond making money or giving it away?

Sanjeev: First, that is essentially what we are currently managing for them but without necessarily knowing where it's going to go or whom it is going to go to. However, if you go back and look at the traditional way of thinking, the wealth is going to be left to the kids. When you talk to the kids, especially in the Bay Area, what you find is that the kids themselves are very aspirational, many a times we have heard them basically tell their parents, "We don't need your money. Mom and dad, we are going to make our own money."

JP: If the kids are not interested in the money that the parents plan to leave behind for them, then are the parents open to changing their lifestyle and making use of that money?

Sanjeev: Some of them start to travel more, for example, give it to other family members, which is very important. Eventually, if the money remains unused, it will probably go to charity. I think it's going to be a real test for the generation of millionaires who made money from the dot com boom days, because that generation is now close to retiring and we'll see what happens with them.

JP: There are two types of millennials—the ones who are working hard and want to make money on their own and are not interested in their parent's money, but then there are others who are managing their parent's money.

Sanjeev: We seldom see the latter—there is just not enough interest in those kids (to manage their parent's money). You have parents who don't want to tell their kids how much money they have.

JP: What is the percentage of people that do tell their children about the money?

Sanjeev: I would say, probably 20–30 per cent do tell their kids how much money they have, at an appropriate age. The dilemma is that, if you have founded and are the CEO of a company, and have made hundreds of millions of dollars, but your kids are may be 5 or 10 years old, what are you going to tell them at this stage, right? However, it's something that does need coaching as these kids grow up. We have held events where we would bring in a psychologist or somebody to talk to these entrepreneurs about the right time to talk to the kids about the money and how you should tell them.

JP: Once these kids come of age and realise that they are going to come into a huge amount of wealth, have you spoken with any of them about what they would do with all that money, once they inherit it?

Sanjeev: Well, there are very few who have said, "I know how much I am supposed to get but it's not something that I am going to count on. It is something I am going to fall back on, but my goal is to try and make my own money." I would say there are probably very few who would actually not do anything of their own in life and just rely on their parent's money.

JP: And is this a cultural thing? Is this very special and peculiar to the Bay Area or to the south Asian diaspora?

Sanjeev: I think it has more to do with the Bay Area because kids who have been born and brought up here, at this stage in life, they are quite American. Now, are they influenced by Southeast Asian culture? I would say so, as well, but I would think that this thinking is much more mainstream.

139

JP: In terms of the philosophy of philanthropy, do you see a pattern here? Are they giving it away to their home country in south Asia, or are they giving it to religious charities? Are they interested in social development? Are they giving the money to social causes, and measuring the social impact created?

Sanjeev: I see quite a bit of money being given to charities within the US. For example, money is given to the graduate school that the entrepreneur or the family may have an affinity with or some kind of affiliation. We also see money going back to India, to schools, which they may have attended or the village they grew up in.

JP: Are these contributions systematically managed by them? Is it self-directed philanthropy or do they give money to other organisations, for example, Akshaya Patra or Sankara Eye Foundation?

Sanjeev: Most of it is still given through, for example, Akshaya Patra, there is also the India Community Centre, OVBI (Overseas Volunteers for a Better India), Sankara Eye Foundation, Maitri etc. There are all these programs to choose from, and they give through charities that support the causes they believe in.

JP: Are there others who want to create their own philanthropic foundation, direct it, and hire people to run it, like Bill & Melinda Gates Foundation and Michael & Susan Dell Foundation?

Sanjeev: We do see that, but I think that at this point the money that the Indian diaspora is giving away is not to that extent. While the idea of a private foundation sounds good and we do have some clients who have them, it is not easy to manage one. You have to give away 5 per cent each year, you have to file your taxes, and all the record keeping that goes with it. We are seeing more and more people who had set up a private foundation, are now going towards setting up donor-advised funds, just because it is lot easier, you don't have to worry about the 5 per cent every year. Overall, it's much easier to work with.

JP: If asked, what advice would you like to give the extremely affluent people you work with, about what to do with all their money?

Sanjeev: I think that is a very good question. As a company, we give away a percentage of our earnings to charity. The clients see that, we invite them to a lot of events where we buy tables in charity events. It's something I believe in strongly. We do coach our clients to set aside money for their own well-being and for their kids but not to the extent that they may never even use all of it. Give the kids a chance to make their own money, whilst keeping their money as backup; and instead move more money towards their Donor Advised Fund or a private foundation.

JP: Any other advice in terms of how you can inspire them to smell the roses—they work so hard to make this money. How are they enjoying that money?

Sanjeev: People enjoy money in different ways. Definitely within the Southeast Asian community, we don't see them buying yachts and planes—though there are exceptions; but for the most part, we have not really seen their lifestyle change drastically, once they have made their money. The only difference we may see is the slightly bigger house, maybe a fancier car, but it is very humbling to see people within the community at parties and events and a lot of times you cannot even tell what this person's net worth is.

From my perspective, the advice I'd like to give my clients and people I know is to take the bite while you are living. I tell them to start putting away money towards charity because there is no point waiting and waiting. You want to see that the money you give away is going to work while you are alive, and you can see the benefits of that.

Professors

Professor Jagdish Sheth, PhD
Professor, Emory University

Professor Srikumar Rao, PhD
Founder, The Rao Institute

Professor Raj Sisodia, PhD
Professor, Babson College

Professor Vivek Wadhwa
Professor, Carnegie Mellon and Harvard University

Professor Jagdish Sheth, PhD

Professor, Emory University

JP: May I request you to introduce yourself.

Professor Jagdish: I am a professor of business at Emory University. I have been teaching for about 55 years starting at Columbia University, MIT, University of Illinois, University of Southern California, and now at Emory for the last 27 years.

JP: May I also request you to tell us the number of books you've written.

Professor Jagdish: Technically, I have written more than 30 books, but my own count would be about 20.

JP: Where did you grow up? What was your standard of living growing up?

Professor Jagdish: I am a refugee from Burma (now Myanmar), and this is before World War II when Japan militarily expanded westwards towards India and took over Burma in late 1940. We just had to run for the last ship and lost everything. We struggled hard for about eight years, tried to settle in different places in India and ultimately, we settled as a family in South India in a city called Chennai—in my days, we used to call it Madras. I came to the United States in 1961 as an MBA student for a one-year program at the University of Pittsburgh. We had no money. I was given a Fellowship. Two families provided me with money to travel to the US and to pay for my living expenses. Then I decided to switch my subject and go for a Doctorate in Behavioural Sciences. I came into the discipline of marketing, the academic side by understanding the psychology of consumers (consumer psychology). That's my background.

JP: What was your perception of money growing up?

Professor Jagdish: I was brought up in a Gandhian family and my own religion is Jainism. Both philosophies strongly recommend that you should not get attached to money because if you get more attached to your material possessions (especially money) the more self-destructive habit it becomes. It is one of the four major self-destructive habits we acquire as human beings. Therefore, one has to learn how to practice having association with money and still

145

be detached. Hence, you are not driven by money as the ultimate outcome, and instead you are driven by some other purpose in life such as giving back or unlocking the potential of others. Money is just an exchange of value and it should not be used as storage value (wealth).

JP: You also got involved with many big corporations as a consultant and board member. Can you describe that journey?

Professor Jagdish: Very early in my career in the US, I got married while I was a doctorate student. We had a couple of children and I was a single wage earner. My university income was not enough for a growing family. Therefore, I began to do extra work beyond teaching the regular MBA classes at Columbia University. I started teaching seminars to industry and that is how I got into the consulting business, became an advisor to corporations and eventually I also sat on the boards of companies, some large ones. One of the largest was Wipro in India and I was on their board for 19 years and their advisor for over 35 years when Wipro was a Vanaspati and soap company. In the advising role, you learn quite a lot. Often, you get to have a one on one conversation with the chairman of the company. Over time, I began to observe that for most people who earn money without purpose, life becomes meaningless. In other words, they are really lonely inside, empty, and they don't know what to do after earning a lot of money. Once they retire, they feel very isolated. That again led me to observe that there is a higher purpose that one has to be driven by as opposed to be driven by accumulation of wealth.

JP: You've also been a consultant to countries, right professor?

Professor Jagdish: Yes, I have been advisor to countries more at the macro level, primarily about positioning the future of a nation. I was heavily involved in the telecommunications industry, and I am the founder of a strategic centre at University of Southern California called the Center for Telecom Management (CTM). I was an advisor to specific departments in government bureaus including the Federal Communications Commission (FCC) as well as Department of Transportation (DOT) during the first energy crisis. However, at a national level, probably the most satisfying has been advices to the government of Singapore.

JP: How has your perception of money changed over the years?

Professor Jagdish: The current obsession of shareholder value is a very recent phenomenon. In my research, I found out that it really began to become the dominant paradigm only after the first energy crisis from 1974 to 1978, when private equity took over many large conglomerates. The only objective of a private equity investor is to create value for their investors at the expense of other stakeholders. There were books written about this ruthless process of laying off people through outsourcing and automation. One of the most popular books was *Barbarians at the Gate*, which discussed how KKR took over R J Reynolds and broke it up to make money for their private equity investors.

This lead to the conscious capitalism movement. My observation was that if a company has its headquarters in a small town where it began its business and if it stays there (even though it may be a large multinational) and the chairman, and the founding family members live in the community itself, that is a great equaliser. Your managers are your neighbours, their children go to the same school as your children or grandchildren, you all go to the same church, and every Sunday it reminds the founders that they are not above faith and God. It is not enough to make money any way possible, and then give it back to the society through foundations, like Alfred Nobel did. He invented dynamite, which is very harmful material, and felt the need to serve society through awards for new discoveries and inventions. Today this will be true of pharmaceutical companies, especially those who provide opioid drugs. They all have foundations, which support social causes. In your day-to-day living, how do you inculcate the view that you are here primarily as a steward to society and the institution, which is your company, rather than as an owner or manager.

My view is that many of the things that non-profit organisations do in terms of governance, in terms of ethical behaviour, is what the private sector should learn just as the non-profits are learning how to be business efficient and productive from the for-profit corporations.

JP: As you look at today's new start-up ecosystem, do you find that that's actually diverging from what you're saying?

Professor Jagdish: Absolutely. In the old days, wealth was inherited. Whether you are a monarch or whether you are a zamindar or a landlord—as a youngster you are inducted into the business and the family values are often given to you—that you are here as a steward of the business and the community. Your role is to ensure the company will be passed on to future generations. This changes the whole value system. In fact, many good monarchs always sent their young children to go and study under a guru (an Aristotle or a Plato in the western world) and go to an academy where the mission of the academy was to make them (through philosophy and ethics)—more human.

When you are the king or the monarch, you are also the judge, the jury, and the prosecutor, and you can do anything to people who are basically servants or in a position of servitude. It was, therefore, necessary to send the younger generation to an academy and make them more liberal, more caring, and more tolerant. I'm a very strong believer that compassion can be learned. This is not just an inherent trait. Compassion can be learnt as you begin to observe or immerse into other people's suffering. The more you observe suffering (and more you live with suffering of other human beings) the more compassionate you become by definition. The more you have experienced suffering and have survived, you disassociate money as the only end in life. That was the old model.

The new model of becoming a billionaire through a unicorn company at a very young age with no values in place (work without values) is more harmful to the entrepreneur, the investors, and the community at large. There are several recent examples of this especially in the techworld. The latest one is WeWork.

JP: The millennials are going to inherit hundreds of billions of dollars over the next decades. What advice would you have for them? In other words, what shall we do with all this money?

Professor Jagdish: Three things—the first thing is to plan now, before the millennials even come into succession. Planning must be done to give away the money for social causes and be engaged in philanthropy with the three Ts—Treasure, Time, and Talent. Treasure is easier to give than putting in your time and talent. If you are a successful billionaire, you have some capability, some talent; therefore, when you are still active in your business take time out to nurture a non-profit, or a social enterprise of some sort. Create one if you have none. That journey will give more meaning in your own life. By the way, I have found repeatedly that those who make a lot of money and don't care for the community, ironically, the community also shuts itself off to the entrepreneur. They don't want the entrepreneur to be involved. They know it's useless to ask him for money because they know he will not give it. Ultimately, the entrepreneur who is successful is totally isolated. It's like Howard Hughes. He became a recluse because people didn't want him in society; it is passive resistance and passive avoidance.

Therefore, the first lesson is giving back to society in the prime of your life. In any case giving while you're alive is more joyful and pleasant than after you are dead. It will give you more satisfaction and meaning to your own life.

Second, you need to inculcate the millennials, (either employees or family members) into what is called servant leadership. Servant leadership is just the opposite of people serving you. Here you serve others—the more wealth you have, the more you go out and serve society. You have to go out to the poorest of the community and give them meals, prepare meals—not just serve them. I think that servant leadership as a philosophy is becoming common now in all the leadership literature as well as in practice in America. Thus, the second recommendation is servant leadership.

The third suggestion is to adopt somebody as your guru. I like the Chinese wisdom that says that when the student is ready, the teacher will show up. You can learn from anybody. You can learn from your children, you can learn from a guru and you can learn from nature; therefore, develop a habit of learning outside of your field. Take some time out, and the more you learn the more you will become liberal in your beliefs and prejudices. The more breadth of knowledge you acquire and read outside of your technical or business comfort zone, the more human you will become. You will understand that the world is much bigger than your enterprise and your wealth and it will make you humble. As I mentioned, compassion can be learned; passion may be more an aptitude, but compassion is something you can learn by immersing into those situations the way missionaries do, I think that's very important.

Professor Srikumar Rao, PhD

Founder, The Rao Institute

JP: May I request you to introduce yourself.

Professor Rao: I live in Long Island, New York. I'm about to head off to London for the first module of my program—it's called Creativity and Personal Mastery. This is a program that is designed to bring about profound transformation in your life. It sounds very strange and exaggerated, but this is a course which can quietly, truly transform every aspect of your life—your professional life, your personal life, your civic life, your spiritual life.

The reason, I can make such a statement is because I draw my materials from the world's greatest masters. They completely understood the human predicament and they came up with solutions that have been tested over millennia, and they absolutely work. The problem is that they spoke in the language and used examples that were appropriate to the time and the geography in which they lived, and that does not necessarily appeal to modern persons in the post-industrial society. I have taken these great teachings, these wonderful concepts—I've stripped them off religious, cultural, and other connotations and underpinnings. I've adapted them into exercises, which people in top business schools, entrepreneurs, and senior executives can relate to. That's my contribution and that's what I do.

JP: May I ask you to give us a little bit of your background?

Professor Rao: I grew up in India and I was a Physics student. I did my MBA at the Indian Institute of Management, Ahmedabad, and then I came to Columbia to do my PhD in Business. After that, I worked in corporations for a number of years. I went into academe and while I was in academe, I developed this course and I moved to Columbia Business School in 1999. Then it simply exploded. I've taught it at many of the world's top business schools. I've taught it at Columbia, at London Business School, at Kellogg, at Berkeley, and at Imperial College in London. It's been written up all over the place— The New York Times, The Wall Street Journal, Fortune, Forbes, Business Week, Financial Times, London Times, TIME magazine— literally dozens of high-profile publications.

JP: There is more and more affluence all over the world, but the distribution of wealth is skewed. I wanted to get your personal perspective on wealth.

Professor Rao: I think wealth is a wonderful thing. It gives you a number of blessings including the freedom to pursue whatever it is you want. But wealth can also be a curse. And when I say wealth can be a curse, I'm not referring to wealth per se, but the attitude that we have towards wealth. If you devote your whole life and struggle to have wealth because in your head—if you have wealth, you will be happy, you will be secure—that is a completely, completely erroneous model and in the process of accumulating wealth, you really lose the only thing you have which is the present—the journey, your life. Don't strive to achieve wealth, let wealth come to you. Each day engage in something, which brings a greater good to a greater community, and immerse yourself in that.

JP: What is your perspective on money and what is your advice to people who are significantly affluent?

Professor Rao: Wealth is energy and you never own energy. You are merely the temporary custodian. You may think that you now have a big bank balance but one day you are going to die and whatever you have accumulated is going to be stripped away from you. It is going to happen. You might as well recognise that now. It came to you for whatever reasons and it will go away from you for sure. You are a custodian, a trustee. Use it to the best of your ability and in my opinion, the most important single thing you can do with your wealth is to help raise a level of consciousness of as many people as you are capable of.

JP: Can I request you to make any specific comment for the Indian diaspora, in terms of what you would recommend they do with their wealth.

Professor Rao: For the Indian diaspora, what I would recommend is—look around you and do two things. Number one: pick an organisation, which is really doing good work. The social problems in India are immense. Find out, do research, pick an organisation that is doing work in this area and support it financially to the extent that you feel.

By the way, I have a general recommendation here. There is an organisation called Ashoka (www.ashoka.org), and it specialises in finding and supporting social entrepreneurs, and they are in a wide variety of fields. Look up the social entrepreneurs or Ashoka Fellows, see what work they are doing. That's a quick way for you to zero in on people who are working in an area that you care about.

The second thing is do something personal. Find a cause, a person who you think is a worthy person, and support that person, invest your time in helping him. It is not enough for you to say, "I have a lot of money and I'm going to give it away." That is a benefit and a wonderful thing to do but for you to benefit, you have to contribute your time, your personal labour, and your love.

JP: Are there things that either you have thought about for yourself or you have advice for your friends who are affluent, in terms of what they should do with their time besides looking after their family and philanthropy?

Professor Rao: I've noticed that many members of the Indian diaspora who become phenomenally wealthy tend to associate with people who are also on the same quest. I think being phenomenally wealthy is wonderful. However, I think there does come a point where you have to transition, not in terms of accumulating but in terms of what am I going to do with all of this that has come?

There is a wonderful verse from Shankara's *Bhaja Govindam*, which says "Satsangatve Nissangatvam."

In other words, if you want to live a fulfilled life, you should associate with sages and wise people and their influence will rub off on you. You will become like the people you hang out with. Be more selective about the books you read, read philosophical texts, which will take you to a different level of understanding of what life is all about. There are many such works like the talks of Bhagwan Ramana Maharshi, for example, or Nisargadatta Maharaj or the books of Anthony de Mello.

JP: What are your thoughts on succession planning? At what point do you transfer your wealth to your next generation and how much should that be?

Professor Rao: It's difficult to answer because great wealth can be both a blessing and a curse. Whether it is a blessing or a curse depends upon the person who gets it. It's not a question of at what point in time, but it is a question of at what point, meaning the stage of evolution of that person. This is something that you have to work out on a custom basis with a well-connected wealth advisor.

I would say that when you have a transfer, you should also have a transfer with certain stipulations built in. When you are transferring assets typically to spouse, children, or grandchildren, there is a portion "this is needed for them to lead a comfortable life without any financial worries" that would probably include a house or a dwelling, a reasonable set income so that they don't have to worry about food and so on.

Then there is the portion beyond that, and that should come with strings attached, "here is money that you are a trustee of, and this money should be used for this purpose", whatever the purpose that is dear to you. There are ways where any of these can be subverted so this is where you have to trust the Universe. Do the best you can, and then forget about it. As I said before—you are a trustee, you can do the very best you can to make sure that you use your wealth in a responsible manner. Ultimately, even thinking too much about this is simply one more fetter binding you to the world. There comes a time when you do have to let go and say, "Okay, I did the best I can, now it's up to the Universe."

JP: When should we tell our children about how much wealth we have?

Professor Rao: That again is a tough one, I'll tell you why it's a tough one, because some children look upon that as, "Yippee! I'm going to be wealthy." They start thinking in terms of consumption and hedonistic pleasures. Others think about, "Okay you know, I'm now a powerful custodian of wealth. I do not really have any pressing financial needs, but I can use it to do something which is important to me." You have to gauge where your child is, as you take that decision. There cannot be a general answer to this.

JP: Millennials are looking for purpose, most of them, many of them — do you agree?

Professor Rao: I would say it's mixed. On average, I think this statement is probably accurate. I have come across many millennials and they are thinking, "Gee, this is wonderful but what is the purpose of what I am doing? And I want it to have a bigger purpose." There are also some who are just striving in mindless accumulation, just like our baby boomer generation, but on average, you are probably accurate.

JP: Any words of wisdom from a Guru like you?

Professor Rao: I don't consider myself a Guru, but I have thought deeply about this. There are many sources of pleasure and there are many sources of feeling joy, achievement and so on.

I ask you to think about two things — this incidentally is from a meditation that I came across by Anthony de Mello, who is a Jesuit priest; I think he is also a realised being. He asks you to imagine that you are very happy because you have accomplished something — you won a tennis tournament, you've been promoted, you've become CEO or whatever, and everyone around you is clapping and saying how wonderful you are and there is acclaim and fame, and think about how you feel. Then think about a time when you are having a quiet dinner or a meeting with a very dear friend of yours and chatting late in the night and you are open, and your friend is open, and it is a beautiful experience. You have no expectations; your friend has no expectations. You are just getting together, and you are having a wonderful time together. Now think about that. Now compare the two and say which would you rather have more of? Are you dependent upon fame, upon others recognising your success, are you hankering for applause or are you willing to be quiet and simply contemplate a beautiful scenic view, mountain, rainbow, oceans, the company of a good friend where there is no expectation on either side, there are no demands?

Which would you rather have more of? Contemplate that because as you do, you start saying, "I'm striving, but what am I striving for?", because if you live your life according to the way I advocate, which to be honest, comes not from me but from the great masters, your striving itself can be your path to liberation if you approach it in the right way.

Professor Raj Sisodia, PhD
Professor, Babson College

JP: May I request you to introduce yourself.

Professor Sisodia: I'm a professor of Business at Babson College in Massachusetts and also the co-founder and co-chairman of Conscious Capitalism, Inc., which is a non-profit that we started a number of years ago to change the story of business.

JP: Where did you grow up and what was your lifestyle then?

Professor Sisodia: I was born in the central state of India, Madhya Pradesh, near a city called Indore. I spent the first five years of my life living in a rural village where my father's family comes from and then two years studying in a school in a little town called Ratlam, while my father was away getting his Bachelor's, Master's and PhD in Canada. Then he came back from Canada, when I was seven years old, and we moved to Barbados, in the West Indies for two years. He was a plant scientist, agriculture scientist and so he moved to Barbados for two years where he worked on sugarcane research and then we moved to California for two years. He was working on wheat research and we spent a year in Canada, then back to India around the time I was 12 years old. I spent the rest of my childhood and young adulthood in India, finishing my high school in Indore and my engineering degree at BITS Pilani, in Rajasthan, and then my MBA in Bombay at the Bajaj Institute of Management. I came to the US at the age of 23 to get my PhD in Business at Columbia University in New York, and became a business professor in 1985; and I've been teaching for 33 years.

JP: Where have you taught in these 33 years?

Professor Sisodia: Three places basically, I started in Boston, taught at Boston University, and then George Mason University in Washington, DC, and then back to Boston for the last 20 years, so actually I've only lived in two cities for three universities.

JP: What was your perspective on money growing up?

Professor Sisodia: We lived in the US and in Canada, in the late 60s; money was never an issue. When I went back to India, my father took a job with the government university. I think his salary at that time in the US was $1,500 a month and from that, he went into a job that maybe paid ₹800 a month. That was the first time he had worked in India. I do remember immediately feeling that money was a problem, that even though we came from a land-owning family, making ends meet teaching in a college on a government salary was not easy. I kind of grew up, with a bit of a mindset of scarcity around money. I remember, I didn't have a radio until almost graduating from college. In hindsight, I think it gives you a good appreciation for money. I mean, nowadays, our kids can demand things and they're able to get them quite readily it seems. A scarcity of money created a kind of appreciation for the things that money can buy; I think that it's something that can get lost, if you're not careful.

After that, I moved to the US at the age of 23. I had a full scholarship at Columbia University, which covered not only my tuition, but also my living expenses, but just barely. I was able to do some tutoring for MBA students on the side and do some other work for professors, research assistants. I was almost a rich PhD student comparatively speaking because I would get $25 an hour to tutor MBAs at a time when the minimum wage was $3. My friends were all working in cafeterias and doing that kind of work and I was being paid much more than that. I had hired some of them to do data entry work for me.

JP: Fast forwarding, share with us your perspective on money and what you do today.

Professor Sisodia: I am a business professor. I also do a lot of speaking, some consulting and I write books, and so money is generated from each of those activities. I've increasingly come to appreciate both, the dark side and the positive side of money. There's a wonderful expression I read in the book called *Shantaram*, which is by an Australian author, but it is based in India about an Australian convict who ends up in the slums of Bombay and gets connected to the underworld, and so forth. But there is a phrase used in there, which I believe, comes from some ancient Indian text. It reads, "If we can't respect the way we earn it, money has no value. If we can't use it to make life better for our families and loved ones, money has no purpose." And I kind of subscribe to that philosophy—in the world of business, profits are important of course and they are the fuel for business, but you have to earn it the right way—because you can make money in a business by squeezing your employees, damaging the environment, squeezing your suppliers, and doing harm to the health of your customers; then that has no value. You're actually not creating value; you're sucking it out of people and that's more of a parasite.

I think money has to be earned the right way, for businesses as well as for individuals. You have to respect the way you earned it and then there is the deployment of money. Money is a form of embodied energy—what you are spending your money on, you are kind of voting for that thing, you're supporting that when you spend your money and when you invest your money. So, when I now invest in things, like this year I invested in some companies, some start-ups, and everything else that I do in that regard, has to be a reflection of what I care about and what I believe in. Money is a form of energy that I'm giving to that particular idea or group of people.

I am writing a book about business as healing. I have invested in a couple of businesses that are healing businesses and they are actually reducing suffering and bringing joy in the world through those businesses. I feel good about that and they're also good business models and good concepts. I think ultimately, I have also learnt in my research in the last 10 years, that businesses that do operate with a sense of purpose, with a sense of wanting to create value and serving all their stakeholders are actually more successful in the long-term as well. They generate more financial wealth, but they also generate many other kinds of wealth. That's the other thing—money is one kind of wealth. There are many other kinds of wealth as well. It's not the only game in town. We act as if money is the only game in town. There are other games in town, money is important, but I think we have to have a healthy perspective on it and recognise its power. It can also do great harm.

I saw this movie, *All the Money in the World* last year. The movie was about J Paul Getty, who was the richest person in the world is the early 70s and yet one of the stingiest people and completely miserable. At some point in the movie somebody says, "Why is he so obsessed with money, why doesn't he want to spend a little bit." He won't let people make phone calls from his house; they have to use a payphone inside his house. The person makes a very interesting observation that it is not really about the money. That money is a substitute for something that's missing in his life. He's trying to use money to make up for a lack of love from his father, lack of respect. Now that money is a substitute and when you're trying to fill a hole of another kind with money, there is no amount of money that's going to fill that hole. We all know a lot of very, very rich yet very, very miserable, unhappy and angry people because that money is not able to make up for what's missing in their lives.

JP: You are currently the founder of Conscious Capitalism, Inc. Can you tell us a little bit about that?

Professor Sisodia: Well, Conscious Capitalism, Inc. is about a movement that we started 10 years ago, the CEO of Whole Foods and me. We met because I had written a book called, *Firms of Endearment: How World-Class Companies Profit from Passion and Purpose*, and discovered a whole way of being, that businesses can operate according to a different paradigm. That they, first of all, have a purpose that is beyond profit, other than profit, they're trying to do something in the world separate to making money. You have to make money to survive and grow as a business, but that should not be the reason for existing. Second, that they create value for all their stakeholders consciously and they serve all of them together—customers, employees, community, suppliers, etc. They are stakeholder oriented; they have leaders who actually care about the people, and they care about the purpose. They're not just driven by power, ego, and money. They have cultures where people look forward to going to work, and culture that is filled with trust, caring, and fun. We discovered this pattern and we found that these companies, in the long-term, actually generate dramatically more financial returns—nine to one over the market as a whole, over a 10-year period. This became a very compelling story to say that the old paradigm of business is all about profit and all about shareholder value maximisation and that you use people and you use supplier to do that. The new paradigm actually is by far a better way because this does not create negative impact on anybody, and it actually generates more wealth as well. Therefore, we said we need to launch a movement to change the dominant paradigm, which is rooted in scarcity, the whole professional economics starts with the presumption of scarcity, and almost a zero-sum way of thinking and business is the ultimate positive-sum game in the world. So, Conscious Capitalism is a global movement—we have chapters in 18 or 19 countries and 38 US cities, where we are gradually making people aware of this alternative paradigm and getting them to adopt these principles and helping them change their business models accordingly.

JP: Is there a connection between Conscious Capitalism and impact investing?

Professor Sisodia: Well, peripherally—in the sense that we're not just about investing. This is about how you run a business. This is looking at all the stakeholders and not only the investor stakeholder; we are even more concerned about the impact on employees or the impact on communities or the impact on customers and the children of employees, on the future, on the environment. We are more holistic. We care about all of those things. And yes, as part of that, impact investing is a good philosophy that is in harmony with this. It goes beyond to how you lead, how you motivate, what kind of culture you create, and all those things within the business.

JP: Do you have any words of advice for millennials who are going to inherit billions of dollars in the coming decades?

Professor Sisodia: Well, I would go back to what I said earlier, the fact that 'you're inheriting this money as opposed to earning it', does make a difference in terms of how you think about it. It can become this paradigm of easy come, easy go; but to recognise that with it comes a lot of power and the opportunity to make a difference. I would say that you have to look within yourself; you have to know yourself, understand yourself deeply. What are your core values? What is it that defines you? In India, we talked about what is your 'swabhav'—your nature, and understand deep down what you're all about, and then bring that to the world. You need to know yourself, love yourself, then be yourself, and express yourself in the world. And now with the additional resources that become available, you can express yourself in the world in terms of bringing about the kinds of things that resonate with you, and using that money as the fuel for that, as energy behind that in order to bring it into being. When you talk about investing, it's really about bringing something into being in this world, to creating not just returns, but impact my legacy as well. So, how can you think about that money as making a bigger difference, not only deploying it or donating it to non-profits, which is great but also investing in businesses. I think it is very important if a business can do something that a non-profit normally does. It's better because then it's not reliant upon donations or subsidies or charity.

So, invest in purposeful businesses with good business models that are trying to address challenges in the world that resonate with you at a deep soul level, and then use your money as part of your investment along with your time and talent, in order to bring that into fruition. There's a very beautiful book that I recommend in this area. It's called the *Soul of Money* by Lynne Twist and it's kind of her own journey through life, as a person who raised hundreds of millions of dollars for the Hunger Project, and has been involved in many other things; her relationship to money and how we should think about money, how we can impact and view money with soul and see the greater power than it normally has.

Professor Vivek Wadhwa

Professor, Carnegie Mellon and Harvard University

JP: May I request you to introduce yourself.

Professor Wadhwa: I am a fellow at Carnegie Mellon University and Harvard Law School.

JP: Where did you grow up and what was your lifestyle?

Professor Wadhwa: I was brought up all over the world. My father was in the Indian Foreign Service, so we were always travelling— New York, Malaysia, and Australia. I was in Australia for a long time, about 20 years, before coming to America in 1980. I have been all over the world and I have been in the US for the last 35 years or so.

JP: Where did you study?

Professor Wadhwa: I did an MBA from NYU and I did my Bachelor's degree from the Canberra University in Australia.

JP: And then post college?

Professor Wadhwa: Post college, I have been working. I worked in Australia for a while and then I joined First Boston in New York City. I moved over here (USA). After that, I started my own company.

JP: What was the company doing?

Professor Wadhwa: The first company was called Seer Technologies and provided systems development tools. The second company was Relativity Technologies, which marketed software for reengineering legacy systems.

JP: As you were growing up and travelling all over the world, what was your perspective on money then?

Professor Wadhwa: I came from a middle-class family and my father worked in the government service. We weren't rich in any way. We were living very modest lives. I didn't inherit anything. It's a matter of earning and building wealth the right way.

JP: Fast forward to today, can you describe a bit more about what you do today, as well as your perspective on money and how it has changed?

Professor Wadhwa: I teach at Carnegie Mellon. I research at Harvard Law School. I give a lot of talks. I teach corporate executives all over the world how to reinvent their companies. I am making more money than I ever made in my life, and care less about money than I ever cared before because my conclusion is that you need enough money to live a decent lifestyle but after that it doesn't buy you happiness, it doesn't buy you prosperity, it doesn't buy you health, it doesn't make a difference. We obsess over it. Obsess over making money and lose sight of the value of life itself, of giving back, helping others, and uplifting humanity.

JP: What is your philosophy on passing on your wealth to your next generation?

Professor Wadhwa: Well, my late wife, Tavinder had very strong family values on it. Her view was that we have to give it to them while we can, while we are alive. She made sure that we gave them all we could when they needed it rather than waiting until we die. And in this way, we helped our children buy their own houses and get on their feet. The idea was to give them everything while we are still alive rather than when we are dead.

JP: You have lived in many different countries, travelled the world and have years of experience teaching so many students. What would you advise some of the millennials who are going to inherit billions of dollars?

Professor Wadhwa: What you do is learn. What would I advise millennials who have a billion dollars? That they put their money aside and remember their humanity. Figure out how you can use that money to help others because the greatest satisfaction is going to come from helping others and from using that money wisely. I mean give it away while you can because you can't spend all of it. You might as well do the most you can for the people and uplift humanity. That will be the greatest reward to have. At the end of the day, people are not going to remember how much money they have in the bank, they are going to remember what they did for others.

JP: What are you going to do with all this money during your lifetime?

Professor Wadhwa: I plan to give it away to my family and other people in need.

JP: What are the fun things you do, especially with money?

Professor Wadhwa: The fun thing is basically spending time with family, travelling, learning, growing, giving back, and teaching. We help others, that's the idea. I don't have that much money that I have to worry about what to do with it. I am not one of those billionaires.

JP: Please share your philosophy and thoughts on giving.

Professor Wadhwa: The only thing I can say is that the greatest thing you can do is to give more than you take and learn to give it away. Don't obsess with hoarding it and earning more, because after a while it doesn't make a difference. The difference between having zero and $10 million is huge but after that whether you have a $10 million or have $1 billion, it doesn't make a difference. You can't live a better lifestyle. Don't obsess with hoarding more and keeping it in the bank, it won't do you any good. It will just make you miserable.

Futurists

Shekhar Kapur
Film Director

Siddharth Sthalekar
Founder, Sacred Capital

Parag Khanna, PhD
Managing Partner, Future Map and Author

Shekhar Kapur
Film Director

JP: May I request you to introduce yourself.

Shekhar: I'm most known as a film director but I guess I'm an occasional film director. I started life as a chartered accountant, but I've been directing films over many years. I've directed Bollywood films, as they are so-called but also extreme kind of marginal cinema in India like *Bandit Queen*, which ultimately propelled me into Hollywood and I started to make *Elizabeth*, which is my first Hollywood film, that introduced Cate Blanchett. Then I went on to make other films like *The Four Feathers* with Heath Ledger, and *Elizabeth: The Golden Age* with Cate Blanchett. I then experimented with television and have just completed a huge series on the young William Shakespeare called *Will* for TNT. I have also been dabbling a lot in theatre. I co-produced *Bombay Dreams* with Andrew Lloyd Webber, which actually introduced A R Rahman to the world. Recently, I have directed a very successful stage musical show in Europe called the *Matterhorn*, which is running very, very successfully there.

I've been directing, producing, and experimenting with film, and I now spend a lot of time at MIT in Boston at the Media Lab, wondering what is the next step in storytelling, where do we go now, how do we adapt new technologies to storytelling technologies like AI (Artificial Intelligence), technologies like virtual reality and augmented reality? That's because storytelling can take every form.

JP: Give us some perspective on how you grew up, the lifestyle, as well as your outlook on money then.

Shekhar: I grew up in Delhi. I studied in Modern School. My father was a doctor. We were refugees from Lahore, Pakistan, that came to India. I remember as a child we never had money, but you know as a child, money doesn't matter at all. You just enjoy yourself and as long as you live in the moment, you're fine. Looking back, I can see the struggles my parents were going through as refugees, to try and establish themselves and ultimately my father—he was a paediatrician—built his life around his talent. My mother used to work also. We became from what was at that time refugee-status of lower-middle-class, to kind of mid to upper-middle-class because of my parents. They worked so hard. They built and borrowed money, picked a house. I cannot remember being poor. I know that my mother was pregnant, and she used to go to work every day because she had to, and you know what Delhi buses are like. Looking back, I think that there was a lot of hardship in the beginning, but as for my attitude towards money then—well, you never think of money when you are a kid. You never actually think of it. You make do because as a kid you're having fun all the time.

JP: What was your journey like after you finished high school?

Shekhar: From school, I went to London to be a chartered accountant. While most people think, "Oh my God! Your parents sent you to London!" Remember that as a chartered accountant you actually worked from day one, you didn't go to university. It's not like when you go to Oxford and Cambridge and have high tuition fees. Instead, you go anywhere you get paid what's called a scholar's stipend. A stipend gives you some perks, you live on that stipend, and that's what I did. Therefore, I became a chartered accountant. I have to say that I was a bit bored with it. I wish I had gone to university instead but back then, all good middle-class Indian boys were either computer engineer, lawyers, doctors or chartered accountant, so being a chartered accountant wasn't my choice, but it gave me the choice to leave India at that time. To me we lived in the dark in India then, because we were cut off from the rest of the world and only perceived the world as depicted in newspapers or occasionally through music. Going to London had completely changed my life as I got onto the main stage of the world.

When I went to London it wasn't the London of now, it wasn't the London of 'everything'. Nothing was valued in terms of wealth. It was so strange. I remember it was the 70s. Those were the days when music had caused revolution in Europe and the days of Woodstock in the US. The days of the anti-Vietnam war-protests in London, which I took part in all the time. It was a wonderful time of actually being socially equal. It was the time of the sexual revolution. I guess I was shaped a lot by all of that. I still live in London, and when I look around and find people talking about money, I kind of get surprised! How can you make money the basic value of your worth? I believe I'm worth what I do. I am worth what I'm thinking. I am worth what I do for the people. I'm worth the amount of love I can give and receive, my heart is my worth, my emotions are my worth, what I give is my worth. It still takes me by surprise when people expect me to state my net worth in dollars. It still shocks me because I go back to the time when I was my own boss, I was 18 when I left, and I was really formed by this idea that money was a by-product. It was a by-product of everything else. I remember three of my best friends—I wanted to be in the movie business, a friend of mine wanted to be writing books or in the publishing business, another one was obsessed with racing and he wanted to be in a pit stop. All three of us did that, and when we meet, not once did we ask, "How much money did you make?" We just did what our passion drove us to do, and I am still doing what my passion drives me to do.

JP: How did you transition to the movies?

Shekhar: To be really honest with you, I was falling into a life that scared me. I was wearing a three-piece suit to work and then I would come home after work and change into my Carnaby Street clothes. At that time anything that the Beatles or Mick Jagger wore, I wanted to wear. Then I would go clubbing; not drugs as much as women and the high life. It was a little scary that there were two halves of me, and they were so separate. Therefore, at 24 I made two decisions. One, that I will never ever do anything again, whether it's work or play or creating—it all has to be the same thing—I will not make a distinction between play and buck. And the second decision that I still follow is that I will never ever consign myself to this little cage that everybody calls a career. What's your career, what are you doing in your life? When are you going to get your pension? How much money are you going to make? I will only follow my passions. That was actually a great decision. What I was leaving was being a chartered accountant, leaving a career. The big question was what to do next? I knew I had to be in the arts because I wanted to express myself in my own way. Actually, my first choice wasn't films. My first choice was to be a roving war photographer. Somehow, that never happened. I was an amateur photographer but then took a trip to India, I let life lead me, and I ended up making films.

3I started off as an actor but not a very good one, but I was in film and television and still am today. That's what I've been doing. I've still not got a career. People still ask me, "Why are you not making more films, you are a film director?" I say, "I'm not. I'm an adventurer. I'm exploring life and I will keep exploring it." Somehow, life has been kind, it's never made me poor. It's not made me as rich as I could have been. Honestly, it's not made me as poor either. I could have crashed very easily but I survived.

JP: How has your perspective on money changed over time?

Shekhar: What value does money have? I remember when Facebook got a $100 billion valuation when it went public. If you would drop the idea of money, you will realise that there is a change. Today we talk about the social impact of Facebook on this world.

To me money is an imperfect device for measuring what worth means to us—social worth, people's worth, emotional worth. It's a really imperfect device—how do you ascertain that the value of a piece of art is worth a $150 million or $100 million? What does that mean? That means that somebody is going to pay $100 million for a painting and put it up on a wall.

Yes, there is a certain amount of money that you need to survive, you need to eat, and you need to have a home. I've lived in several very big houses in my life and I've also just lived in one room. In Sri Lanka, I saw this beautiful beach, and somebody said, "Hmmm, I wonder how much that property is worth?" What does that mean? Do you want to swim, do you want to walk on the beach, and do you want to admire it? All you're doing is saying I wonder what it's worth in terms of what. Money? What is this measure called money? I have never understood it. I've never understood why we're so addicted to it.

JP: We've got a bunch of millennials who are going to inherit billions of dollars in the next few decades. Any advice you would like to give them?

Shekhar: My advice would be to give away as much money as you can. Give it away because if you hold on to billions of dollars saying, "Okay...what do I buy with it?" then it means nothing. You're going to destroy your own salt. The moment you try and save it and hang on to it, it becomes a burden you carry. How do you unload that burden? Give it away with joy, just give it away. Do something joyful and live a joyful life. I would never ever be able to measure my worth saying I have got $1 billion in my bank or my shares or my company is worth a $1 billion. I would never do that because then suddenly you're looking at something that actually has no worth, to look upon yourself as worth $1 billion, you're saying you have no worth. To look upon yourself as a human being, that is a part of the universal imagination, joy, and love, there's worth in that. If you're going to inherit $1 billion—unburden yourself because the thought of $1 billion in your bank will never be enough. Tomorrow you are going to want $200 billion...it's never enough! The more you think about it, the more you want, the more you're getting yourself into a cage and imprisoning yourself. Unburden it and let it go. It's not yours.

JP: What is your philosophy on giving?

Shekhar: If you open your heart, you'll find your own philosophy on giving. I'm not going to say you must give it to this charity or that charity or you must give it to these people. It's an instinct—giving as much as receiving is an insight. If you do it with honesty, you'll find a way to give it.

Siddharth Sthalekar

Founder, Sacred Capital

JP: May I request you to introduce yourself.

Siddharth: I am 36 years old. Born and brought up in Mumbai, I studied at Bombay Scottish School; spent a large chunk of my childhood and my 20s in Mumbai, it's pretty much my home. I was brought up by two lovely parents who were very strong professionals and have been inspiring figures for me. Growing up, I was definitely a 'good kid' because I excelled at science, maths, academics—it was a system that really worked for me.

Materially it was a modest to very comfortable upbringing but at the same time I think the privilege of having so many loved ones around me was something I really cherish. I did my engineering from Mumbai University. Post engineering there was a pivotal point in my life where I had to decide between going to a university in the US, like Columbia, or Georgia Tech versus going to IIM Ahmedabad. I chose to go to business school in India, in Ahmedabad and that was largely because of a very strong, romantic connection I felt with India and because I felt India has something to offer to the world.

While in business school, the years 2003–2005 were very strong moments for India's journey because capital markets had started transforming the landscape. They had started creating some tremendous value and I wanted to be part of that. I could see how markets or capitalism had the potential to solve some very serious problems in India like communalism, poverty, lack of physical infrastructure. For me, that was tremendous because from business school I ended up heading one of India's largest trading desk for the next five years and that allowed me to see how money operated at a tremendously large scale. I'm talking billions of dollars flowing through a trading floor—you could see how the system worked at one of those trading floors. It was a focal point for the economy because you could see how decisions are made and how money is channelled. I was 28, and I felt it was a real gift to be heading such a large desk at a very young age. I remember around 2008–2009, the time of the Wall Street crisis, sitting at these focal points where the economic system was fragile and at the same time some serious corrections needed to be made. The economic system was designed in the 1930s and 1940s 70–100 years ago, and it needed to be iterated upon quite significantly. I had a lot of questions, but I didn't have too many answers.

That's why I decided to take a radical step, which was questioned by a lot of loved ones around me, but in 2011, I decided to move to Sabarmati Ashram in Ahmedabad. It was a community founded by Gandhi in 1918 from where the Salt March took off. For me, it was really important to be part of that community and understand the economic system in a very different light. Those four years, from 2011–2015, I would say were foundational and very educational but in a different way.

JP: How did you arrive at the decision to move to Gandhi Ashram?

Siddharth: In 2010, I decided to leave work and for six months I was travelling across the country. I read a lot. I was 29 when I came across Gandhi's autobiography for the first time. I think the authenticity of it was very inspiring and so I decided to visit Gandhian communities around the country. I remember, a very interesting person named Venkat from GiveIndia's Joy of Giving movement, connected me with Jayeshbhai Patel at the ashram. The first day of my first visit to the ashram pretty much indicated to me that I needed to spend some time as part of the community that was embedded in Gandhian values. I was curious about it, that's how I decided to move to Sabarmati Ashram.

JP: You were there from 2011–2015. Can you please describe those four years?

Siddharth: My early days in Gandhi Ashram were about minimal material possessions—how many pairs of clothes do I need? How simple can I make my material life? As part of the community, I was contributing and volunteering. I was running a gift economy restaurant called Seva Cafe. I was living within a community. I could see that the community was also taking care of me in simple ways like housing or food or helping me navigate my life.

A lot of what I am doing now with Sacred Capital, which is helping build a distributed economy, came from Gandhi's thoughts and writings on how distributed economies like India can thrive and function.

JP: What is a 'Gift Economy'?

Siddharth: Several experiments were conducted by ServiceSpace, which gave shape to projects like Seva Café. Seva Café is a restaurant which is run by volunteers and guests are told it's up to them to make a contribution for the food that they have been offered. The contribution that they make allows this generosity to be paid forward; it is not a transaction because food is being served, the guests are not forced into paying; it is in fact the choice that they make, and that choice starts building different kinds of capital. That's very important because gift economies and gift culture helps build ties in society and helps amplify social capital.

JP: What do you do today?

Siddharth: Distributed economies don't always have the benefit of overarching regulatory systems to guide interactions. They rely on underlying reputation so people can seek each other out and engage in new ways. In the late 1930s, principles of distributed economies were articulated by Gandhian economists such as J C Kumarappa and furthered by E F Schumacher in the west.

The crux of their work was this—if you want to promote local economies, you need to focus on building social fabric. Without this fabric, interactions between people are not possible. In other words, in distributed networks, the focus shifts away from material capital (i.e. money) and moves towards social fabric, or reputation. Sacred Capital, the organisation that I have founded is building the foundations of the 'Reputation Economy'.

For those who are not familiar, let me explain distributed ledger technology and blockchain. This is a technology, which allows new forms of record keeping. In the past, records had to be maintained by a bank or if it was a land record it had to be maintained by the government or a large entity. In the case of my data or pictures it had to be maintained by a large platform like Facebook. But because of distributed ledger technology we can maintain this information in a distributed way. This is bringing a transformation in the way people organise themselves in social networks. They can now decide what is critical to them, and what they wish to keep a record of. There might be a group of 10 or 20 people who say, "I want to measure how punctual someone is or how honest someone is?" Or it could be, "How many coins did Sid give Jayesh?" Because this design for punctuality or honesty or how good a driver I am is maintained on a distributed ledger, it is now immutable and so it starts earning money-like qualities. That's why we say this is the new wealth.

Wealth not only has to mean money in my bank account or how many Bitcoins I have or how many US dollars I have. For example, Sid is considered to be a food expert or a great speaker by his community—this is also a form of wealth; Sid may have good insights on the Gandhian economy—that is also a form of wealth. As distributed ledger is immutable, it's like money in my bank account. My money in my bank account can't be extracted away from me without democratic process. In the same way, individuals are now gaining a sense of ownership and control over their reputation.

JP: What is cryptocurrency?

Siddharth: Distributed ledgers allow people to keep records. Sid gave Jayesh five coins, and these coins were created by Sid and Jayesh. It's just a measure of record for what they did for one another. In the past, we had large governments who were maintaining this record of things like, Sid did 10 hours of work for Jayesh, so Jayesh owes him a $1,000. The question is can we start maintaining these records of our accounts among ourselves? That in essence is cryptocurrencies. It is, very specifically, a record of material capital between different people.

JP: There are few well-known cryptocurrencies, tell us a little bit about them.

Siddharth: One of the popular ones is Bitcoin. The whole conversation around distributed ledgers and blockchain was really spawned off in 2009 by this PDF that was published anonymously about a coin, or a design for a coin called Bitcoin which allows people to maintain a record of who owes whom what, without a centralised authority. Bitcoin was one of the first cryptocurrencies. Ether was an iteration of an advancement of this in 2014–2015 and Ether actually allowed us to create contracts between people without necessarily depending on a centralised authority.

JP: With this new form of economy, how has your perspective on money changed in these past few years?

Siddharth: When I moved from Mumbai to Singapore—in the past, my material capital was ported in seconds but other forms of capitals like social and cultural capital had to be re-built in Singapore through informal networks. Porting those from one network to another, or for the ability for social capital to move around the world and unlock value in different projects is still not designed in our economic system. Distributed ledgers and blockchain allow us to do this very seamlessly in the new economy while preserving the value that is embedded in them, and so, my understanding of money has evolved. I can say material capital is important, however, reputational capital, and by that, I mean social capital, these other forms of capital, cultural capital, the quality of the air that I breath, natural capital—all of these are also important. If we design an economic language for all of these other forms of capital, then we don't have to convert everything into material capital. Thus, my definition of wealth has expanded.

I think money, the way you are seeing it today was designed 100 years ago. It was designed keeping in mind the needs of humans 100 years ago. I think this is a question that I and several other millennials around the world face. I understand that hundreds of billions of dollars that millennials are about to inherit won't necessarily solve the problems that millennials are facing, which is climate change, degrading social fabric, lower mental health, or wellness. Different problems in the world can't be solved by material capital alone. They need cultural shifts, they need social fabric, and I believe that's what we as millennials need to tune into. The problems that we will face in the next 10–15 years need a nuanced understanding of these other forms of values. I need a certain amount of material capital, but I also can hold a certain amount of value in social, cultural, intellectual capital through reputation systems.

JP: What words of wisdom do you have for millennials who are going to inherit billions of dollars in the next few decades?

Siddharth: First—Urgency. I do think the last few years have shown us the urgency of some of the world's problems. We don't have more than 5–15 years to solve some of these problems because they could lead to catastrophic consequences.

Second, we have to think in a tremendously different way as compared to the previous generation and that's because the problems that our parents and previous generations were facing and solving were very different. We have figured out how to build roads but if we really wanted to be effective, I mean sustainable for the planet, and actually include billions of people in the world, then we need a multi-dimensional wealth system.

Parag Khanna, PhD
Managing Partner, Future Map and Author

JP: May I request you to introduce yourself.

Parag: I am a resident of Singapore. I have been affiliated for several years as a senior research fellow of the Lee Kwan Yew School of Public Policy, here in Singapore. I am the author of a number of books that address the intersection of geopolitics and globalisation. I write about megatrends—some people call me a futurist. I am an academic. I have a PhD from London School of Economics, Bachelor's degree and Master's from Georgetown University as well. I was born in India. I grew up in Abu Dhabi, New York, and Germany. I've lived in many places, including Washington, Berlin, London, Geneva, and now I call Singapore home.

JP: Growing up, what was your perspective on money?

Parag: I think my family is a very typical middle-class immigrant family story—enough income to have made it out of India. My parents worked in professional class and service sector jobs and moved to the Middle East and then United States, into finance. We lived in typical immigrant neighbourhoods like Queens in New York and my parents made their way, saved a lot very diligently, and got us to Westchester which is a very established and recognised set of zip codes outside of Manhattan, where I grew up for a number of years.

The way I think about the trajectory of real earnings and income in the first 20 years of my life is relating my parents' earnings being greater than the rate of inflation, clearly learning a lot about savings and money management and I think that's very typically an ancient immigrant story. I think it definitely carries lessons that I internalised as I grew up and I thought about never really wasting for no reason. Just as one doesn't waste food for no reason, I think it was equally logical in my house not to waste money for no reason and to think about the cost of most things most of the time. Not in a way that you felt onerous and restrictive but in a way that simply felt intuitive, logical, and sensible.

JP: Fast forward to the current day, what brought you to Singapore, and what is your perspective on money today?

Parag: What brought me to the city of *Crazy Rich Asians* where everything costs more than everywhere else in the world? Obviously, not a desire to save the better part of my annual income because that's not possible in this town, but I have learned some of the principles that I live by, that have consequences for how much one spends or that is worth paying for convenience, for example. Singapore in particular is a place that affords you fantastic conveniences in terms of quality of life. You pay for it. You pay high rent or cost of owning a house, you pay a lot for your children to go to good schools, and you pay a lot for transportation or owning a car. On the other hand, you have domestic help at low cost, and support, which allows you to spend as much quality time with your children and family as you can. Logistically there is public safety, law and order, and the airport is well connected to such interesting places that you can travel to at a very low cost and have very enriching family experiences that are worth spending on. So, you spend on time, my perspective is the ultimate cliché, but time is worth money or rather the balance in my view is that time is worth more than money. I spent the premium of money to buy time. Either in the form of paying other people to do things for me that create more time for myself to do more higher value-added things, either more lucrative things or have more quality time with family. I truly put more of a premium on time than money today.

JP: What do you sense in terms of the future of money in your life?

Parag: Unfortunately, this is not the kind of situation where one has full control. As someone who works in analysing the global economy I am very, very attuned to how volatile the world economy is. We are in the situation where the younger you are the less you can have confidence that you ever saved enough. In fact, in my next book I am writing about generational change, accelerating generational change and what I identify is that my own generation, micro generation you might say, people born in the late 1970s grew up in an extremely privileged set of circumstances in years. It was a time of growth in the world economy, time of post-cold war world triumphalism and we were teenagers in 1990s. We have now saved enough cash despite the turbulence in the world economy and the economic down turns. We saved enough to ride out the storms whereas people younger than me, they are very, very attuned to the fact that for them there is far greater degree of insecurity. Due to the fact that I am now caring for people that are younger than me, namely my own children, I do sense on their behalf that one cannot simply say I have saved enough, because we are not old enough to say well I have only X number of years left on earth, I know how much it will cost to live each year and to maintain the cost of the house that one already owns, like baby boomers. I think about not just my own individual point of view but from the point of view of a household that's of course multi-generational. As much as I think, my family, my wife and I have done a good job of saving, I don't think that we have saved enough. That's because there is no longer a sense of enough, and that's not a different kind of attitude than someone who is simply earning money, multiplying capital recklessly for the sake of it just to have more. It's really a reflection of the defensive paranoia about the state of the world today.

JP: Any words of wisdom for the affluent and wealthy, but also for the millennials who are going to inherit billions of dollars in the coming decades? The fundamental question is, what shall we do with all this money?

Parag: Let me give a couple of answers. The first is more macro but I think it's relevant because ultra-high net worth individuals, whether they are millennials or retirees and those who manage family assets and wealth are also people who are influential. I want to make a point that global stock of capital is approximately $300 trillion today. It's about four times the actual real GDP of the world economy and most of that is public and private debt that hasn't been sufficiently steered towards productive investments. The first thing that one can do with one's wealth is not necessarily spending it but to use the prestige and the influence that one has as a wealthy person to shape their current and future patterns of investment to take all that debt that's accumulated in our global system and to make it work for the world economy as a whole because we have moved into a world with a very high degree of inequality between the haves and the have nots. Even as the international income gap has been reduced, there is clearly a very large, about 50 per cent of each country's population, that falls below the median income line and those people are clearly struggling. I think that having savings and debt directed towards the betterment of the conditions of the bottom 50 per cent of every population is the single most important challenge in public policy in the world today. Those who have means should use that influence accordingly.

Now, the reason we are in this situation is because we have a market failure in public policy. We don't have smart governments making those investments. Singapore is one of the only exceptions in the world and it's too small to be representative of the world. My suggestion is that for those who have extraordinary means or wealth, they should do their part to invest in human capital as much as possible. Actually, there are many places to improve the quality, there is physical infrastructure, the cost of living a decent life whether it's 3D printed housing or mobile phone connectivity has dipped lower and lower and lower. One can spend money to provide those basics to as much of the world's population as possible and fortunately the falling cost of technology is making it possible anyway. I think what remains is the gap to be filled—that of human capital, investing in each other. For every person who is inheriting wealth, who is sitting on wealth, who has the opportunity to say, here are five ideas of social enterprises or businesses that I wanted to launch but I haven't, now I am going to take all of the unemployed people or under paid people, all of the skilled but under employed people around me and around the world and put them to work on this idea. Give people ownership, give people stake, give people something to do and they are going to wind up not only remunerating you by running this successful business, but they will actually increase the size of the world economy in the world economic pie and make the world a better place in the process.

JP: Any specific words of wisdom for the Indian diaspora.

Parag: This is the time of extraordinary wealth creation in India. The Indian diaspora is considered numerically the second largest in the world, after China, but it's far more globally dispersed. In fact, a fun fact: there is a lot of focus on geopolitics on the presence of the Chinese in Africa. There are six times more Indians in Africa than there are Chinese because there was this thing called the British

Empire and it re-circulated Indians all across the Indian Ocean. It didn't do that to Chinese people. There are more Indians everywhere by and large, except for Southeast Asia where there are more Chinese. I think that being a member of the Indian diaspora is almost something of special responsibility because we are a large number of the most globally distributed people from any one nationality and that is quite unique in the world. I think that means that there is something of a global Indian community. There are things that the Indian diaspora can do for itself to maintain the standards. Growing up as an Indian American, for example, at a time in 1980s, there weren't as many Indians in America and certainly not as wide or deep as they are today. In my case, there were two Indian families in my town for much of the time I grew up. By the time I moved out for college, it was eight or nine families; and now there are hundreds of families. The larger the population group, like Indian Americans, the more diverse it's going to be. Not everyone is going to be a straight 'A' student. Not everyone is going to be a straight arrow.

There is a lot of responsibility that we now need to take on for ourselves to make sure that the next generation works as hard as the previous generation and it doesn't lose sight, it doesn't get complacent, lose sight of values, lose sight of objectives; I think that is critical. For wealthy members of the Indian diaspora, to nurture the next generation diaspora and be role models is extremely critical. You know there is pejorative term in America called the 'model minority' which means a minority that is largely conformist to the existing hierarchy, but actually in America today Indian Americans have the position of very high prominence in government, in politics, business, basically all across the board. Therefore, there is a real responsibility to the role models to not be docile and conformist but to be leaders. And to be a leader of your own community, the community has to follow your footsteps.

Impact Investors

Vineet Rai
Founder, The Aavishkaar Group

Vikram Gandhi
Founder, Asha Impact and Professor, Harvard Business School

Rajeev Srivastava
Founder and Executive Chairman, Basil Partner

Varun Sahni
Founder and Managing Partner, Impact Investor Partners

Impact Investors

Vineet Rai

Vikram Gandhi

Rajeev Sivasankar

Varun Sahni

Vineet Rai

Founder, The Aavishkaar Group

JP: May I request you to introduce yourself.

Vineet: I belong to Varanasi. My father worked for a state government as a hydrogeologist. I was born in Jodhpur in 1971. I was an average student in all sense of the word. After graduation, my aspiration in life was to be in the Indian Army. For some strange reason, the Army rejected me at the interview stage. The rejection from the Service Selection Board carries a very positive message— they say you are meant for better things. It was probably the biggest failure in my life, but being a happy go lucky person I moved on. A friend's father guided me to appear for the Indian Institute of Forest Management (IIFM) entrance exam, and inspired by the beautiful architecture of the IIFM building and the lure of a full scholarship made me join IIFM.

JP: What did you do post forest management?

Vineet: I will start with an anecdote on my first experience about earning, which was during the IIFM days itself. During forest management I interacted with batch mates, 25 of them came from different backgrounds and for each money had a different meaning. Different. I was earning in training, and it introduced me to the corrupting power or invisible influence of money. If you earn money for the first time, it starts making you do things that are new. I enjoyed sharing lavish tips and I really enjoyed giving the money as tips from my little earning. I enjoyed the look of surprise on the face of the rikshawala, when I gave him twice of what he asked. Right or wrong, but it was exciting and I enjoyed sharing the money with those who I felt had a limitation in their life. It was not conscious and I was not being charitable. I just enjoyed the idea.

I joined Ballarpur Industries after IIFM and spent three years in remote forests of Odisha, in Eastern India. I got married and was advised by my wife to find a job which is slightly more urban.

IIM Ahmedabad was looking for an academic research associate and so I left my forest. I met Professor Anil Gupta who offered me to work with him on a research project at IIM Ahmedabad, so I spent one year with him. After the project ended, Professor Anil Gupta

185

directed me to India's first agri-incubator in 1998 called GIAN (Grassroots Innovations Augmentation Network). I was offered the role of chief executive, and ran that incubator for three and a half years; it was a government of Gujarat initiative and I was barely 26 when I joined. I was very lucky to be the CEO and those four years taught me the most. My job was to convert innovations done by farmers into business. During this incubation process, I started understanding the importance of capital i.e. money in converting ideas into business. For someone like me, born in a government service family who doesn't understand the concept of failure and the risks associated with failure and money—the meaning of risk and its connection with money dawned to me a little late, when I was about to turn 30.

JP: Take us through your journey, from then to where you are today.

Vineet: Money that can take risk is very critical for any change to happen. With this idea that money is much more critical than ideas, intention, mentoring, and support, I quit my job to find money. To my surprise, enough people were interested in the idea of risking their capital with a person like me who had no experience to use that capital. My takeaway was that if your intentions are good, there are enough good people in the world who are willing to participate in helping you bring about change. I always believed nobody wants to part with their money for utopian ideas like making the world a better place; to my great surprise that's not true.

Once I got the money, I realised that investing that money is even more difficult. Taking risk on someone else's money means this person has trusted you, and by investing that money with someone else you have to transfer that trust to somebody else. That skill is completely different and requires you to have a very strong heart—worse, which I learnt later, is that once you invest, your ownership on that money is minimal, now you cannot control the money and its destiny; you now have to live with somebody else's thoughts of its utilisation. Mr Vishnu Varshney, CEO of GVFL, a pioneering Venture fund in India, told me about a theory he used to christen 'The God and Dog' theory. He told me that until the time you sign the cheque, you are God for the person seeking your money. But once you sign the cheque and the money is transferred, you are the dog in the relationship. Worse, you are a dog that can only bark, can't bite. My experience has been that money has a lot of meaning, but in itself, it is nothing until you associate purpose with it; and, once you associate purpose with it, money can be a very powerful tool for change.

JP: You have been the pioneer for social impact investing and Aavishkaar. Can you take us through that journey?

Vineet: I started with the belief that money can make a difference. I learnt that business can actually be a powerful change catalyst. I tried to deconstruct poverty and richness and I realised all rich people did business. In my very naïve, natural intelligence thinking I believed that those who do business become rich. It seemed making poor people rich is easy if they can engage with business. Businesses needed money and I actually thought that if I can get money that wants to help business work with poor people, I will achieve my goal of changing the world. Today, in a very broad sense, all that's essentially what is known as impact investing.

I started with trying to find very nice people who would do these businesses because you associate business with hard decision makers who may not have the heart to work with poor people—a wrong belief that took me long to correct. Good people, well-meaning people, well intentioned people can be great cheerleaders but not necessarily agents of change themselves. I discovered this distinction between just good people versus those who could be agents of change when my investments started failing. I faced serious struggle between 2004–2006, as companies that we invested in struggled to scale and deliver any real change and did not go anywhere.

I also started realising that business as a force of good can only work if the good is in the business and not just in the human intention that is outside the business. Integrating the idea of impact within the business was far more important than having a good guy leading it. That was my learning and the person who should lead a business must actually be a good businessman and a good person, and not just a good person. Being good and being a businessmen are not exclusive set. It just means that a good person must have business skills and at Aavishkaar that became our new social set for discovery of an entrepreneur that can be a catalyst for change.

The other thing that I learnt in my journey of Aavishkaar is the discipline of investing. Venture capital and private equity actually looks for scale. You are not in the business of creating a profitable company alone, you're in a business of creating a fast growing, very scalable business which should at some point of time make money but need not necessarily be making money all the time. Now this distinction is not easy to comprehend for a forester as it is counter to logic of being financially sustainable quickly. I tried to understand this investing idiom and applying it to the idea of impact and sustainability. What we realised is that given the large population that needs to be impacted one must not ignore scale. We may arrive at the idea of scale in different ways but scale and its importance cannot be ignored. The other learning I have is that sustainability at institutional level is not as important as it is at unit level. At the basic unit level if you are sustainable and impactful you must think about scaling up and that is how venture capital and private equity create wealth.

As an impact investor, we need to be cautious of the challenge of large failure that can leave millions distraught and hence we cannot go after the type of scale that private equity or venture capital seeks. Being responsible becomes a more demanding obligation while adopting the venture capital model to impact investing—that is my other learning. I also learnt that there is subtle expectation difference between investing your own money and when you are driven by an investing model that is time constrained like venture capital and private equity or even impact investing. As a fiduciary money manager and impact investor you are not interested in owning a business but generating value and impact through scale. While as the proprietor, you are interested in owning the business, controlling your destiny, and also nurturing it.

As impact investor or just investor, you have to understand the distinction. Value creation, which is creating impact and wealth together, necessitates scale and limited time horizon means the rate of growth is equally critical. Thus when you choose a model of impact investing that borrows from VC/PE model—scale, size, and growth rate are critical things to be aware of and internalised.

JP: Can you just give us some speeds and feeds about the Aavishkaar and Intellecap companies?

Vineet: I started in 2001 with personal capital of ₹5,000. I was supported by some of the young Indians, including the author of this book, Jayesh Parekh, and some others like Anantha Nageswaran, and Arun Diaz to reach $1 million of assets under management by 2005. In 2002, I also borrowed from my wife ₹1 lakh ($2,200 at exchange rate in 2001) to start Intellecap—an ecosystem builder which I thought was critical if I need to bring about change. Between 2005–2010, we went from $1 million to $100 million of assets and some good work in building ecosystem through Intellecap.

Between 2010–2019, we have transitioned from being just an impact investor and ecosystem builder in India to an impact platform operating across Southeast Asia, India, and East and West Africa. Today we manage close to $1 billion in assets and offer entrepreneurs equity, debt, and advisory services, and are backed by a strong group of shareholders that include a foundation, a trillion dollar fund manager, and two European banks.

Our uniqueness is that instead of focussing just on money we have focussed on the idea of building the ecosystem of impact. The Aavishkaar Group today comprises of a technology-led inclusive finance company called Arohan, SME lending platform called IntelleGrow (renamed as Ashv Finance), FinTech company called Tribe, advisory management consulting and impact investing advisory firm called Intellecap, and impact investing funds under Aavishkaar Capital. Our focus is to serve the need of low-income segments through entrepreneurial intervention.

Given the absence of real impact capital at scale, Aavishkaar Group is striving to become a pioneering impact platform that offers deep impact. We have identified an asset under management of ₹50,000 crore or $7 billion as our aspirational goal of mobilising dedicated impact capital delivering deep impact across Asia and Africa.

JP: How has your perspective on money changed?

Vineet: I hold the view that money is not a lead intervention to do anything including making an impact. However, I do believe now that you cannot ignore money and it is a necessary condition but not sufficient condition in the equation of impact and change. Money follows passion and commitment, but it is fearful and cannot deal with new ideas generally. Hence, you have to learn to attract

189

money without scaring it. Trust, humility, and persistence are some critical factors to attract money to even very utopian ideas. If you are a science student, you know that a non-conductor like rubber or wood can break the electrical circuit. Money managers are those non-conductors and your passion is filtered out by them easily; if you associate your passion with trust, humility, and perseverance you may be able to communicate with people with money and thus can transform into becoming a conductor of money.

You have to also know that your self-belief is far more critical to bring about a change. Self-belief aided with clarity of thought are two critical aids in success and both are within and not outside you.

My personal learning has been that it is good to meet people, hear their views, but when you act it must be your own idea. If you have a good idea, act on it without worrying about money and if you are good at some point of time money will chase you.

JP: There is so much growth in Aavishkaar and in you, compared to the humble beginnings. Going forward, what do you plan to do with all the money in your own life and in the life of Aavishkaar?

Vineet: All my earnings are institutional and reside within the operating group. My personal asks or ambitions are quite small as we continue to live in our old house in the suburb in Mumbai and we do not have any big asks. If I do have significant capital, I would like to use it to push real impact by making investment that are not seeking short term return. I would want to back entrepreneurs who are bringing about real change on the ground and cannot be funded by impact funds. Making money is a noble act but using this money to deliver a more equal world free of basic suffering may be a truly noble use of the money. When I have wealth, I would continue to push to help brave young entrepreneurs who are challenging conventional wisdom and are being naïve in their thinking to aspire to make the world a better place to live in for the coming generations.

Vikram Gandhi

Founder, Asha Impact and Professor, Harvard Business School

JP: May I request you to introduce yourself.

Vikram: I am a senior lecturer and a member of the Harvard Business School where I teach in both the MBA and Executive Education programs. I am also senior advisor to the Canadian Pension Plan Investment Board and founder of Asha Impact, which is an impact investing platform, currently focussed on India.

JP: Please share with us where you grew up and your journey in life.

Vikram: I grew up in Mumbai. I spent the first 25 years of my life in Mumbai except one year when I was running AIESEC, which is an international organisation in Brussels. Otherwise, I spent 25 years in Mumbai before I went off to business school in the US. I grew up in a middle-class family. Both my parents were immigrants from Pakistan and had to start all over again. My dad didn't have much education and started off as a salesman going around cities spending nights at railway stations. Essentially, I grew up in an environment where all my parents' hard work and focus and some connection got me to a good school, called The Cathedral and John Connon School in South Bombay.

I grew up in a middle-class, focussed, hardworking, "get on and go about putting your head down and getting things done" type of family—but there was also a focus on trying to do good and philanthropic activities. One of them, on which I spent a lot of time from when I was 10 years old, was a place called Asha Dan, which was part of Mother Teresa's orphanage in Byculla, South Bombay. I used to spend a lot of time there on weekends, in terms of reading, hanging out with the kids there as well as learning from them and teaching them. It was great fun and that was my first exposure to philanthropy.

JP: Where did you go to college?

Vikram: I went to Sydenham College here in Mumbai. Along with college, I also did my chartered accountancy. I used to go to college—in India as you know going to college is a little bit of an iffy thing, you don't have to actually attend that much, but I did. I also had the opportunity to go and work at a company called

191

Lovelock & Lewis, which was Coopers and Lybrand in India, to do my Chartered Accountancy.

While I was in college, I helped set up this organisation called AIESEC in India, which is an international association of students, where students are exchanged to work abroad. One of the people that I approached for support was Mr Ratan Tata, who became a big supporter of AIESEC and gave me a chance to get to know him pretty well. After I graduated with a BCom and completed my CA, I worked as his executive assistant for a couple of years on a whole bunch of projects. He was the chairman of Tata Industries at that time which was Tata's company for starting new businesses. I helped set up Tata Finance. I did a lot of work on an agricultural joint venture that the Tata's set up. Those two to three years I was an executive assistant, but I was also like one of his younger project guys. Then I applied to Harvard Business School. I got in and I went to do my MBA there from 1987–1989.

JP: After that did you come back to India or did you continue to work in US?

Vikram: I stayed back. In the late 1980s, the opportunities in India were not the way they are today. I didn't have that much capital, so my parents had borrowed a lot of money to pay for my MBA. I worked at McKinsey in New York during my business school summer where I was assigned to an investment banking project. Growing up in Mumbai, I had no idea what investment banking was, but I worked on a project for an investment bank that was very cool. I had a finance background that involved marketing, structuring, and things like that.

Rather than going back to McKinsey, I joined Morgan Stanley in New York. My career with Morgan Stanley lasted 16 years, but I was in New York for five to six years in the mergers, acquisition, and pre-structure type of group. Then one day the CEO called me and said, "We need to develop business in India. We have a little bit there already and we've got some issues and problems. We need somebody to go there and help them fix it." I was 32 years old and we had three little kids. I talked to my wife and we thought it was a cool opportunity to go and help build the business at such a young age. I came back to India for three years to help build Morgan Stanley in

India and then went back. I did a bunch of different jobs at Morgan Stanley and then went to Credit Suisse.

JP: Then one day you decided to come back to India?

Vikram: Credit Suisse was in the US and in Hong Kong. In about 2009–2010, I was in a senior position and was reporting to the CEO. I had worked for 24 years in investment banking and had been fortunate enough to catch the ultimate bull market in the financial services, having completely stumbled into it and created a fair amount of wealth for myself. From a career standpoint, I was capped out, I was not really enjoying it, I was getting bored. I grew up in Mumbai, I built up Morgan Stanley and I kept my Indian passport— never gave it up—I wanted to come back and do interesting and different things. That's why I quit in 2011.

I came back for a couple of years just to explore. I moved from Bombay to Delhi because I felt working in different avenues in the government may be an interesting thing to do. I started working with Sam Pitroda, the Congress government, on a whole bunch of things. I got involved with the Grameen Foundation, and through some connection, I got connected to Muhammad Yunus, before he got the Nobel Peace Prize. I got quite involved in the Grameen movement, I am still on the board of the Grameen Foundation. I got involved in this area of impact investing, and while it was coined by The Rockefeller Foundation in 2007, it's something that I felt was a great way to bring my business principle, my business acumen, and my experience to solve a problem beyond donating capital to NGOs.

JP: What is your perspective on money? Tell us about the genesis of Asha Impact, and what you do there?

Vikram: When I came back to India, I thought, why don't I set up my own impact fund? But I didn't want to do a fund because I didn't have the patience or time at this stage of my life going around fund raising, so I hired a team. I hired Kartik Desai and few other people, decided I would allocate X per cent of my portfolio—my investment portfolio not charitable portfolio—to this area, with the objective to generate private equity venture capital kind of returns but with an impact lens on it; and that anything I do has to have both financial returns and impact returns.

I called it Asha Impact because Asha Daan, in Mumbai, was the first charity I was exposed to, and the first good thing I did in my life. Then I did some research as to what the word 'Asha' means apart from aspiration and hope—it means 'hope' in Swahili. I set that up and the team started originating deals and made a few investments. I talked to Pramod Bhasin. He was very keen and joined. We did that for a couple of years, it seemed to be working well, and then we expanded the circle to another six people. It's not an angel network. It's an impact investing, small little network, which essentially originates deals. We have done about 12 transactions in the last three and a half years, even exited one at a lucrative return. The team originates deals and if Pramod and I, one of us or both of us, decide to invest then we take it to the other members of the circle. It's working pretty well and is now at a stage where we are figuring out how to grow it? Do we change the format? We have a mix of good and not so good investments, but I think all of them have been high impact, which is very heartening.

JP: What is your perspective on money today and for the future? The question is, what shall we do with all this money?

Vikram: I like the title of your book because I think it's very relevant. While I was setting up Asha Impact, I also started spending more time at Harvard Business School (HBS). I realised that the millennials really do think differently. In my age, if I am not from a wealthy family—the first 25 years of my life I will focus on education, next 25 years of my life I will focus on my career, wealth creation etc., and then I will focus on giving back, and try to do some good. However, that's not the way millennials think today. I felt there was a big need to teach millennials about impact investing but there was no course at HBS. Therefore, I developed a completely new course at HBS, where I teach millennials about impact investing.

We don't have to sacrifice financial returns but it's important that capital can make a difference. You have to focus on bringing proper investment disciplines to the environmental factor, social factor, governance factor—the whole ESG thing, income equality, gender equality, and that whole spectrum—into the public market and the private market. There is a bucket of investing and there is a bucket of more effective philanthropy. How can you use interesting financial tools like social investment bonds to make philanthropy more effective by focussing on outcomes as opposed to just spending on outputs? For me, the key statistic is that $40 trillion of wealth is going to be transferred from the older generation to the millennials in the next decade or so.

JP: Beyond philanthropy and social impact investing, do you have anything else that you want to share with us in terms of what shall we do with all this money?

Vikram: It's not only about social investing. It's about investing with a mission in addition to financial returns. The UN Sustainable Development Goals (SDG) has become kind of a north star—they have identified 17 issues the world needs to focus on, or else the world is going to be in deep trouble. All of the analysis suggests that there is a deficit of $5–$7 trillion to reach these goals by 2030. This has to come from the private sector. And so, you look at all the big professional money managers, they all focus on this— BlackRock, Vanguard, State Street, pension funds. We have a fiduciary responsibility but if we don't actually do something with this money, we won't have a world to live in. This has to be front and centre, that's why the course I teach is called 'Investing in the 21st Century: Risk, Return, and Impact'.

JP: Beside investment and philanthropy, how do you spend money and enjoy life?

Vikram: I enjoy giving, doing philanthropy but at the same time I enjoy life, which I think is important too. I have a good standard of living. You don't have to become a hermit to do good in the world, and at the same time you don't have to splurge to be happy. I think having a happy balance is the key for me and that's how I live my life.

Rajeev Srivastava

Founder and Executive Chairman, Basil Partner

JP: May I request you to introduce yourself.

Rajeev: I come from Uttar Pradesh, I was born in a very small village town called Deoria, but I grew up in Mumbai. My father is a medical doctor, he was in the armed forces for nine years, and then he was in the Indian railways. I studied at Sardar Patel Engineering and Sydenham Institute of Management Studies. I spent the first four years of my career at TCS and then worked in the US, at iGate, and then decided to start my own business in 1996 and have been doing that business ever since.

JP: How many years did you spend in Mumbai?

Rajeev: I was in Mumbai for 20 years of my life. I lived in Pittsburgh for four years with a company called iGate. I started the iGate Singapore operation and a year later decided to start my own entrepreneurial journey. That happened because a spiritual person prodded me to do so. Initially, I wasn't interested but when he gave me a vision to start a business and allocate half my ownership to charity—that actually excited me more than just business per se. Then through the business, I went back to the US and I lived there for 10 years in Pittsburgh, Pennsylvania.

JP: What were you doing in Pittsburgh?

Rajeev: This was my own business called Apar Infotech. Since the US was the biggest market, it grew rapidly, and we finally merged with another company and did a NASDAQ listing in 2004.

JP: Can you give us the quantum of that?

Rajeev: Apar Infotech started with seed funding of the only capital that I had, which was $150,000 and then we got an investment from a very unusual source—my brother-in-law. It was a little dangerous to get into a business partnership with him. My brother-in-law and I were joined by this concept that whatever shares we would have in the company, both he as the investor and me as the CEO, had this common goal—to offer half our shares to charity. That kept us together, took us through the journey where the company grew all the way to $90 million. In 2005, I left the company.

I thought, may be the grass is greener on the other side, and went to the investment side of the business.

JP: Describe your journey from 2005 onwards.

Rajeev: From the end of 2005, when I left Apar/Ness, I first invested my own money into technology services businesses. I took the approach of investing in entrepreneurs who are not just looking at business to make money but have some purpose, as well. And only after seeing that those companies did well, did I get into creating a fund-like structure in 2010. I still continued with my utopian idea that I only want investors who will not just try to make money from the investment but also give something back to their respective charities. Therefore, when you have this kind of a vision you don't attract too many investors, but it worked fine. This journey continues and in August 2018, I raised an institutional fund with institutional investors. The fund that we have created, with me as a managing partner and 100 per cent owner of the fund management company, the vision still remains that 35 per cent of our carry fees is allocated to charity. Somehow, my belief has always been that by having some kind of purpose all through the journey, both as an entrepreneur as well as in the fund, it drives me much more, it drives the other partners more. Even in the entrepreneurial journey, the kind of people I could attract was great, because by working in a set up like this, these professionals were indirectly giving something back to society. I managed to get investors who could see that besides the successful business track record of the General Partners (GP) these GPs had a higher purpose besides just making money.

JP: I would like to understand your perspective on money growing up, that ultimately led you to these philosophies?

Rajeev: Growing up, we were a family of four children—three brothers and one sister. My father had just his government salary to support all of us. We were a lower-middle-class family. We never had a car, we always used public transport. However, I could see that 90 per cent of others who were also in government service had other ways of making money, so many of them were quite well off. But my father's values and ideals have always been to be honest and be happy with whatever little you have. I did learn a lot about the value of money and also about never doing something incorrect or unethical. I think by my parent's blessings, by their good wishes we completed our education and today we have achieved some amount of success.

JP: What is your fund called?

Rajeev: My fund is called Basil Technology Partners and it's $175 million fund with three large institutions that have backed us, and one investor is a family office. The fund is into technology services and we take controlling equity in these businesses and we are fairly hands-on trying to help these businesses grow, but I am very happy that my colleagues and general partners, all of us are united on the goal that we work hard for our portfolio companies. All of us are certainly looking to make money but each of the partners is attracted to giving part of their wealth to charity.

JP: Please do elaborate a little more on that structure?

Rajeev: The structure of the current fund is such that I am the 100 per cent owner of the fund, but the general partners and the managing partners have allocated a total of 35 per cent of the 100 per cent carry to charity.

In the next fund, I am not going to stay the owner. The ownership will move to a professionally run trust that will have 20 per cent of the carry fees allocated to founder-connected charity and 20 per cent to other GP decided charities with the balance 60 per cent going to GPs. And I am confident that I will be attracting a lot of professionals who are even better than I am, and who will continue this belief and who resonate with the same philosophy. Our hope is that more funds globally look towards bringing a higher purpose into their ethos as well.

JP: One part of your life is Basil Partners and the other part of your life is Artha. Can you please tell us what Artha is about?

Rajeev: The Artha platform is basically trying to create a network of professionals and entrepreneurs who have a higher purpose to their business. Artha Forum is now a network, which has had events all over the world, and it is inspiring more and more entrepreneurs. Several entrepreneurs have now allocated 10–50 per cent of their ownership to charity and each of the entrepreneurs have grown their business three or four times in value, even while having this vision.

JP: Are you also running some events around Artha Forum?

Rajeev: Artha Forum conducts events in Singapore regularly, as well as in Dubai and Silicon Valley. We have members like Damodar Reddy, who was the first Indian to list a semiconductor company on NASDAQ. His new businesses are all allocating half his shares to charity. He is 74 years old and he came to Artha Forum in 2013.

JP: Can you describe how the events take place?

Rajeev: The events are held in hotels. We had one event in Dubai where the topic was 'Plain Living, High Thinking'. These events are held in proper business forums and we bring in professionals like Ronnie Screwvala from UTV, who has spoken at our events; we had Mohandas Pai; we had Ajay Piramal; we had Marci Shimoff, who is the author of *Chicken Soup for the Soul* books; we had Amit Chandra (Bain Capital) who was on the Tata Sons Board. Mostly, the Indian ethos is to be very private about sharing what they are doing in philanthropy, and I appreciate that, but somewhere we have been able to request the panel members to come out and share their story so that many more youngsters will take to this path.

JP: Do religious or spiritual gurus also come to Artha events?

Rajeev: At all our events, we ensure that there is somebody from the spiritual tradition who has absolutely nothing commercial to gain or lose from this, but he says things based on the ancient scriptures when India followed the model of what we call conscious capitalism or dharmic capitalism. When a spiritual person says something, then it really percolates into the hearts of people and change happens because greed and money is not something people can easily let go. At all our events, we have spiritual teachers who say things with a lot of spiritual depth and with deep realisation, because they are deeper practitioners.

JP: The question is, what shall we do with all this money? What is your perspective on money for the future?

Rajeev: With respect to personal wealth, all through the journey of gaining wealth, I have always looked at it like this: 50 per cent will stay with the family and 50 per cent goes to charity. Even with the family, the same culture is expected to continue.

To me whatever wealth I have been able to create, either goes to charity, or it continues to create more wealth. This platform that I am creating, if the Lord desires, will continue to grow. In a small limited way we are trying to follow the Tata model where over 60 per cent of Tata Sons is owned by charities and this unique business model has led to significant growth in business and also generated so much for various charities in education, health, sports, and more. Wealth has grown in this unique structure and produced leaders with a deep sense of character and humility like Mr JRD Tata and Mr Ratan Tata. We hope that many business leaders will also set up similar structures for their own family, following the principle of 'earn with integrity and spend with compassion'. The world needs more role models like Tata in business, and to evolve from the current greed based capitalism to conscious capitalism.

Varun Sahni
Founder and Managing Partner, Impact Investor Partners

JP: May I request you to introduce yourself.

Varun: Let me start with an introduction of myself with experiences that have shaped my thinking and whom I am. At very young age I grew up between India and the UK. Growing up in Bombay, when I was 10 to about 20 years old, there was a deep sense of numbness and almost apathy towards people's surroundings; there was a lot of wealth living amongst immense poverty and most people I interacted with had a worldview that was fairly narrow from a perspective of their own lives. I think that really affected me to the extent that when I was in college, I decided that I wanted to spend summers in rural India and to see what the other side of life is.

In the early 90s, I spent time in villages in a South Indian district called Kadapa, which is a quarrying centre for granite. I spent summers over there with a not-for-profit called Oxfam—probably in 1995–1996. I tried to understand how small businesses function, work with farmers, work with artisans and that was an eye-opening experience for me because it really taught me about human struggle and taught me both about equality and inequality and what money and opportunity can do to people's lives. In the 1990s, I got really interested in looking at how innovation and change in micro economies in small businesses was functioning across India which was all being led by the not-for-profit sector, however, it could not really scale due to structural limitations of the sector. The for-profit sector, which on the other hand is purely profit maximising and in the 1990s it yet didn't realise that you don't have to profit-maximise to be profitable. I think that's a lesson we are learning today and has now become mainstream thinking.

I didn't want to join an investment bank or a consulting firm. I wanted to push my limits and that's why I landed up in Yemen in the late 90s and I worked in Sanaa and Aden, in not-for-profit, looking at gender issues. I came back to India and between early 2000–2005, I worked with both a US based NGO called Care, as well as with Unilever in India. When I was in Care, I could see that the corporate sectors were starting to look at low-income markets, and C K Prahalad had written the book, *The Fortune at the Bottom of the Pyramid.*

People were trying to figure out distribution into those markets. The whole institutionalisation of micro finance had started in those markets. I worked on setting up fairly large businesses in those markets with artisans and farmers to look at value chain and provide them better value for their goods and products. I consulted with Unilever to build one of the world's largest rural distribution platform called Shakti, where we set up distribution to hundreds and thousands of villages in India and learnt a lot about if capital is not a constraint, what is the constraint and how learning execution is more important than capital in building large-scale businesses.

During that time horizon, philanthropy as a concept had moved from pure grant to this whole venture philanthropy model. I had the opportunity to be the first India director of Acumen from 2005–2010, where I was part of the global leadership and portfolio team, where over five years I saw probably 3,000–4,000 businesses across India and Africa. The experience taught me a lot about pattern recognition and about how to fail and what do you learn from failure. That pattern recognition helped in thinking about how to build businesses at scale in low-income markets and how you can use different forms of capital effectively for providing affordable and high-quality goods and services to low-income markets. That is how I was shaped as an individual and how I thought about the use of capital in our world.

I did that for a number of years until 2010, when I with my wife, Nadia Sood, set up our own holding company called Impact Investment Partners, in London. The idea of Impact Investment Partners was to look at different forms of capital to address the societal issues and over the years, we did some very interesting investments, some very interesting work. We then decided to take our collective experiences and build our own companies, which we are doing at present with our business CreditEnable, which is a financial technology company facilitating affordable credit to SME.

This is a large, global societal issue and we are working with a diverse group of individuals and institutions to address this credit gap challenge that small business face worldwide.

JP: Where did you grow up?

Varun: I grew up a bit in Bombay and then a bit in the UK. I ended up in a pretty good school in India called The Cathedral and John Connon School. I frankly did not enjoy school and felt stifled in a traditional classroom environment. I was pretty much a terrible student until university and my education really started when I started exposing myself to other environments.

JP: Where did you go to college?

Varun: After Cathedral I attended St. Xavier's. After Xavier's, I went to Columbia University in the US.

JP: What were you studying at Columbia?

Varun: At Columbia, I studied International Affairs, Political Economy, and then I was at the London School of Economics as a Chevening Scholar. I have been fortunate to be a TED fellow and Asia Society Global Young Leader. I built for the first time my own business as an entrepreneur. In the late 90s, I got together with two friends in India where the economy was opening up. The three of us ended up building a hospitality company, restaurants, and bars, which today is about 40–45 restaurants and bars across India, a company called Impresario. I saw the whole cycle of promoter, investor, putting a little bit of capital, the pain of short term failure, picking ourselves up again and eventual exit in seven years; that experience I had was probably in part some of the best education I could have ever had.

JP: What was your lifestyle growing up?

Varun: As I was growing up my standard of living was, in hindsight, very good, but whilst we were growing up, we never thought about those things. For example, we only went out three or four times a year when my parents would take us out for birthdays. I grew up in a fairly austere environment where money was not treated frivolously but then there wasn't money to be treated frivolously, but otherwise I think I didn't really want for any basic things.

JP: What is your view on money today?

Varun: In my view, money should fundamentally be used as a tool to benefit society, number one. Number two, I believe capital has many personalities that affect human beings. I think capital when used for high returns in a hedge fund drives very different emotions in someone then when capital is used for grant and philanthropic need.

I think how money is used actually affects peoples' personalities in a very dramatic way.

JP: Going forward, whatever affluence you are going to have with all these investments, what will you do with all this money?

Varun: My view is that we as individuals have to be more aware of the world around us. I think one of the challenges we face is a globally structural challenge in democracy, where as individuals we are a silent majority and quite apathetic until something shocks us. I think a large part of the world is like that. In my view, if capital was not a constraint, I really want to believe that each of us is politically and socially active, but I think the incentives are not clearly understood or defined. How do you make every individual say, "I do want to vote, and I should vote; and I want to think about what I am doing in my vote, about the choices I make in the world."

I would like to see capital be used to rethink and to figure out how to incentivise ourselves, as individuals, as a tool to make us more active in the choices we make politically in this world. I am a big believer that that is a massive reason why the world has ended up where it is today. A world where, as individuals, we are not really standing up for what we believe in as much as we could or should before the fact—it's usually after the fact of things going wrong and then we only have ourselves as a human race to blame for that. There needs to be a change where the incentive systems in our world need to be rethought and unlocked and I think capital has a significant role over there.

The way the capital is distributed is also very different in different states. There is a question about what is the ideal size of a welfare state? If you look at how capital is distributed in Northern European economies versus how it is distributed in large populations, there is a question to be understood in terms of how money can be used more effectively for the welfare benefit of a large number of people. And for me, that means stop spending the amount that we do on defence and arms, and instead, start putting money back into healthcare, education, housing, and feeding people.

JP: Please talk about your thesis of social impact investment.

Varun: My thesis of social impact investment is that primarily it needs to be commercially viable, cost effective, and it needs to essentially benefit a large number of people. I am not a believer in the idea that philanthropy per se is an answer. I am a believer in the need to be profitable without profit maximising as an investor and really benefit the largest number of people.

JP: How do you differentiate the conflict between economics and impact?

Varun: Without economics, we are not going to have impact. It's more about defining what the balance is. This also goes into decision-making and the corporate structure. I think one of the challenges with economics and impact is when you have a pure for-profit private limited structure that corporate structure itself makes you a shareholder, and the owner of capital thinks very differently, they want to purely maximise profit. On the other hand, in a not-for-profit structure the opposite happens. There is a need to rethink some form of corporate structures, it may not be co-operative, but I think there are partnership structures that the world is seeing, maybe producer-owned partnership. There are many examples, there is John Lewis Partnership—where you have economics and impact, and the stakeholders—the owner, the worker, and the community are aligned. I think the challenge is really in us identifying the correct structures to be able to think of how to balance economics and impact.

JP: Any final word of wisdom?

Varun: No. No words of wisdom. For me, life is a miracle and hopefully we get to live it to our fullest human capability, to benefit each other with respect and love.

Social Impactors

Rohini Nilekani
Founder and Chairperson, Arghyam

Mritunjay Tiwary
Founder and Trustee, Akhand Jyoti Eye Hospital

Karl Mehta
Founder, Code for India, PlaySpan, and EdCast

Ami Doshi
Director, Frontier Investment Management Company

Latika Thukral
Co-founder, iamgurgaon

Bina Rampuria
Board Member, Magic Bus Singapore

Rohini Nilekani
Founder and Chairperson, Arghyam

JP: May I request you to introduce yourself.

Rohini: I grew up in Mumbai, in a normal, middle-class family. My parents transferred to us values about wealth that are more to do with giving than with consuming it. My maternal grandfather was known for setting up colleges and giving to various institutions. My paternal grandfather didn't have much wealth, partly because as a lawyer he was less interested in making money than settling disputes out of court. But he shone the light on the right path. He was part of the first batch that responded to Mahatma Gandhi's call for volunteers in Champaran in 1917. He helped set up Gandhiji's first ashram in Bithiharwa, and stayed there for months along with Kasturba Gandhi and others, helping the locals on education and sanitation.

JP: What was his name?

Rohini: His name was Sadashiv Soman, but everyone called him Baba Saheb. He is mentioned in Gandhiji's autobiography. That's the kind of legacy we grew up with. We always understood that there was a societal responsibility that we all carry.

JP: Where did you study?

Rohini: I went to couple of schools, then I went to Elphinstone College in Mumbai, after which I did a postgraduate diploma in Mass Communications at St. Xavier's College and became a journalist. For the first few years, I was writing for Bombay Magazine and then freelancing for India Today and other publications. I joined Sunday Magazine, and then when the kids came along, I had to take a break.

JP: Growing up, what was your perspective on money?

Rohini: In urban Bombay middle-class life, we didn't think that much about money, honestly. We had enough for everything that we needed. We were quite busy deciding what to focus on, what we wanted to do with our life. My mother was a very strong personality and encouraged her three daughters to do well for themselves, to be ambitious, to study well, and to plan for a career even though she couldn't have one herself. She was a teacher and she always took tuitions from home almost until the end of her life. She was always creatively and productively engaged, and she encouraged her daughters to be the same. She had a keen interest in politics. We didn't think much about money; we had enough, and we didn't need much. We weren't hankering for it. We really never compared ourselves to anybody richer even though we were in Bombay. Personally, I now realise that it was because of the relatively good public infrastructure in Mumbai. We had good learning institutions, good public transport, good spaces for art and culture, safe public spaces where we could travel alone even at night. That is so important, and reduces the need for extra disposable income.

JP: Today you're are a very affluent person. How have you come to where you are now?

Rohini: In 1981, when Infosys was set up by my husband and others, we were just married. In fact, just before we got married, he asked me, "Should I do this? Should I quit my job?" I didn't know any better luckily, so, I said, "Of course, yes." We were young and we could afford to take a risk, so they started Infosys and I invested whatever little money I had at the time, partly given by my parents, partly from my savings, the princely sum of ₹10,000 in Infosys in those very early days. And since Infosys became so phenomenally successful, I became phenomenally wealthier alongside and independently. Nandan often says, "I am an accidental entrepreneur." And so I became accidentally wealthy and an accidental philanthropist.

JP: What is your perspective on money today?

Rohini: It took me a while to get used to this kind of wealth because of the middle-class background I described earlier. I was always leaning a bit towards the left on the political spectrum, so I was a little suspicious of the wealthy as I grew up and then I became wealthy myself, so I had to deal with that. It took me a while and then I realised that wealth can be an opportunity to achieve the same goals that I had always dreamt of. I always felt I wanted to live in a society which is really looking out for the weakest. That is the kind of society that I thought would make me happy to be a part of. Then I realised that wealth could be one vector to make that happen though it's not easy. Once I dealt with that, we began to use our wealth for larger societal gain and of course, I started making small grants and later much more strategic grants. It has culminated in our joining

The Giving Pledge last year where we have pledged to give away at least half our wealth.

JP: Apart from giving grants, do you personally give time to your projects?

Rohini: I have also been a serial social entrepreneur. I co-founded Pratham Books where I wanted to help democratise the joy of reading to millions of children. In the 10 years from 2004–2014, when I was the founder-chairperson of Pratham Books, we had already reached millions of kids with local, indigenised content in multiple languages at an affordable price. With a personal endowment, I also set up Arghyam, which means 'offering' in Sanskrit. In 2005, Arghyam started focussing on the water sector. For 14 years, we have supported NGOs around the country especially, in participatory ground water management. India is facing a serious water crisis. Arghyam has, I hope, been able to positively influence the sector and we intend to do more. Other than that, Nandan and I, along with Shankar Maruwada have set up the EkStep Foundation in 2014, where we are working in the education sector with the goal to enable access to learning opportunities for 200 million children. We are using technology as the backbone to achieve that. Other than that, I support work in various things, such as environment, governance, independent media, justice, and gender—especially working with young men and boys, and a few other sectors.

JP: What is The Giving Pledge?

Rohini: The Giving Pledge was set up by Bill and Melinda Gates and Warren Buffett. Basically, the idea is that the extreme wealth in the hands of very few people needs to get out and so they encourage people to make a pledge. There is nothing that you sign. People pledge and publicly make a commitment to giving away at least half of their wealth.

JP: That's not specifically only to the Bill & Melinda Gates Foundation?

Rohini: Not at all. The money can be given anywhere by the people who committed the pledge. It's nothing to do with the Gates Foundation. Nobody asks questions about where it will be spent, to whom it will be given—it's just a public commitment that the wealthy will give away their money to whichever cause they want to. It's nothing to do with their foundation. I can continue my philanthropy in my way. It's just that by making a public pledge you are accepting responsibility for that wealth and for its purpose to create social benefit. It is an important signalling for society.

JP: From the day you began giving, you wanted to create a thesis of impact. Is that thesis coming through? Is it more outcome oriented or is there also a journey in it for you?

Rohini: My philosophy has always been that in the continuum of samaaj, bazaar, and sarkaar (society, market, and state), we need to ensure a strong samaaj. Markets and the state are created to serve society, not dominate it. My focus is entirely on the samaaj sector. I believe that we are not just consumers for the market nor are we subjects for the state. We are citizens in our own rights, we co-create good markets, and we must co-create good governance. In all the work, I do and all the things that I give to, I try to support ideas, individuals, and institutions that help build up civic capacity in the samaaj space, in the society space. We need moral leadership; we need institutions; we need grassroots work. We need to build strong societies to keep market and state accountable for the larger public good. That's been my philosophy for work and giving.

JP: What's the journey been like?

Rohini: The journey has been exhilarating and humbling. We have such a vibrant and innovative civil society in India, though it is renewing itself now and is also under much pressure. In whichever sector that I choose I identify good people who have high integrity, high commitment, and a long-term perseverance to achieve the goals that they have chosen in the context and the way they see it best fit. It's really a journey and so long as we keep meeting some of the markers on the road, I am happy. I feel that outcomes are very hard to achieve, and I understand that. So long as we are headed in the right direction, I am kind of okay with it. I understand that we will occasionally fail, and that philanthropy is extreme risk capital. I understand that we are investing where markets won't, and states can't. For example, in water through my foundation Arghyam, we have made significant impact on the ground in creating lots of communities that are managing their water more sustainably. We have achieved tremendous policy impact over the years.

But we were very patient, and worked alongside our partners. Sometimes donors can be very unreasonable in the impact that they want to achieve, and I try not to be like that. I try to build a relationship of trust.

JP: A part of your wealth goes towards philanthropy. Is there any other use of wealth that you can share with us?

Rohini: We want to create a large impact through building public institutions. India still needs to build out its intellectual infrastructure. Both Nandan and I support several institutions in the social sector; institutions of learning and institutions of research. We have supported the Indian Institute for Human Settlements (IIHS), which is building out professional capacity to nurture an urbanising India. We have also supported Bangalore International Centre (BIC), which is a hub where people can come and learn from each other. I also support the Vidhi Centre for Legal Policy. Well run public institutions are a strategic and long-term way to deploy wealth. Some of these institutions do a lot of evidence-based research for policy advocacy, so that of course impacts millions of lives because good policy and good laws make a huge difference to society. I think that's the forward impact of giving away wealth wisely.

I also think there is a social signalling; we live in times of extreme inequality. I don't think it is good for any country or any society, to have so much disparity. India and the US are extreme outliers in this. We don't know enough about China and Russia. But in India and the USA, the pattern of extreme inequality means that very few people control a lot of the wealth, have garnered tremendous resources and consequently, power. Today's technologies enable even more of that and the way markets are structured it allows continual accumulation of wealth by the wealthy. That's not very good for society, it's not good for social justice, and it's not good for future generations. I look at wealth and giving in that context. I also try to understand the distortions of power that can creep in from our ability to give. That is why I try to create a lot of voice and diversity in my philanthropy portfolio.

JP: Beside doing charity or giving or contributing to society?

Rohini: I don't call it charity. I call it strategic philanthropy.

JP: Okay, so besides strategic philanthropy how else do you spend your money, besides giving it away?

Rohini: Honestly, we live extremely comfortably. It is of course, rather relative, but we don't live very indulgently, and at least until now, we have avoided splurging on private planes etc. But of course money is extremely useful. There are two big things that we spend on—travel and health care. It enables me to travel whenever I want, however I want. It enables me to be very comfortable about the fact that myself, and the people around me can afford any health care that they need. These are the two big things that I can think of that are most useful. We don't live very extravagantly but we certainly live very comfortably, and we are very grateful for that.

JP: Going forward in your life, what will you do with all this money? Will you keep the money for your family or give it all away? What is your philosophy about passing down wealth to your next generation?

Rohini: My husband and I have already given to our children what we think is their rightful share of our wealth. Since we have made The Giving Pledge, we have to focus a lot on our philanthropy and it is going to be a tremendous uphill task to give that wealth in our lifetime.

Even if, God forbid, something were to happen to us soon, our children will uphold our commitment. I am not worried about that, but it is not at all easy to give away so much money in a meaningful and an effective manner. It takes a lot of hard work. Both my husband and I spend a lot of time on that.

JP: Do you feel that your perspective on money, going forward, will remain the same or is it going to change?

Rohini: One can never predict the future, but I don't expect too much change in our thinking. As I told you some of us have become so unreasonably wealthy that it will take generations to use that wealth, to finish that wealth, unless something really catastrophic happens. I don't see our attitude towards wealth changing, because with God's grace and also because of structural flaws in society, some of us have far too much money and so, we can afford to live well and give away wealth.

JP: Millennials are going to come into hundreds of millions of dollars in the next decades. Can you please share your wisdom with them?

Rohini: I would say that we have given the millennials a very rough legacy because of climate change, due to which they are going to see a lot of upheaval in their lifetime. I would ask them to not focus on the money so much, though you can't prevent that, as some of them will be very ambitious in a monetary way. I would advise them to stay curious, stay connected, and stay committed as citizens. That's where the meaningfulness of life unfolds. Wealth is one thing. Take time to define your own attitude towards money and wealth. Understand from research that it's not just wealth that produces happiness but how you deal with the wealth. That if happiness is the general goal then wealth is not going to be the first thing that is going to create happiness. Think through, read about wealth, read about the meaning of wealth, read about whether constant consumption will add or subtract from the quality of your life. There is so much new research on this. Depending on how you deal with your wealth, you can make or break your own happiness. And practice empathy. We get wealthy due to accidents of fate. Millennials should remember that sometimes when you are very wealthy, your life becomes disconnected from others. But as we know increasingly well, our fate remains entwined with the rest of humanity. Try to understand how interconnected we have all become. Then once we internalise this, our monetary situation becomes a creative opportunity.

Mritunjay Tiwary

Founder and Trustee, Akhand Jyoti Eye Hospital

JP: May I request you to introduce yourself.

Mritunjay: I am a Bihari hailing from an affluent business family and was born and brought up in Calcutta. After my graduation, I joined my family business and helped my father expand his distributorship business. I have been a keen footballer, having played first division football for Mohun Bagan in Calcutta and had always thought of making some impact on society.

In 2004, during a chance visit to Bihar, I saw a girl being sold off due to poverty and they let her go into bonded slavery or prostitution. Earlier, India shining for me meant the performances of the Bombay Stock Exchange and foreign exchange reserves. This visit actually changed my whole perspective and forced me to reflect on two questions—Who am I? What is the purpose of life? Or, what does success truly mean for me? I started on what, in Hindi, we call shodh yatra, the journey to find myself, and how I could contribute. I came to this village of Mastichak in Bihar and spoke to Pandit Ramesh Chandra Shukla ji, and started Akhand Jyoti 12 years back under his chairmanship. I volunteered to spend three or four days in a month to come to Bihar and support any good cause so that I could get some solace in my journey to find myself.

I was struggling to find a work-area to focus on but a chance event at the local district hospital at Chapra, Bihar changed that. I met this 45 or 50-year-old blind farmer who was with his 10-year-old daughter; he was turned away from the district hospital because there was no eye surgeon in the setup. He explained that his eyesight has been diminishing from the last 8–10 years, and since the last two years he couldn't see anything at all; importantly, this girl who was with him was in school until two years back but was pulled out of school to take care of her blind father. After that meeting, I found out that blindness was a big issue in the low-income states of India, primarily in states that are steeped in poverty. I also found out that if we were able to give sight back to a blind person, it also restores his income and dignity, thereby helping him come out of poverty. The added

216

effect is that the caregiver, mostly the girl-child, goes back to school thereafter ensuring her education. I also realised that if we were to take the states of Bihar and Uttar Pradesh together, they would form the third largest country in the world after India and China in terms of population. Primarily these states are agrarian; it is well-known that the farmer never retires and that he retires only when he dies or is incapacitated. Blindness is the biggest cause of incapacitation.

With this in mind, 12 years ago, I started the Akhand Jyoti Eye Hospital in the village of Mastichak, which is one and half hours' drive from Patna, the capital of Bihar. When we started, we had paucity of resources and I was new to eye care but one thing was very clear—I really wanted to make a dent on blindness, which was prevalent in the state. It was also very clear that Akhand Jyoti would only work in the low-income states of the country, primarily because we want to reach the unreached and make maximum impact. Therefore, we started with Bihar because of our conviction that if we could crack the code in Bihar, we could do it in any state of the country easily.

We started with 10 beds and very limited resources but with the help of a very committed team, we were able to reach the level of 60,000 surgeries by the sixth year itself. We built a new hospital, which helped us move up to 300 beds in 6 years. One thing was absolutely clear in my mind—that the hospital will also be a platform for bringing bigger societal change, which for me was gender equality. We were aspiring for gender equality because most of the states have strong patriarchy and the girl child is the most marginalised, not only in terms of economic exploitation, but also in terms of social discrimination. I started wondering how we could integrate girls in the hospital system.

Eight years ago, it hit me that if we could use the game of football to draw out girls from their houses and then offer the parents an incentive that if they allow their girl to play football, we would take care of her education and skilling as an optometrist and give her a fantastic job. Optometrists are support clinical staff in an eye hospital. It worked albeit slowly but since 2010, we were able to build up quite a base of young girls who started coming into the system and understanding the culture. Most importantly, they were the ones who would be groomed to do two things: one is helping in the eradication of blindness by restoring people's eyesight, which was the main issue; but they would also serve as inspiration for more girls to come and seek not only an alternative career but also to resist gender inequality, dowry, domestic violence, and all the other malaise which exists in a strong patriarchal society. This program, which we called Football to Eyeball, is primarily an education, skill development, and empowerment program. We take girls when they pass their O level standard 10, they come into the system and go through a basic optometry course and are trained in English and computers. Then they come into the main three-year course, which they pass out and get jobs where they start earning the standard market pay; this is five times what her entire family's income would have been, prior to her joining Akhand Jyoti.

The Akhand Jyoti mission and vision is very clear. By 2022, we want to eradicate blindness from Bihar. The World Health Organization defines blindness as inability to count fingers from a distance of three metres in both eyes. Our entire focus is on prioritising the blind patient rather than just doing the number of surgeries. Till 2022, we want to make Bihar free of blindness, and then move on to the other low-income states of India; and to do this we also need to triple the number of girls we have in the system. Over the next four years we plan to complete 500,000 surgeries, 80 per cent of them free. More than 300 girls will be in the system who will be helping us out in this endeavour. Most importantly, when these 500,000 people regain sight—it will also free up their caretaker girls to go back to school. Apart from that, we intend to build the world's first Centre of Excellence in eye care, in a rural area. Our Medical Director has completed more than 100,000 surgeries and over 50 per cent of our doctors have done more than 20,000 surgeries. Over the long run, we hope that Akhand Jyoti becomes a masthead of eradicating blindness from India's poorest states, but at the same time, it also uplifts women and girls in the effort.

JP: What was your perspective on money while you were growing up in Calcutta?

Mritunjay: Prior to coming to Akhand Jyoti, for me the barometer of success was mainly centred on the Sensex and foreign exchange reserve. I always felt that money was important, but maybe I just couldn't get my priorities right. Because I always feel, as my guru says, that we must remember that in the ultimate analysis we are temporary custodians of the wealth we generate, whether financial or intellectual and the best way is to use it for people who are less fortunate. That chance to visit Bihar actually forced me to think about money and success. One day everyone has to leave this world, so, when you have to go away, why not make an impact and leave the world? This visit to Bihar completely changed my perspective — we could have many desires but we should try to cap our personal ambitions and try to give more food for thought to our soul and find a purpose in life. I am a great believer in Mark Twain's quote "The two most important days in your life are the day you were born and the day you know why." I found my 'why' at Akhand Jyoti, and my 'why' is empowering girls, and my 'why' is giving people sight.

JP: You grew up in a very affluent family. What is your perspective on money today, and do you still have a successful business and lifestyle?

Mritunjay: My family business is based in Kolkata. We are C&F (clearing & forwarding) agents for eight companies and I have restricted the business, wherein I don't have to give much time. I don't want to become a millionaire or a billionaire. I am happy because that amount of money satisfies the basic needs of my family. I guess now my kids have understood that they have to make their own mark, I have done whatever I could do as a family person, but now it's time that I devote myself to others.

JP: All of us want to have some money for the welfare of our family, and we want to pass some of the funds to our next generation. What's your perspective?

Mritunjay: I agree that in today's materialistic world you do need savings; you need to look out and plan for the future, but to an extent. I would say do enough that would cover your family. Then think of reformation, think of trying to inculcate and pull up more people to

219

come up to a certain benchmark; in fact change the thinking process itself. The savings should be there, but not beyond a point. I think it's better to share your wealth with people who are less fortunate.

JP: Millennials are going to inherit tremendous wealth in the coming years. Any advice about what they should they do with all this money?

Mritunjay: I personally think that one of the big issues with millennials is the need for instant gratification. Whether it's due to technology or other factors, people have been getting things instantly, have lost the understanding of what exactly hard work is, and why exactly toiling is important. Everyone wants to be at the top, but they don't want to go through the pain of that journey of going to the top. I think that it is about getting your priorities right. It is about understanding that we are in a world, which is not isolated. It is to understand that when we were born, it was not stamped on our back that we will become millionaire or billionaire, or that you will become a software engineer or a doctor.

The important thing is to become a good human being. It is more difficult to become a good human being than becoming a doctor or an engineer. Millennials should toil for what they want to achieve in life. Strive to go to the top but you must take the pain of actually climbing to the top and getting your priorities right. At the end of the day, when you go away you need to make a lasting impact. When you pass away and would be having a cup of tea with the Almighty and looking down you will probably find lots of people praising your achievements. I think that should be something that you should gun for—the eternal acclaim the world gives you due to the legacy you leave for people who were not your family.

Karl Mehta
Founder, Code for India, PlaySpan, and EdCast

JP: May I request you to introduce yourself.

Karl: I have lived in Silicon Valley for the past 24 years. I came to California just like most immigrants—as a student, and then I stayed back for opportunities. I have been building companies in the technology space since. I have built four companies. The fourth one is ongoing, EdCast, and the previous three companies, two of them were venture backed, and both had successful exits. MobileAria was backed by Mayfield Fund and was acquired by a public company, Wireless Matrix. The next company, PlaySpan was backed by Menlo Ventures and SoftBank, was acquired by VISA. That pretty much enabled me to retire at the age of 39 before hitting 40, which was a very fortunate event.

I worked on many non-profits after that. I worked at the White House; I became the first Presidential Innovation Fellow for President Obama, and did nationwide as well as global work with the USAID, especially on the bottom of the pyramid. I wrote a book about the bottom of the pyramid called *The Financial Inclusion at the Bottom of the Pyramid*. It has received some very good reviews including from the Bill & Melinda Gates Foundation. It's pretty satisfying as it is being used as a textbook in some of the colleges in the US.

I started a couple of non-profits—one of them is Code for India, which has become the largest non-profit for Indian American techies in Silicon Valley—people just like me who have technology talent to give back to India. The foundation, Code for India is now one of the largest with 5,000 software engineers of Indian origin, and it has been backed by some tech elites like Satya Nadella and Sundar Pichai; it is also supported by the Prime Minister of India. That's going very well and there is another non-profit that I founded when I was in the White House called Grassroots Innovation, which does more charity in my adopted land, the United States, where we work with under privileged people and disadvantaged communities, especially in lower income neighbourhood, where we help them with vocational education, to help them find jobs. All that work helped me lead into my current company EdCast, which although it's a for-profit company, its mission is to use education as a tool to uplift the people at the bottom of the pyramid to rise above the poverty level. From my own personal experience, education is the greatest equaliser and it's the best tool to get out of poverty.

JP: What was your perspective on money growing up?

Karl: I grew up in Bombay. My dad was an entrepreneur and he had many ups and downs in his business. He had no funding, there was no venture capital back in those days; banks did not give him loans. He had a hard time trying to keep his business afloat, pay the bills, and put food on the table. Growing up in Bombay, my childhood was quite difficult. My dad died when I was only 16. He was the only bread earner of our family and he passed away very early. My brother and I, we had to do many odd jobs and pay for our college but throughout that time we learned the value of money and hard work, how hard it is to earn and how difficult it is to keep up in life. The value of money was very strongly established—that money is a very precious energy and it has to be earned. You cannot have a mindset of entitlement that somebody is going to take care of you; somebody is going to give you money. You have to work hard, you have to earn money, and you have to stand up for yourself. We were poor but we had a very strong sense of understanding that we did not want to become financially dependent on others.

JP: Now that you are such a successful entrepreneur, how has your perspective on money changed?

Karl: Due to my own upbringing, I have a certain bias in my view of the world. I have that capitalist view that we can't have a society of people who are dependent on handouts—I do have more of a capitalist view than a socialist view about money. I have done many different non-profits and I like helping people at the bottom of the pyramid but all my projects and initiatives, whether it's my book or my two non-profits, none of them are designed to give handouts like what a socialist society or government does. I don't believe in that because it never builds up people. I believe in teaching people how to fish as opposed to giving them a fish. For example, Code for India is not for writing cheques to poor people; we try to solve the problem using technology, and that will help them rise up on their own. I am very optimistic that every person who needs money to survive or to take care of their family and themselves should be capable of earning money. My view and my role is more of an enabler to get them the tools—the kind of tools that I was able to accumulate for myself that got me out of poverty and got me to stability and comfort. I feel that we should be able to do that with the help of technology for everyone.

JP: How are you utilising your wealth effectively?

Karl: I don't think I am utilising my wealth effectively. I admit that there is lot more that I can learn, and I can use money in a much better way than money just sitting in a bank account and earning or multiplying, if it is multiplying, I don't know. I know that it can be put to more effective use, I keep thinking about ideas. I am always amazed when I hear non-profit ideas which are very innovative and that use philanthropic money to do innovative things and give people tools and help them with that money. Kiva, for example is an innovative concept. I love giving loans on Kiva to a vegetable seller in Africa and it feels so good and you know you are not giving a handout; you know that they are taking loans and running their small business and feeding themselves and their families.

That's my view of the world, that we need a lot more concepts like Kiva that unleashes money from people who have a lot of spare cash sitting in the bank. I am personally not going to use even 1 per cent of my money before I die. Most likely, my family is taken care of—they don't need, probably, more than 10 per cent of money that I have. What is the best way to utilise wealth for the upliftment of overall society? The more ideas we have like Kiva, which are scalable, aspirant, honest, and really have a network effect the better things will get. However, currently, these types of ideas are few today but hopefully we can have more ideas in the future.

JP: We all want to keep some money for our family's comfort and welfare and some money for the next generation—have you thought about that? Besides that, what do you want to do with your money?

Karl: I mean that's what we all do in terms of financial planning. You take care of yourself and your family. That is number one because you don't want to be dependent ever on society after creating wealth—that will be stupid. I have taken the traditional path of creating a family foundation, and our foundation writes many cheques to a number of non-profits here in Silicon Valley, from Pratham to Mount Madonna and many others. Then I have two of my non-profits, as

I mentioned earlier, Code for India and Grassroot Innovation which are both supported pretty much exclusively by my foundation. That's basically what I am doing, and I am always open to new ideas and innovations that can do more and use the extra money that I have effectively towards the betterment of society.

JP: Do you have any advice for the millennials, who are going to inherit large sums of money, about what to do with all this money?

Karl: For the millennials—I have a son who is 22 and has just started his life after graduating from USC (University of Southern California)—and the advice I would give to my son or to everyone is that you have to take care of yourself in terms of basic necessities and not be a dependent on society. Then, create wealth that you can distribute and share. The more you give, the more satisfied you are going to feel inside. You have to have the dual mindset—build a for-profit enterprise that creates great innovation and wealth but the second side of the same coin is to think about some scalable non-profit or support some existing scalable non-profit, like Kiva, that can help the rest of society, because they are part of you, you are part of them. If they are not growing you are not growing, fundamentally because we are all interconnected, we are all part of the same consciousness. If the rest of the world is not growing and if there is a lot of conflict, poverty, and unhappiness in the rest of the world, no matter how nice the glass house is that we build for ourselves, we are never going to be happy.

Ami Doshi
Director, Frontier Investment Management Company

JP: May I request you to introduce yourself.

Ami: I live in Dallas, Texas. Born and raised in Singapore to immigrant parents from India, I moved out of Singapore to pursue my under graduate studies in Connecticut. I went to Wesleyan University to do my Bachelor's in Anthropology and International Development. I went on to do my Master's in International Affairs in Economic and Political Development, with a focus on micro finance in New York at Columbia's School of International and Public Affairs. After graduate school, I worked at UBS as a fixed income research analyst, covering fixed income for emerging markets, specifically Latin American corporates in oil, gas, and paper. While I was at UBS, I realised that investment banking was not my calling. My heart was always in social finance, and I learnt that I needed a career that was in line with my personal values and mission—it just didn't fulfil my heart and soul much.

Fast forward, a few years and a few other jobs later, I moved to Dallas, Texas in 2005, where my husband, Ravi Patel, grew up. We've been here for 14 years now, and have two kids, a 9-year-old girl and an 11-year-old boy. I started working for a social enterprise that developed a crowd-funded platform that works with low-income women in India through micro loans and micro finance. I was inspired by the impact of the program and started a non-profit organisation called Opportunity Plus, to support micro finance programs and financial literacy for low-income female entrepreneurs around the world. We support two programs here in Dallas. Here we work with low-income women entrepreneurs in the Hispanic community who don't have access to traditional low-cost capital.

While managing the non-profit, I also worked for a community foundation called Communities Foundation of Texas (CFT) as a Donor Engagement Officer. I managed a portfolio of donor advised funds and was responsible for prospecting a diverse range of new individuals, families and corporations to become CFT fund holders. I had the opportunity to work with individuals, families, and their professional advisers on philanthropic intent and how to use their assets in the most effective and efficient way to get the impact that they are looking to create in the community. I also have my

Chartered Advisor in Philanthropy, which has helped me gain the knowledge and tools to help my clients articulate and advance their highest aspirations for self, family, and society.

JP: I want to ask you to give us some background on two other things that you did in life. Can you tell us about ProPoor and Milaap?

Ami: ProPoor was my first foray into the non-profit world. I think it was 1997–1998 and I had the distinct pleasure of working with you, Jayesh. We wrote a paper, which you presented in Helsinki, Finland to get funded. We had the idea to create an online portal for non-profit organisations across South Asia, to give them a digital footprint. The platform would allow someone from North India working on a project that impacts women entrepreneurs to have the opportunity to learn and share their best practices with someone in Sri Lanka, for example, or allow donors to be able to find these projects, or perhaps for other non-profit organisations to collaborate with them. I believe it was 1998 when we started building the platform, which we called www.propoor.org, which was sold, or rather handed over to CharityFocus many years later.

Years later, I worked for Milaap, which is a Singapore-based social enterprise. They created a crowd funded micro-lending platform, and I helped them establish a US office. We raised funding through impact investments as well as grant dollars towards micro finance organisations across India, using high risk capital to invest in micro finance, in solar, in water, female entrepreneurship, and energy projects.

JP: What was your perspective on money growing up?

Ami: I grew up in a home where cash was king. I guess that is the Singaporean way. I grew up associating money or cash with security. My father was an entrepreneur, my mom was a homemaker, and we lived a very comfortable life growing up.

JP: You spent the last 20 years in the US. Did your perspective on money change as you shifted base from Singapore to America?

Ami: I left Singapore when I was 17, before I was an adult and managing my own money. I think my relationship with money really developed here in the USA. I had a hard time with the idea of a credit driven society. When I was in graduate school the idea of living on a credit card or using a credit card to build my credit was a very foreign idea, but of course, that's just the way life is here and you have to manage within this system.

JP: Both you and your husband are working, so, what is your perspective on money going forward?

Ami: I am a planner. I like to know that we have a plan, both a financial and a personal plan that we can work towards. I would like to pay for our children's undergraduate education. I need to know that we have a roadmap, and have addressed our financial futures to ensure that we are not left vulnerable during our later years.

Something that is often on my mind, is the need to simplify and minimise my footprint and my wants, just to not feel so bogged down by my belongings. I'm always trying to simplify and trying to find ways to want less, to spend less on material things and spend more on experiences and put away money.

JP: Shed some light on your famous Diwali parties.

Ami: Ravi and I started having our Diwali party, I guess a year before we left New York. This is our sixteenth year, we've had one every year since we got married. We started it with eight people, four couples in our small NYC apartment, and now I think the maximum number of people we have hosted is almost 300. Since setting up my non-profit, Opportunity Plus, we have hosted it as a fundraiser. We have an incredibly dynamic group of people that come together once a year and are very inspired to do something. When I set up the non-profit, they came to me and said you have the platform now, let us help to do something important, let's use this energy, and create some impact.

JP: In your job with CFT you come across all these affluent people. Based on that I want to get a perspective on the question—what shall we do with all this money?

Ami: I really did have a very unique job and I feel very blessed to be able to partner with people that are truly very civic minded, people with means, people with lot of aspirational wealth. This is the most philanthropic city I have ever known. CFT powers the largest giving day in the country, or possibly the world, called North Texas Giving Day. This was our eleventh year, and the community raised over

$50 million in 18 hours for over 2,900 non-profit organisations in the North Texas area and pledged to volunteer over 600,000 volunteer-hours to their favourite causes. This is a platform to help donors in our community give towards local non-profits impacting the North Texas community. That's a lot of money. This is a very, very giving community and that money is not just from a handful of very wealthy families—it is really the culture here. From that perspective, it has been a real pleasure to partner in this space with these families. The pervasive culture here is that to whom much is given, much is expected.

JP: Can you also describe what people are doing with their money?

Ami: In the philanthropic space?

JP: In general, you see so many affluent people around you. What are they doing with their money?

Ami: Dallas is like a mini LA. There is a lot of money in this city—old and new money. There is a lot of focus on creating systemic change and trying to address the root cause of a lot of the challenges that the city faces. Despite the amount of wealth here, there is an incredible amount of social and financial racial inequity, with wealth focussed in very specific communities. At the same time, people live large here. They give big, but they also live large. As they say, everything is bigger in Texas.

JP: Any final word of wisdom?

Ami: I feel like I have a lot to learn from the people I've had the opportunity to work with. A lot of these families that have made a lot of money and are in the position to give very generously but started in a very small way. I think what I am learning from them is to live a simple life, that's how some of these families have developed such tremendous wealth, as well as the family's internal culture of giving. I've recently moved into a wealth advisor role with a boutique investment firm. I'll be working mostly with women and minority clients as well as philanthropic families who are transitioning wealth across multiple generations, and want to pass on not just their wealth, but also their values and legacy. I think my background in the non-profit space and the opportunity to have worked with some incredible philanthropists in Dallas, has given me a unique perspective on aligning your wealth with your values.

Latika Thukral
Co-founder, iamgurgaon

JP: May I request you to introduce yourself.

Latika: I have been a resident of Gurgaon for the past 22 years. I used to work with Citibank for 18 years and was a senior vice president. In 2009, I quit my job and co-founded an NGO, iamgurgaon, which works on making Gurgaon a better city to live in.

JP: I wanted to get a bit more insight into your past.

Latika: I came from a very humble background. My father used to work for a government organisation. I worked with Citibank for 18 years. In the initial years of starting my career, my husband and I struggled to earn our livelihood and raise our two sons. Ten years ago we decided that we were financially stable enough to survive on one income—which led to my decision to quit my job. The motivation behind this decision was partly to spend more time with my boys who were in middle school at the time, however, it also gave me the opportunity to work towards making a difference through iamgurgaon. This is what I have been doing for the last ten years where we are working with the government and people all across the country in many ways to improve green spaces and facilitate better living conditions for people in Gurgaon.

JP: As a family you have grown from strength to strength and Mohit has done extremely well. What is your perspective on money?

Latika: I don't know what 'extremely well' is or what our net worth is, and I would not get into that, but I can say that we live a very comfortable life. There is nothing that I really want to buy. I come from a very middle-class family, so I have those values where you cannot spend money on a whim; and there is nothing that I really want to get. One of our son studies in the US and another son studies in India. We are able to live a good life. We travel reasonably well, in a way that's luxurious. I can just say that there is nothing that we may reasonably want that we cannot have.

JP: Coming back to iamgurgaon, can you please tell us the genesis of it?

Latika: iamgurgaon started 10 years ago. I am one of the co-founders of iamgurgaon and when we started, I did not think it would become as big as it has today. I thought I would spend half a day and do something for the city. However, today we are a nine-member core group and are working on very large projects. We have revived 380 acres of forestland, which used to be a mining site and today it has become a young forest where we have planted saplings and created a habitat with the help of 70 corporates who have funded us. We have many other projects—such as the 'bundh' where we have revived a 5.2 km walkway, which flows next to a storm water drain and cuts through the city. This project has been compared to the High Line in New York or many other projects, which are restoration of wasted spaces that are lying around. I must mention that all these projects have happened with the help of the government of Haryana and corporates who have provided financial support to make this happen.

JP: From being a successful executive, your husband, has become an entrepreneur. What is your perspective on money in the future, what do you plan to do with your money?

Latika: The way I look at it, when I gave up my job, we did do away with one income and lots of people said that I gave away my job in the prime of my career, and that that's the time one build's net worth. My response to that is, yes, with that money I would have bought another house, but more than that, there is nothing more I could do with our standard of living because they are what they are. I mean, what more can you improve? You can buy some more jewellery or bags or whatever. But there is nothing more you can do with it.

When Mohit took the decision to become an entrepreneur, there were two reasons. The money is one part of it and the other part was if you don't do something now it will be too late, he is 53 so he wants to do something on his own and he wants to prove that he could. Obviously, when you want to become an entrepreneur, you want to make more money than what you would have made in a corporate job.

I think both of us believe in giving back. He is going to work on setting up a university. Plaksha, with many other co-founders who will contribute to that university and this is collective philanthropy; so they are taking out money from their own personal wealth and contributing to a university with no expectation of financial gain.

In our mind, we are very clear that we want to give back in whatever way possible. I have been giving back by not earning and contributing in a big way and Mohit is continuing to work on building this technology driven university. It is on the lines of Ashoka University and will focus on collaboration with various reputed international universities.

JP: Being a socialite in an affluent place like Delhi, can you give us that perspective on money?

Latika: What I see all around us is that people are chasing money; for what purpose I don't know—whether it is for building more houses or buying more apartments. For me, wealth means living a good comfortable life, while using your resources—in terms of time and money—to help people in order to contribute to people's welfare. I don't know what I can say for other people. Everybody has their own path to follow.

JP: Any final word of wisdom?

Latika: Whatever money we have, I don't know whether it is enough for the future or not. I have no idea, but I know for a fact that we are going to enjoy our money and we are not getting too worried about what we are going to leave behind for our children.

Bina Rampuria
Board Member, Magic Bus Singapore

JP: May I request you to introduce yourself.

Bina: I am a 52-year-old Gujarati girl from Calcutta, India. I grew up in a semi-conservative vegetarian family. My upbringing was very normal. We were very happy when we sat on the floor sometimes for our meals.

JP: Describe the Rampuria family.

Bina: The Rampuria family is a very well-known family from Bikaner and they are almost treated like royalty there. There is even a street named after them called Rampuria Street. All the Rampurias lived on that street in their heritage homes, which are now turned into heritage hotels. They have old wealth and are culturally rich. The family eventually moved to Calcutta. My father-in-law was a successful entrepreneur. He created the famous Air-conditioned Market 50 years ago, in his early 20s. Looking at him and my husband, who is self-made, inspired me to see this quality in others.

JP: You married into a very affluent family. I want to know your perspective on money, before and after marriage.

Bina: Before I got married I needed very little. I was a very simple girl. But even then I was crazy about my clothes, shoes, bags, etc. I got a job so I could cover my expenses.

Then I got married into the Rampuria family, and for them I was somebody that they couldn't connect with because I didn't come from the same background. I had a different attitude in life, I was too carefree, and I would say what was on my mind. For them the use of money was in education, culture, travel, investments, jewellery, shawls, and all that. That was a different perspective for me, as I wasn't exposed to it. When the shawlwalas would come, my mother-in-law would teach me about toosh, pashmina, and the difference between good embroidery and average embroidery. I learnt from them and I realised that I was a quick learner. I always watched people when I wanted to learn something and how they do things—that was part of my education because I wasn't exposed to any of this.

JP: Did you spend the money and enjoy yourself?

Bina: Not initially. I didn't want anyone to say that I married for money. No, it took me a very long time to start spending money.

JP: You live a good life. Describe your standard of living?

Bina: It's amazing. Also it's a matter of perspective. For me, the value of money is the flexibility—whatever I can spend on myself, on the things I like, or when I want to do something for someone, I have the freedom to do it. I like that. I just want to have that free spirit in me, knowing that I have the option and can do what I want with it. I have always been like that.

JP: How do you spend your money?

Bina: Spending money on materialistic things is very easy. I still love my bags, shoes, and clothes. I spend money on them because I love them, and I have realised that I only have a few more years to do what I want. I love to travel, and I love to invest in people. I like to give them the opportunity if they have the potential. Let me share it with a story. It was a tiny gesture but it's a story.

I was in Ahmedabad just last week and I met a really young guy. He was holding a plastic bag, while I was waiting outside my car for a friend. He comes up to me and offered to polish my shoes and I said no. I was a bit reluctant because all this makes me feel bad—that I am making somebody else do my dirty work. He said, "Please get it done. If you give me some money, I can feed my sisters at home tonight." Very quietly I sat in the car and gave him my shoes because I didn't want to be seen making him do this work. Then I told my daughter, who was with me, to give him her shoes as well, so that I can give him more money. I asked him about his family and what they did. He told me he didn't have a job and that he went around polishing shoes. On a good day, he earned ₹300 to ₹400 and that provided them with food for the week. I asked him why he didn't set up a shoe polish stand and he said that the box of polishing supplies etc. would cost him about ₹6,000 and he didn't have that kind of money, he never had enough to save. I decided to give him ₹5,000, while ₹1,000 would be out of his own pocket. Now I don't know if he really did any of that, but for me, I think I did my part. I believe in people. I did offer him money without polishing my shoes because I didn't want him to and he said, "Sorry, I can't take your money if you don't let me polish your shoes." That assured me that he was not just looking for easy money. He wants to do something. It was my job to give him that opportunity to let him find a way to earn more money so that his sisters and his family can be fed on a regular basis.

So, in the end I was happy to give him a chance to find a platform as per his skill-set to try and change his life.

JP: Can you describe a few of the charities that you are helping?

Bina: Well, I am a big part of Magic Bus. I am on the board of Magic Bus and it has been my biggest passion for the last eight years. I am inspired by the founder who is British but lives in India and helps change lives of many children growing up in the slums. It's deeper than just sending the kids to school. It's about childhood to livelihood. At the end of the full programme, that child has a job and is a tax payer and not a burden on the country. It's also about gender equality and many more important social issues. I help raise money for them in Singapore. It is so fulfilling.

I am also part of Singapore Repertory Theatre (SRT), in Singapore for the last three years. I love art and culture. We need more art and cultural stuff in Singapore. I just joined the Singapore Film Festival, which is a platform for south Asian films. Let's see how I can contribute. I am also a co-founder of Gala of Light, which supports two of the local Singaporean charities. This is the first year. Hopefully, it will also get some recognition. It is supported by prominent local personalities. I am happy to contribute to the society that has shaped the past 25 years of my life. I owe it to Singapore.

JP: What happens going forward? What will you do with all this money?

Bina: Firstly, it's not that much but we are not taking it up there (pointing to the sky) in the end. I always wanted to give my kids the education that they deserve. We just want to set them up, but we definitely don't want to give them more money than they need. I want to keep some money for Gautam and myself, and in case my kids need it in an emergency; but the rest of it, I definitely want to do something to generate more money, so that I could support the charities I work for. I would like to either invest in a small business or with people who will help me multiply my investment. I am also always happy to help different charities and anyone that asks me for help.

Millennials

Jasprit Bumrah
Bowler, Indian National Cricket Team

Sarvesh Shashi
Founder and CEO, Sarva Yoga

Kamakshi Malhotra
Principal, SAR Group

Anushka Shah
Founder, Civic Studios

Richa Dsouza
Executive Principal, Basil Technology Partners

Siddharth Sachdeva
Machine Learning Engineer, Roam Analytics

Anisha Kataria
Family Office Member, Pantheon Holdings

Jasprit Bumrah

Bowler, Indian National Cricket Team

JP: May I request you to introduce yourself.

Jasprit: I play for the Indian National Cricket Team. I am 25 years old. I grew up in Ahmedabad, Gujarat. I completed my schooling at Nirman High School, Ahmedabad. I represent the Indian National team in all three formats of the game: T20 (20 overs), ODI (50 overs), and Test match (5 days). At the domestic level, I represent the Gujarat team and I play for the Mumbai Indians franchise in the Indian Premier League (IPL). I am a right-arm fast pace bowler.

JP: Give us your perspective on money as you were growing up?

Jasprit: As a child, the concept of pocket money was non-existent. We did not receive any fixed amount of money as children. However, from the little money I would manage to receive, I would go and purchase tennis balls like most kids at that age. I always believed in saving money. I realised the importance of money at a very young age. If I would receive ₹10, I would spend only ₹4 and save the remaining ₹6. One of the few sources of income for me was the money we would receive from relatives when they would come and visit us. This money would also be spent mainly on tennis balls as I did not have too many other expenses as a child.

One memory that I have from my childhood is that after we would be done playing cricket, most of my friends would go out to eat snacks and have cold drinks, but I would always give that a miss and return home instead. I liked to save my money rather than spending it on food and cold drinks. I never really wished that I had more money as a child. The only time that happened was when I would have to wear the same pair of clothes for all my matches. If those clothes would tear then I would have to get the same clothes stitched up and wear them again. I would have to wear the same shoes irrespective of their condition—more money would have given me more options.

JP: Now that you are so successful, how has your perspective on money changed?

Jasprit: My approach towards saving and investing money remains the same. I still follow the same policy of saving ₹6 and spending only ₹4. I don't like to incur wasteful expenses and the money I earn is saved in my bank account or invested in mutual funds, property etc. I recently purchased a new house and most of my expenditure is towards the expenses of my family. I like to get the best things for my mother and my sister and I want them to have a very comfortable life. My mother often donates and helps out old-age homes, schools for the blind, and other institutions on my behalf, when I am away on international duty. I like to help people who are in need since I have the resources now and can provide for the less fortunate.

On a lighter note, all that money spent by me on tennis balls as a child is now spent on buying shoes for myself. I love buying new shoes and having a good shoe collection. I also like to give my shoes to cricketers in Gujarat who do not have good cricket shoes. I believe that a good pair of shoes can completely change an athlete's performance and help an athlete in achieving the best results.

JP: What is your perspective on money in the future?

Jasprit: There are two causes that are extremely close to my heart, the first one is that I want to provide for the education of an orphan. I truly believe that educating a child is the best form of charity that one can do. Children are the future of our country and every single child deserves a good education. The second thing I would like to do is to provide for senior citizens in old-age homes. I want to take care of senior citizens and help them in whatever way I can. Like I mentioned earlier, my mother does these things on my behalf but at some stage in my life, I do want to take this up myself.

One of the thoughts I had as a child was to write a book at some point in my life. Writing a book myself is very much on the cards in the future. I want to share my story and the little anecdotes that have taken place in my life with everyone.

Cricket has made me everything that I am today. Whatever I have is all because of cricket, the person I am is all because of cricket. I want to give back to this beautiful game in whatever way I can and it is something that I will be doing in the future.

JP: What advice would you give to wealthy millennials?

Jasprit: According to me, every wealthy millennial must use their money very smartly. Make the right investments, save money, and understand the best ways in which they can multiply their money.

In today's time money plays a very crucial part in everyone's life. There is a need to be realistic while spending money. It is important that they find a balance between spending money and saving it. They must fulfil their dreams by all means but not by finishing off all their money in one go. Savings has always been a very integral part of my life and I would urge all millennials to make savings a habit. I personally believe that when you are helping others out, spend with your heart, but when it comes to investing, always use your mind and invest your money intelligently.

Sarvesh Shashi

Founder and CEO, Sarva Yoga

JP: May I request you to introduce yourself.

Sarvesh: I am 26 years old. I was born in Kerala, brought up in Chennai, was fortunate and largely grateful to nature and the world to be born in a very, very well off family. In the south, my dad runs about 16 to 18 different companies across the country in different verticals. I was a professional cricketer for the longest time, actively playing cricket in the Tamil Nadu First Division League. I was fortunate enough to travel with the Rajasthan Royals and Kochi Tuskers as an official net bowler.

JP: Tell us about your growing up years, where you went to school and your family background.

Sarvesh: I think the biggest claim to fame for my family background would be my dad's company—the company that bought over the entire scrap of the World Trade Center. We auctioned it out almost completely.

I studied in Chennai at Chinmaya Vidyalaya, until the fifth standard. Then, considering we were living in a really large house and I was unconsciously very spoiled, my dad put me in a hostel from sixth to seventh standard at Chinmaya International, a residential school in Coimbatore. I came back to Chennai and studied at Chettinad Vidhyashram from eighth to twelfth standard. I joined Loyola College just to play cricket, but I haven't completed college yet—so, it's a college dropout story.

JP: Growing up in an affluent family, what was your perspective on money?

Sarvesh: I have been fortunate enough to always get what I wanted. My ninth standard birthday gift was a car. My perspective on money is that money in itself is essential, but not because people say that they are motivated by money to earn more money, but it's the lifestyle that money brings that motivates you.

JP: Was there anything in particular that transformed your life?

Sarvesh: Yoga really transformed my life at 17. My dad took up yoga classes, which he wasn't able to complete, and he said,

"Sarvesh, just complete these 8–10 sessions that are left because we have paid a lot of money." I started doing a lot of sadhna; I got silent for 10 days and did the vipassana. I have also gone completely silent for 40 days. I am doing something called the Panchsheel, known as the five precepts, for the last nine years. It has been a fantastic journey for me—understanding life in a different perspective altogether. It taught me a lot of things like gratitude. What is anger? What do emotions do? What is attachment? This also resulted in me having a different perception towards money and lifestyle. Yoga has taught me how to have balance in my life, and that has changed my perception of money, luxury, and lifestyles.

JP: Please describe the business that you are in now.

Sarvesh: Well, at 21 when my dad said, "Sarvesh, I think it's time that you get into my business because we are a large company with a turnover of $200 million; so, you have to start helping me." But I couldn't do something that was not from my heart. For one month, I did go to my dad's office. It wasn't my cup of tea. The best reason, at 21, that I could give him to not get into his business was that I was starting my own.

Yoga has really changed my life and I wanted to change people's lives. For about 600 million people in India under the age group of 30, I wanted to be a catalyst and provide a tool to empower them in embracing happiness, a healthy lifestyle, and being grateful, because sleeplessness, anxiety, obesity, and depression is increasing in today's world and is becoming a global epidemic.

That lead to the birth of my yoga and wellness start-up called Sarva. The word Sarva means complete, whole. The tag line is 'Yoga, Mindfulness & Beyond' which is the core of our business; 'mindfulness' is meditation which is being aware, knowing your breath; and 'beyond' stands for anything, for example, you might not like to do yoga but love music; we will infuse our own form of music for different purposes. I had one studio in 2013, two in 2014, three in 2015, and in March 2016 we had three studios in one city. We received our first investment in March 2016. After that investment, from three studios in one city, to April 2018, in about two years, we went to over 70 studios across 30 plus cities in India. We are one of the largest chains of yoga and wellness studios in the country.

JP: Who are your partners and who are your investors?

Sarvesh: Mr Harsha Bhatkal saw that what we were doing is not just yoga. If I have to give you a parallel, it's how Zumba created dance into a movement, how Starbucks created coffee into a culture. Harsha saw our secret sauce, that we were giving yoga a whole new twist. He has a friend called David Giampaolo, who's rated as one of London's most influential and most networked person by Time magazine and Financial Times. David Giampaolo led and was the chief architect of our friends and family round. Jennifer Lopez, Alex Rodriguez, Malaika Arora, Rajinikanth's daughter Aishwarya Dhanush, Shahid and Mira Kapoor, Satveer Singh Thakral, the managing partner of BC Partners, the president of Warner Brothers studio, Mark Mastrov, who is the owner of 24-Hour Fitness and known as the Steve Jobs of fitness, and Bill Roedy, the former chairman of MTV; they all have invested in the company and so have you, Jayesh.

Sarva's vision statement is 'Connecting 7 million breathes'. We are doing good and we are making a living out of it. It's a profitable social venture.

JP: What is your perspective on money today and for the future?

Sarvesh: I think money is just a function of necessity or what people want. For example, whether you are travelling in a Mercedes or a Honda City, your intent is to reach the destination. Your intent is not wrong in travelling in the Mercedes or taking a private jet, but my personal thought is that one should not live for others. One should not do things simply to impress others. For example, you don't need to travel by private jet just because people will see you. I have no problem travelling in a bus but then my intent should be humble if I am travelling in a bus. I should be the same person if I am travelling in whichever car, however much money I have—I think the personality of a person should not change no matter how much money a person has.

My perception or perspective on money, after doing a lot of yoga, will continue to remain the same—that money is a necessity to fulfil your aspirations, but that aspiration should not take over oneself—it should enhance oneself and should definitely have his or her value system in play. I think the motivator is never money, it is about what you do with money. Money should not motivate you to do things which will harm anybody else. That's going to be a concern, whether it's too little or too much, anything that will harm anybody has to have a different perspective to that.

JP: You have come from a very affluent family and now you are building a solid business on a global scale. Fast forward 5–10 years, you are going to be incredibly wealthy, wealthier than you are now, so I need to ask you this question, what shall we do with all this money?

Sarvesh: I am not going to give away everything and walk away to the Himalayas. If I have more than what I need, I would love to make a social impact that is not for profit. My dad always says, "In charity, what the right hand does the left hand should not know." I would do it without anybody knowing. I would like to provide some kind of help to people, not just for poverty, in terms of providing them with housing and clothing, but also leading them in the right direction. Whatever I can do to make people's life better I will do after ensuring that I am happy because I think your personal happiness is very, very important to make anybody else happy; but charity should be done without anybody knowing, that's the most important thing. I don't want to be seen as this guy who is making a name doing a lot of CSR (Corporate Social Responsibility) social activities. I am not for that at all.

Kamakshi Malhotra

Principal, SAR Group

JP: May I request you to introduce yourself.

Kamakshi: I grew up in Delhi, India. I am 25. I moved to the US right after graduating high school and I studied Chemical Engineering at Georgia Tech. I took up a job with a Fortune 500 company in Singapore and started doing something completely different from what I had studied. I spent six months doing retail strategy and then moved on to build their global e-commerce strategy. But it was all very high-level conversation. We spent too much time deliberating and much less time actually implementing. I felt like I wanted something a little more exciting and hands-on, so I started to work in a B2B e-commerce start-up. I was employee number three there, after the co-founders. I worked there for about a year and half before moving to Ncubate (our family office's private investment arm). This year I got into INSEAD, and plan to join the July 2020 batch.

JP: Why INSEAD?

Kamakshi: I short-listed a couple of schools based on a very simple criteria. Basically, I chose to do an MBA because I wanted concentrated but fast-track experience. I grew up in an entrepreneurial setting and nobody has gotten an MBA in my family. So, I definitely realise that I can learn by doing everything an MBA can offer me. But it was all about the timeline, so INSEAD's 10-month program seemed perfect. In the long-term, the dream is ideally to do something on my own, for profit, but with a social impact. While picking a school, this social entrepreneurship angle was important to me, and INSEAD fit right in. Of course, the aspect of enormous cultural diversity, and gaining some experience in Europe, all made INSEAD the best option for me. I feel very grateful to have gotten in.

JP: Tell me a little bit about your family and wealth?

Kamakshi: I grew up in a very typical middle-class setting. We lived in a small house—my grandparents, parents, brother, and I. My mother always ensured that we were very aware of the deep disparity in standards of living of people around us, and both my parents taught us to be grateful for what we have. She would always tell us that the biggest lesson she learnt from her father was to look at people less fortunate than yourself, to remain satisfied and content in life.

My brother and I had a very comfortable and fun childhood. We didn't get to spend much time with my dad, but that also sensitised us towards the kind of hard-work and dedication it took to build a company from scratch. In 1988, my father started a company called Luminous Power Technologies, in the power backup space—UPSs, inverters and inverter batteries. He and my uncle spent many years on growing the company to a point where it attracted some of the largest private equity players in the Indian market. CLSA came on board in the early 2000s. Luminous was a household brand—all my friends recognised it, and I felt very proud to be associated with it.

At some point around 2010, my dad had a little bit of a health scare. He realised, that for a long time he had made the business his priority and not so much his family, friends or his health. It wasn't a very balanced lifestyle. So, he decided to take a step back and re-evaluate things. That is when he took a call on selling Luminous to Schneider Electric in late 2011. When this liquidity event happened, we set up a family office and a charitable trust and that's where my mom jumped in. She has always been very passionate about improving the condition of primary education in our country, so my parents picked three key focus areas for the trust—primary health, livelihood, and primary education.

JP: Has your father, Rakesh Malhotra retired completely now?

Kamakshi: Not at all. I don't know if he is ready to completely retire, but he's definitely taking out time for things outside of work now. We sold the majority stakes in 2011, and in late 2016, we sold the rest of our stake in Luminous. Back in 2012, after selling this majority piece, he started another business with my uncle called LivPure. It's in the water and air purification space, building a platform for purity, health, and wellness in India. Then in 2014, they started another business called LivGuard, which is also in the energy storage space, doing everything from automotive, solar, and electric vehicle, to inverters and inverter batteries.

JP: You are going to get an MBA, but you have been involved in the family business to a certain extent and into the family office, as we call it. What motivated you to be part of that?

Kamakshi: I think from a very early age we saw my dad build this company. We were always aware of the fact that it takes a lot of effort to build what he has built. I asked my dad once what his motivation

245

was, to build what he was building, instead of doing a slightly less stressful job, like most of my friends' parents. He said, "What we're building here supports over 1,000 families directly and many more indirectly. No office job could give me this sense of fulfilment. But it's also a massive responsibility that I'm taking on. Can you imagine being the source of bread and butter for 4,000 people?" This really stuck with me and I think it was also the reason why I wanted to become an entrepreneur myself. I felt that it was a socially responsible thing to do.

Besides that, my father has always spoken to us openly about what it really meant for us to have access to an opportunity of this scale—a platform of this scale. Of course, he'd always add that it was up to us to choose to take advantage of it or not. We talk a lot about how wealth erodes across generation because of poor succession planning, and lack of open communication between different generations. While we're not quite there yet, we have definitely had multiple rounds of open communication about the options on the table and challenges that await my brother and I. Getting involved with the family office instead of the main operating business was a great decision. It has allowed me to dip my feet into the business as a whole, while focussing on what I enjoy doing most—being around fast-paced innovation and extremely smart people. It has also allowed me to build connections with some of the key people I will be working with, if and when I join the business in a different capacity.

JP: Do you and your brother know how much wealth your family has?

Kamakshi: Yes, we have a fair estimate.

JP: At what age did you find out?

Kamakshi: In terms of details, just recently. When I first decided that I would move full-time and work with the family office, I spent a lot of time understanding our family constitution—what was the rationale behind it and how my dad was thinking about the wealth. This was really important for me because our risk appetites could be different, our motivations (though mostly aligned) could potentially be different, and our plans on how to preserve or grow the wealth could be different. I also spent a significant amount of time analysing the overall portfolio, which gave me a pretty good picture of the kind of platform we were managing.

JP: For the first time when you heard about the quantum of wealth, what was your reaction? What went through your mind?

Kamakshi: Actually, not much. I think because the Luminous deal was very out-in-the-open, the press covered it in detail, I was aware of the ballpark figure already.

JP: During your college years, you must have been aware that you are taken care of and you don't have student loans.

Kamakshi: Absolutely, especially in college in the US. I worked part time and did lots of things, but that was always by choice. I saw a lot of my friends having to think about how much they are going to spend on food, conveyance etc. I was blessed enough to not have that as a concern.

JP: Now what is your ambition with that wealth?

Kamakshi: We have these two operating businesses and we have the family office piece. The ambition is to make each of these pieces into billion-dollar platforms 10 years down the line or before I cross 40.

JP: Where is that ambition coming from? Why do you need that much money?

Kamakshi: I don't think that I need that much money at all. In fact, money has never been a big motivator. A big part of the motivation comes from my inherent sense of responsibility. Everything that I have today is something I was simply given because of somebody else's hard work. It is now my responsibility to make sure that, at the very least, I do my best to preserve what we have, and then do whatever I can to grow it. The numbers are just targets I have set for myself based on my judgement of the potential of each of these businesses. Like I said earlier, I always wanted to do something with the social angle. The value system was engrained in me by my parents. I truly believe that we have chosen some of the most relevant industries to be operating in. That, along with an organisation of dedicated, passionate people, it's only fair to strive to build this into a multi-billion-dollar platform, doing lots of good for the people of our country and beyond. This will, of course, in turn help build the charitable trust activities as well, through which I hope to be able to have significant impact.

JP: A certain amount of your energy is devoted to giving away that money. Can you take us through that journey?

Kamakshi: Back when we sold a part of Luminous, we set up this charitable trust in my grandmother's name, whom we lost a couple of years ago. My mom has always been passionate about doing good for our country. She took the responsibility of figuring out how to focus on a few things because we were always clear that to make a sustainable, long-term impact, we would need a streamlined approach. We eventually picked three key initiatives that we were passionate about and decided to really get involved with them. These were primary health, primary education, and livelihood. To give a quick idea, we adopted two schools in the northern part of India—one that works with blind students and another that works with under-privileged female students Another key initiative is in the primary health care space, which is based out of Kolkata. They are called Rural Health Care Foundation and they provide healthcare facilities for ₹70 to people across rural and urban parts of West Bengal. For us, it's important to understand the key processes of the organisation, where we can add value, and how it will generate sustainable impact in the future—much like any other investments we make in the for-profit world.

JP: You said that at INSEAD you would like to look at the social entrepreneurship track, please tell us about that.

Kamakshi: What I want to do through our family office, besides the philanthropy piece, is to either invest in social impact funds or have some sort of allocation within our own portfolio towards socially impactful start-ups and entrepreneurs. I'm particularly passionate about mental health and related technologies. Perhaps at INSEAD, I might even get an opportunity to build something of my own in this realm.

JP: What are the fun things you do in your own time, especially with all this wealth that is available to you?

Kamakshi: I have no flamboyant taste at all. In fact, I am very stingy when it comes to spending. What I do spend is on travel. I have always done that. My whole family loves travelling. We each keep count of the number of countries we've travelled to and my mom has created this beautiful wall in our house that has a world map with magnets from every country she and I have been to.

I started travelling by myself when I was in college and try to take a few short trips for fun every year. Besides that, my favourite thing to do with free time is dance. I am a trained Kathak dancer and have been teaching for about six years now. Over the years, I have learnt many types of dance forms. If I could only do one thing all day, this would be it. I also like spending my time doing something hands-on and creative whether it's arts and crafts, or sketching, painting, things like that. I feel like there is a lot happening in my brain that comes out through these channels.

JP: But these things don't cost money. What are you going to do with all this money?

Kamakshi: I have a brother; he does his bit. But jokes aside, neither of us spends much, and we get that from our parents who do not have flamboyant tastes themselves. I mean, we do live in a nice house in India and in Singapore. We travel everywhere. We take family vacations. It's not like we don't splurge ever so often, but there's no crazy spending on cars, wardrobes, or anything like that. We're very mindful of what we spend on, and really think about value for money before making any steep purchases.

JP: Are you religious or spiritual?

Kamakshi: I am spiritual but not religious. My parents never forced any of their beliefs on Yash and myself, but we were taught to be respectful towards everyone's beliefs. About two-three years ago, I got involved in this meditation technique called vipassana. I went for my first 10-day course, two years ago. I was so frightened, I had no idea how I would manage: a) without technology, b) without talking or looking at anyone for 10 whole days. But I got through it, and it truly added value to my life. I went in hoping to get lots of answers to things that bother me in life, but I didn't really come out with that many answers. I guess it only made me realise what my real challenges are and they manifest themselves on a daily basis. Unfortunately, I'm not very disciplined about my practice anymore, but I turn to in moments of distress.

Anushka Shah

Founder, Civic Studios

JP: May I request you to introduce yourself.

Anushka: I am currently based between Boston and Mumbai. I work as a researcher at the MIT Media Lab in Boston and I also run a production firm, Civic Studios in Mumbai. I am 27 years old and I am originally from Mumbai.

In terms of education and work, I went to an International Baccalaureate (IB) school in Mumbai and then went on to do my undergraduate at the London School of Economics in UK where I studied Government and Economics. After that, I spent about four years in Mumbai, working with different non-profits largely to put myself in places and communities that I did not get exposed to while growing up. I worked in slums and prisons in Mumbai, in villages in rural Maharashtra, and with a political party for about a year. I went on to study my Master's in Applied Statistics focussing on Media Analytics at NYU (New York University); since then I have been working at MIT for the last three years.

JP: Post NYU how did you get into MIT and Media Lab?

Anushka: The relationship between citizens and government is something I am curious about. When I was younger I saw it as an efficiency problem—there was a society, there was a state that society had elected (in a democracy), but the two didn't often work well together because they didn't talk to each other much outside of elections. As I grew older, I came to define this 'talking' as civic participation, and became more cognizant of the complexities of it.

That was one of the reasons I studied Economics and Government at LSE (London School of Economics). It's also the reason I chose to do the non-profit work after coming back from LSE because growing up in a place like Mumbai, especially in a neighbourhood like Bandra, it is very easy to live in a bubble that has little to do with how most of India lives. That exposure, the different types of communities, economic classes, and social groups, gave me an insight into different lifestyles and different ways that citizens interact with the state, especially my experience working with a political party. All of these experiences gave me a better understanding of the citizen-state relationship.

I came out of the experiences with three problem statements: (a) as citizens of India, we know very little about our democratic institutions and how the state at large functions; (b) whatever we know makes us mistrust our politics and public institutions; (c) as citizens we don't believe we have the power to change or improve our institutions. Colloquially, this is what we always keep saying, "We need to fix this system; the system is broken." However, we have very little imagination of where that fixing begins.

My thesis was to see how media and specifically entertainment— films, television shows, digital content with their overarching reach and influence in India—could become a means for improving civic participation in India. Could we tell stories about our public institutions? Could we humanise them and provide an insight of bureaucrats, policy makers, and politicians to give citizens a better understanding of how they functions? Could we narrate the history of different social movements in India and the important role of activism, protests, and petition? Could we represent experiences of minorities on a larger screen?

I went on to study quantitative media metrics at NYU to get a closer understanding of media influence. That's what led to my job at the MIT Media Lab and specifically within a group called the Centre for Civic Media. A lot of the work there was about exploring civic participation and the role of the media; in the three years I have been at MIT we have been using an open-source platform that we created to study the digital analytics of news in the US, India, and other countries around the world.

About six months ago, I went back to the original idea of entertainment media. I established my own project at MIT called Civic Entertainment and that has also led to the founding of the production house in Mumbai called Civic Studios which aims to produce such entertainment for Indian audiences.

JP: You come from a very affluent family; can you give us a bit of perspective on what money meant to you growing up?

Anushka: I was born in 1991 and that's the same year that my parents' pharmaceutical business really began its trajectory of growth with the market opening up because of the liberalisation reforms. I think for my sister and I, we have been very privileged and lucky to be supported by this economic comfort; and so kind of like Maslow's pyramid it has given us the luxury to pick professions that don't necessarily require financial success and that can be in a non-profit or low-profit space. I think this has been a boon in so many ways, but I also think because of the resource availability my management and understanding of money is not very skilled—it's something I'm learning to do more of now.

Having said that because my parents grew up in middle-class themselves, they never allowed us to take money for granted. While it was always available for education, travel, etc., we still have to spend it wisely. Until I was earning on my own, my credit card was linked to my dad's, so if there was any unreasonable expense it's always something that I had to justify, which helped me be more accountable. A funny anecdote is that there were two different times my dad tried gifting my mom a designer bag, but she secretly asked me to go and return them. She couldn't quite internalise a practical item costing so much. I think it's things like that that have shaped my perspective about money.

JP: Fast forwarding to today, tell us about Civic Studios and what you are doing there. I also want to get your perspective on money today and going forward.

Anushka: Civic Studios as of today is in its very early stages. We are still in the process of our first few projects. We have dedicated the first year to creating research around the impact of entertainment and organising events and conversations on this.

We have broken our work into four verticals; each one of the public institutions—the judiciary, executive, legislature, and the fourth one being the bureaucracy, even though that is not really a separate wing. Our first project is about the judiciary, and what citizens can do to strengthen the judiciary by focussing on specific issues, in this case it's domestic violence and sexual harassment. At the moment, we have a team of about six people across the US and India.

The source for financing the Civic Studios will be philanthropic funding and private investors. We have set up this as a for-profit company and believe that to have reach our entertainment has to be genuinely good and must respond to the market.

JP: My question to you is what will you do with all this money?

Anushka: I think we can all contribute to a better world in different ways depending on our individual resources like education, skill, time, or money. For me, that is the basis of my education and skill in civics and media through Civic Studios and MIT.

Outside of my professional work, the access to the wealth I have is not mine, but the family's wealth. As a family, we realise that to deploy this effectively it has to be done in a structured and strategic manner, so we have set up a family foundation. My sister who has worked in impact investing leads this effort. Each family member takes care of two or three non-profits that are listed within the foundation. We support about 20 at the moment. We work across healthcare, education, and governance wherein we have invested in the gaps.

Personally, in my analysis, the three issues that are the most urgent to your question about issues to spend this money on specific to India are: i) caste, ii) political leadership, and iii) climate change.

First, caste—it's the single defining factor of how we are organised as a society in India. If we don't break the foundation of our inequality, everything from our GDP (Gross Domestic Product) to our humanities suffers. There's lots to do in this space, but that's better understood by listening to members of the oppressed castes and caste activists who can best inform us where and on what interventions the money or other resources and practices should be deployed.

The second, political leadership—because for any issue that we care about, from education to health care—to see improvement at a systemic level, you need political will to create a new legislation or implement an existing one. For this, you need good, qualified people, and a system that incentivises good qualified people to join. We need to support organisations like Association for Democratic Reform that has made it mandatory for candidates to reveal their education and criminal background.

The third, climate change—because this is by all measures so, so urgent. There are several publications, documentation in the whole field of climate change, communication that is telling us what we can do to change this in a large way at a systemic level—from pushing consumers and companies to adopt eco-friendly practices, to contacting their elected representatives to sign the right international pacts and treaties.

These are just three areas of importance according to me. Because ours is a family foundation, the areas, organisations, and interventions will be decided in a more collaborative manner.

JP: Over the next few decades millennials are going to come into tremendous wealth. Do you have any words of wisdom for your friends?

Anushka: I'm still learning so no words of wisdom as such, but some open thoughts. I think it's easy to underestimate the challenge of investing money into social causes—my sister says the problem with charity is that we always think of it as charity. If we think of it as something that's over and beyond our responsibility, then we also end up applying ourselves in a limited way to it. But if we consider it part of our key responsibility then we take it more seriously. Like any other venture, we have to read, research, and educate ourselves before we can do anything.

I also don't think it's about necessarily setting up foundations or supporting non-profits—it could be making your own professional or business practices more responsible, which can often involve spending more money as a business, for example, paying labourers in a manufacturing business wages to help them not just have a living wage but pull their next generation out of the poverty cycle, or spending more on eco-friendly packaging even if we haven't quite discovered the most cost-friendly materials. It will probably affect a business' bottom line, but we need kinder perspectives, both within businesses and investors.

While in the next few decades millennials around the world will have a certain population with a lot of wealth, there will be another population of millennials that will suffer as technology and automation threatens jobs and authoritarianism affects migration, good governance, etc. I think we need to be smart with spending towards this inequality because in the end we all gain socially, politically, economically, and hence personally from that.

Richa Dsouza

Executive Principal, Basil Technology Partners

JP: May I request you to introduce yourself.

Richa: I was born and raised in Bahrain, in the Middle East. While I am of Indian ethnicity, I tend to hesitate every time I'm asked where I'm from because I am never quite sure where to begin—it's the classic 'third culture kid' problem. I'll be turning 27 in April.

My parents are originally from Mangalore, in the south of India. Even though I was born to a Catholic family, I didn't have the most traditional Catholic upbringing. This is largely due to my dad's experiences in his 20s, when he moved to Bombay for work and came across the Hare Krishna Gaudiya Vaishnava movement. He was very interested and drawn to the philosophy. He later married my mom, and they agreed to keep their religious beliefs to themselves and peacefully coexisted. However, when it came down to how my younger sister and I would be raised, my mother insisted that we followed Catholic practices, especially to appease our extended family members. My dad, being the non-interfering person that he is, was very amenable to this. So, growing up, going to church every Friday morning became the norm, but at the same time, I was constantly exposed to my dad's spiritual practices, like his meditation rituals and his beliefs—I found that quite interesting. So, gradually, I found myself being drawn to these philosophical aspects of spirituality and Hinduism, like reincarnation and karma. I was always a very curious kid so, to me, these concepts were the answers to questions I had been searching for, for a long time.

JP: Can you please give us a bit of perspective on how you grew up and where you studied?

Richa: I went to an international school in Bahrain and when I was 18 I moved to the US. Growing up in Bahrain was a very unique experience, because I was exposed to so many different cultures at school, and still got a glimpse of the local Arab culture outside of it. Given my childhood experiences, I knew at an early age that I wanted to learn more about business, so after graduating from high school, I attended The Wharton School, at the University of Pennsylvania, where I majored in finance and management.

I was in the States, in Philly, for four years and then I moved to New York. I worked there for about three and a half years. My first job was at Citigroup, and a few years later, I worked at a smaller boutique bank, both on the public side. I reached a point in my career, where I was thinking about what I wanted to do long-term and the idea of investing was definitely appealing to me, but on the private side. However, at that point, Trump got elected, and there were a whole set of immigration issues and concerns surfacing. So, for a non-American, getting the right job at smaller financial institutions became increasingly challenging. I had to make a tough decision with regards to whether I wanted to stay in the US versus progress in my career, and maybe expand my geographical search and pursue other opportunities. In the end, it was a no brainer for me—my career was important, my growth, and my future were also equally important. So, I left the US, which was difficult because having been there for seven years, having an established friends' circle, and a life there, leaving all of that and diving into the unknown and taking that plunge was definitely a little intimidating. And temporarily, since I didn't have a job or any other opportunity lined up, leaving meant having to go back home to Bahrain, and live with my parents for a little bit. Initially, I really wasn't sure how I felt about that—going from being independent, self-sufficient and having the freedom to make my own choices and decisions to temporarily relying on my parents. It just didn't sit quite well with me. In hindsight, however, this period of uncertainty turned into a blessing in disguise, where I got to spend time with my family, re-evaluate what I wanted to do with my life, regroup and refocus.

JP: As you were growing up, what was your perspective on money and what did it mean to you?

Richa: I largely attribute my perspective on money to how I was raised. Prior to starting his own business, my dad used to work at an IT company. One thing I always noticed that remained constant was just his general mentality towards money—respect it and value it, no matter how much or how little you have. He always put our education first. He made sure we had access to the best education possible at the best private school, and he never compromised on this, even if that meant sacrificing a certain kind of lifestyle and cutting back on certain luxuries for him and my mom. While my sister and I never really had any demands, we've always been quite simple in that sense, my parents have always tried their best to provide us with a comfortable life.

When my dad transitioned full-time into his business, we initially had to be more mindful of expenses, but that was never really an issue because my parents had always instilled in us the notion of valuing and respecting money. Till this day, even though we don't have any financial concerns, the values our parents have taught us are just ingrained in us, so certain financial decisions and choices that I make very much factor in those values—it's also because of my perspective on the nature of money—it's here today, gone tomorrow. I've seen this happen around me several times. Having said that, I don't believe that people shouldn't have fun, and hold back from enjoying certain luxuries, it's just that I believe in also having a sense of responsibility and respect when it comes to spending money.

JP: How has your perspective on money changed?

Richa: Circling back to what I said about the philosophy and the principles of spirituality that I've come to adopt, I believe in having more of a long-term approach to life. You asked me how I feel about money today. To be honest, I don't think my views on money have changed all that much. I still treat money the same way I used to. Going back to the luxury aspect of spending money, while I do like indulging every now and then, I don't necessarily feel the need to, just because I have access to it. I guess it's just not something that I derive a great sense of happiness or excitement from. Of course, I understand everyone's different; some people enjoy buying things for themselves or for others and I don't think there's anything wrong with that. Personally, it doesn't give me a sense of fulfilment. What I've come to realise is, that even if I've had my eyes on something for a while, once I buy that particular item, the thrill is gone, it just evaporates…it's just such an ephemeral experience. I guess over the years, I've come to understand that the concept of chasing temporary happiness is quite pointless. Because, in my opinion, there doesn't seem to be a limit or an end to this chase. Instead, I feel that you need to have a certain higher purpose in life, if you truly want to be happy. That's definitely a sentiment that I'm trying to espouse.

Going forward, I want to find a way to rope in my professional background and utilise my skills in an environment where I can give back to the community, to society and just be in a place where I can be at my most productive and feel a true sense of fulfilment. I think the ability to assess my contributions and see them actually pan out is something that would be extremely fulfilling, because as a results oriented person, it's something measurable which is motivating. I often think about being involved in impact investing or with some kind of a socially responsible fund with an ethical initiative. More than just being affiliated with a charity, I'm interested in being able to create a business model that's able to self-sustain. Again, it's a long-term approach. These are still just initial thoughts. I don't know how I will get there just yet, but you have to start somewhere. It's like what my dad always mentioned to us growing up, the hardest part is starting—once you start, the momentum builds up, and you find yourself on the path again, moving from point A to point B and so on.

JP: You grew up in Bahrain and then went to Philadelphia. You now live in Singapore—what is your perspective on your family's affluence and wealth?

Richa: [Laughs] I often struggle when it comes to talking about this candidly. I've never really felt comfortable with putting myself in a bucket when it comes to wealth, because I generally dislike labels and being placed in a box—I've just never looked at myself as rich or poor. At any point, my relationship with money has mostly been as a means of getting from point A to point B. You enjoy life, sure, but money is not something I place that much of an importance on from a materialistic standpoint.

Having said that, and at the risk of sound cliché, I believe that if I am privileged enough to have access to capital and certain resources, I would feel a strong sense of responsibility to deploy it in a meaningful way, that adds value to society and contributes positively. As I previously mentioned, I don't have a concrete game plan as such, yet, but the overall goal is to be able to do something productive and impactful with money versus solely using it for personal enjoyment and gain.

JP: So, the question is, what shall we do with all this money?

Richa: That's the million dollar question, right? I wish I had a more solid answer but I think that a good starting point would be me, and others in my generation, at least beginning to think about ways in which we could meaningfully utilise the resources available to us. Giving a little bit more thought as to where our passions lie, what our goals are, and how we can move closer towards those goals. I think that's a mentality that I would be an advocate of. I guess my next steps are trying to connect with individuals who are in a similar headspace, sharing our thoughts, ideas and experiences, and using that wealth of knowledge to move closer to our personal goals. That's my roadmap on a very high level.

JP: Any final words of wisdom for your millennial friends?

Richa: Don't stop thinking. I've always been an over thinker and an over analyser, and while that's held me back at times, it has also allowed me to consider things that most people don't think about. It's about taking a moment and just re-evaluating your life from time to time, checking in, monitoring your progress towards your goals — I believe that having some kind of direction is very important. Of course, life pulls you in different directions and that initial path is going to keep changing. My goals have changed throughout the course of my life, and I'm certain they will continue to do so — it's a constantly evolving process. It is the idea of having some goals in place and measuring your progress towards them, seeing how you can improve on them going forward and learning from your mistakes.

Siddharth Sachdeva

Machine Learning Engineer, Roam Analytics

JP: May I request you to introduce yourself.

Siddharth: I just graduated from the University of Chicago and I am working as a machine learning engineer in the Bay Area.

JP: Tell us a little about your growing-up years.

Siddharth: I grew up in very fortunate circumstances. I was born in India. I grew up in New York and New Jersey; lived in Singapore for three years; went to boarding school in Massachusetts, then went for college in Chicago, and now I am here in San Francisco.

JP: How is Silicon Valley?

Siddharth: It's dope. My favourite part is the number of immigrants that are here as well as the diversity of immigrants that are here.

JP: What I want to understand first is your perspective on money?

Siddharth: I see money entirely as a tool. I think it's very important as a tool to solve problems, but it can easily blind people as a goal in itself because of its cultural significance.

JP: You have lived a charmed life and come from a privileged background. You grew up in United States and also in Singapore. Do you have an understanding of the amount of wealth your family has?

Siddharth: Yes. We are easily in the 99.9999 percentile.

JP: Are you aware of it?

Siddharth: Yes, actually in some sense, I think I am fortunate because we are so well off that I understand I am well off. I think it's interesting, I meet a lot of people who classify themselves as upper-middle-class because they are surrounded by people exactly like them. And the only reason I am maybe a little different, is because my mom runs this foundation, where I go, and I have seen her work in slums and with street children, all over India. I think that people define how much money they have in terms of whom they spend time around. I think that I have been lucky in the sense that I am able to understand how fortunate I am.

JP: What would you do with the money, if your parents gave you your inheritance today, instead of later?

Siddharth: I would invest in a cause I believe in. I would keep some portion of it as investment for my first business. But most of it I would invest in what I feel to be the most promising climate businesses, businesses that create technology that has a real chance at changing the way we use energy and tackle the problem of climate change.

JP: A part of the money will be reserved for your own welfare, the welfare of your family and of your next generation. Is that accurate?

Siddharth: No, not for the next generation. I am not even certain if I will have family or a next generation. I think that money is an enabler for me to take a risk to do something I believe in. I think that is quite valuable and so that is what I will use it for. I don't think I need that much money for that.

JP: Coming back to the original question — you get all the money now versus, let's say 30, 40, 50 years from now...what will you do with it?

Siddharth: I think that it depends on the amount you are considering. I'd rather take the small portion. Actually, no, I'll take all of it now. That's because both the options that I am interested in, the discounting rate is very high. The problems of the world right now are quite time-sensitive, that's why I'd take it now. I think that taking a risk in terms of starting something that I believe is something I am most well positioned to do within the next five or ten years.

JP: Have you convinced your parents to give you all the money now?

Siddharth: I have been trying to convince my parents to give the money away, not to me, but still give it away. They give quite a lot, but being young and idealistic I always try to push for more.

JP: Your parents have two children. Assuming everything is divided 50:50, what would you do with your share of the money if it comes to you today?

Siddharth: First, I should emphasise that both my parents and I have agreed that there will be no guarantee of me getting anything and there shouldn't be, as such a thing would ruin my life.

I have made enough in whatever jobs I have been in so far and am leading a comfortable life. I don't want to buy a house. I don't want to buy a car. I think these things take more time than the value of the investment that they are. I think the only valuable investment, if you have money, is to build a business or to invest in someone else's business because I think those are the actual things that can improve the world, and which will have a genuine impact in improving life. I can rent an apartment, I can take an Uber, and I don't need to own it.

JP: If you could actually start something with all this money, and grow that social enterprise, what kind of projects would they be?

Siddharth: One project that I have already started was using technology to improve political discourse. There are multiple ways—we can do this informed by research on how humans process information. If we can create the right interface, for example, for reading political news, for discussing controversial opinion—if you can create the right medium for that, then maybe, we can improve the quality of our conversations, the quality of our politics, and the quality of our society's abilities to collectively solve problems. That's one example of a product that could potentially make positive social change.

The second thing, the reason I am so passionate about it is because I think it's extremely time sensitive, is climate change. You can solve health care in 50 years, you can solve economic stagnation in 50 years—but if we screw-up the climate, which seems we are likely to do—that's permanent. I would set aside most of the money for that, because I think that for any of the other things in the world, we have to solve that problem first.

JP: Tell us little bit about the start-up you are working at.

Siddharth: The start-up works on health care AI (Artificial Intelligence). Essentially, the goal is to make use of unstructured data to improve health care decisions.

JP: Is this a long-term play for you?

Siddharth: I think it's a long-term play in multiple ways. I believe in the core thesis of the business. I think the team is amazing and will teach me a lot. They give me a lot of freedom and ownership in my work. I am able to do a lot of interesting things. It's a problem that matters to everybody, but if I were starting a business, I would not personally start in health care, but I think it's the perfect job for me to have.

JP: People out there are worried about millennials, especially millennials with affluent parents. Folks like you are very few and far between. You come from a very affluent family, you don't have to do anything, and you can just enjoy, chill, and have a party for the rest of your life. What is the motivation and ambition that drives you to do more?

Siddharth: I think it's pretty simple. I have seen very clearly in my life that an abundance of money is no guarantee of happiness. That living a happy fulfilling life, beyond a relatively very low baseline of how much money you have, has very little effect on the quality of your life, the quality of your relationships, the quality of the extent to which you can follow your passions. I have seen that money is deeply overrated. A lot of kids with rich parents agree with me, but a lot them who don't agree, aren't necessarily, in my opinion, very happy, which is a controversial opinion but it's the opinion that I have.

JP: You are on this journey, on this path where money is important for a good quality of life, but not for happiness. For you, happiness comes from having a purpose.

Siddharth: I think I'm lucky. Because of my life circumstance— basically, no matter what I do, I am going to be fine. I think digital technology is also a big part of it. So much of the interesting things in life are free or close to free, such as learning resources, entertainment, and communication. Relationships are free, and they're the key to a meaningful, happy life. These are the two things that are most interesting in my life. I already have a job that pays more than enough, more than I think I would need in order to live a happy life, apart from fulfilling purpose. I think, that the only thing I see money as valuable for is fulfilling purpose, which could be building a business or creating an organisation that solves some problems. That to me is very valuable and it needs money. I am not trying to say that money has no value, but I think that the reason many people care about having a lot of money is to spend on luxury goods. We live in a world where everyone has most of them. They just have a regular version of it. I mean, how different is a Ford from a Ferrari? The difference is not that much. If you show those two cars to someone 300–400 years ago and asked them to choose, they would probably pick the Ford because they can take their kids in the car. Our sense of value for things is warped by cultural competition, which is affected a lot by money. Maybe it's different if you have kids because you might want to buy a big house or an expensive education for them, but even in that case, most of the smartest kids I know are that way not because their parents spent a lot of money, but because they read to them when they were young. Like I said, most of the important things in life are free beyond a reasonable baseline of money that I am far past.

Anisha Kataria
Family Office Member, Pantheon Holdings

JP: May I request you to introduce yourself.

Anisha: I am 23 years old. I was born and raised in London and then moved to Dubai at the age of nine, which is where I spent the majority of my formation years. I studied at Dubai College—a British curriculum school and then attended college in America at New York University where I majored in Business Studies and Sociology.

JP: And then post college?

Anisha: Post college, I worked in New York for a year as part of my OPT (Optional Practical Training), for a brand management company, Bluestar Alliance. They specialised in acquiring fashion brands, and had marketing and licensing rights for them, which was really interesting. So, I did marketing and branding there for a year before moving back home to Dubai, just two months ago, and have since joined my family business.

JP: How did that transition happen?

Anisha: Well, a lot of it was due to me wanting to return home after five years because it had been a while. I also wanted to connect with the family business, understand what it's all about, and eventually figure out how I can add value to it as well.

JP: What was your perspective on money growing up?

Anisha: Growing up, money was never really at the forefront of our minds. We knew it was something that was hard to obtain, from the stories we heard about the hardships our parents and grandparents faced. We never really knew how much money we had or where it all came from, but we always knew it was hard to earn. I remember the sacrifices our parents made, and the long work trips our father had to take.

JP: But you grew up in affluent circumstances?

Anisha: I did. We lived in a very affluent neighbourhood growing up. And when I compared myself to friends or people I went to school with, I would find that a lot of them were similar but I would also see some who had different background as well. It gave us a good perspective, and made us realise we were in a good environment.

JP: What are you doing now? How has your perspective on money changed?

Anisha: Over time, once you learn more and hear more stories of how the money was created, it gives you that mental value. Obviously, we will never know the physical value of it because we can't re-live what our parents did. We know that money is very valuable, and our perspective has changed over the years learning more about it and now we want to make use of that and in our generation add more value to it. That's part and parcel of why I joined the family business, that's where it comes into play and allows us to do that.

JP: Do you know how much money you and your family have?

Anisha: To be very honest I have an idea, but growing up I didn't know the exact amount and I think I am happy not knowing or letting it get to my head.

JP: You are the beneficiary of this wealth, so have you started formulating some ideas on what you will do with all this money?

Anisha: The way I think about it is in two dimensions. One is what our parents' objectives are in terms of giving us that money to look after and adhering to those, but creating our own in conjunction. And the second dimension is what we can give back to the world or what the world needs, and for me that would be philanthropy and sustainable development practices, which I think a lot of other millennials are thinking about now, especially since our circumstances are changing and there is a lot of damage that could be repaired.

I think it should be divided in a calculated way. Some that's invested or gained upon over time, and some that's given to others for certain causes that could add intrinsic value over time. To me it's more about dividing it in ways that can multiply the value of it, whether it's physically, intrinsically, or mentally.

JP: Have you thought of how you would handle philanthropy?

Anisha: Spending time and investing in different sectors like healthcare, education, sustainability, and anything that can have a positive impact on people's lives or community's lives. The first would definitely be health care and education because those are fundamental and it allows people to have a good standing in life, coupled with impact investing for different causes.

JP: At 23 and coming from an affluent family, what are your thoughts on materialistic spending and experiential spending?

Anisha: I like both to be honest, because I have passion for both. I love to spend on travelling or experiences that involve memories with family and friends as those times are invaluable and teach you so much, but I also like to spend on clothes, shoes, and things a lot of other girls my age like. Whenever I spend, I definitely think twice before doing so. If it's something that can't be appreciated, then there is no point spending it or no value gained, and therefore doesn't make sense.

JP: Does knowing how wealthy your family is affect your motivation and ambition to make money?

Anisha: I think it definitely gives us a need to prove ourselves to our parents and to others. Instead of just simply living off what we were given, I want to multiply it and add value to it as well. It also inspires me to use it as a platform for my personal goals and passions—that's definitely what I would want to do.

JP: Any words of wisdom to other millennials like you?

Anisha: We as millennials need to look at our current situations and use our time and resources to improve them in an efficient manner. We don't really have the luxury of time. We are definitely surrounded by more destruction than ever before, whether it's to do with resources, humanity, or geopolitics, and I think to combat these we need to improve our collective consciousness and invest in positive and constructive causes. Do what makes you happier and a better human being.

Intuitives

Varin Gill
Self-Transformation Guide

Suzanne Toro
Spiritual Guide

Karishma Gill
Spiritual Awakening Teacher

JP: May I request you to introduce yourself.

Varin: I live in Kuala Lumpur, Malaysia, which is my hometown, that's where I was born. I spent a good 18 or 19 years of my life there before I went to the UK to pursue my Finance degree. I began my career in finance in the UK. Eventually, I discovered I was not motivated by the job I did. I pursued it for money only. It fulfilled my physical and mental needs, but it lacked an emotional aspect, which I now understand is the need of the soul, true wisdom and the intuitive aspects of the human self. I had a need to 'feel' life and express myself using knowledge that I never learnt but I already knew, such as tarot, energy healing, sound healing, yoga, pranayama, self-love empowerment, and alchemy (the latter is the science of how you are the force creating your own life). I have now learnt and teach all the above to assist people to become the best version of themselves.

JP: Tell us about your journey.

Varin: It's been a journey of searching for this formula that exists in human beings, what is it that makes us do what we do? The book, *Sapiens* totally breaks down the fact that your life is not even yours. It's a set of biases that has prevailed from time immemorial, power after power, survival of the strongest and what you at are the back of all that. Therefore, I learnt to meditate at university. When I started my job with Arthur Andersen, the work that I was doing was just something I did nine to five, as I never fully related to it. If I compared how life was 20 years ago and what is available now, in terms of spirituality and solutions to the soul, there is so much but I believe it is still not even 1 per cent of the spiritual knowledge that actually exists in this world.

I went to Dr Deepak Chopra's centre as my first step into self-discovery because I found his book and I read three or four of them at the time, and I was very inspired by him. I went to learn primordial sound meditation at The Chopra Center in La Jolla, California, when I was 24. I was the youngest person in that course. Everyone was over 40. Dr Chopra himself was shocked to see me there.

JP: What is your educational and professional background?

Varin: I went to the University of Manchester where I studied Economics and Finance, Bachelor of Economics. I had a first class there. I guess that allowed me to get a job in the UK. I worked for Andersen until it dissolved because of the Enron scandal. The division that I was in became Ernst & Young.

JP: At such a young age, you had experienced life in at least three countries—Malaysia, UK, Singapore, and now back to Malaysia. I want to understand your perspective on money having gone through so many different countries and cultures. What is your personal view on what money is and what it means to you?

Varin: Money to me is a resource. It is a power; it is an energy that gives as much as you give it. For instance, you go to the bank and you withdraw $100, you are empowering that money to give you what that $100 is actually worth. Every time you have money in your hand, you always have a choice. You are so conditioned to do just what our social situation is allowing us to do.

JP: What does this energy of wealth and affluence mean to you?

Varin: To me it means the ability to change the future in many ways. For example, with that $100 you could do so much. With $100,000, you could do even more. I mean, literally, every time you have money, every time you think of money, you think of how to spend it. It means you are changing something in your life or in somebody else's life. Everything becomes a little changed by this thought process.

JP: If there was a sudden windfall and you got $50 million, how would you change your life?

Varin: I would first look after my parent's requirements. Then I would begin on my spiritual journey. I would look at what is the latest research on the value of the soul. I have read so much about how in Egypt, the power of our soul can actually energise an entire city for years. If we are able to mobilise the human body and the soul together, it creates an energy source, and there is so much data available out there. Whatever is the latest, I would make that research user-friendly for people. There is a lot of data available that we don't take seriously, because we think it is alien, or hundreds or thousands of years old and mythical. Why do we not focus on doing research? I believe that there is not enough money being put in that direction. I believe the human soul has the potential that is far from being tapped and that's where I want to put all my money into.

JP: Between material and experiential, you are more focussed on the experiential, specifically soul research. How would you go about doing that?

Varin: I would want to see people who have already started in that direction. Dr Chopra is someone that has been doing research for a long time. He is known as the 'Guru of Hollywood'. I would want to see what medical science is proving with regards to this. I would also go and see the Dalai Lama because in Tibetan Buddhism, there is a lot of ancient text. I believe there is a lot of knowledge and research in this area that has been done by Egyptian researchers as well.

JP: What else would you do with the $50 million?

Varin: I would give $2 million to the #MeToo movement. I would want to give $2 million to educating girls, the girl-child specifically, any kind of organisation that's supporting the education of girls, that's something I want to donate to, and I would like to give $2 million to organisations looking to bring back the lost knowledge of the divine feminine. It's called the womb wisdom. There is actually a lot of work that has been done on the subject. That's what I would like to focus on.

JP: What's the rationale behind each of them?

Varin: The #MeToo movement is something that has really picked up since the end of 2017, and it's taking on a different shape. It's actually bringing back a kind of self-honour that I think women have lost over time. The whole world uses sex as give and take, instead of sex as an ability to actually experience real joys for your physical body. This reduced the status of sex in life and the #MeToo movement brings back the honour that associates with it. Right now, at times, it does seem to be some kind of power game, but I think the outcome is a positive one and I would like to see the funds going towards making it a positive outcome.

The cause of the girl-child, I think that's self-explanatory. I think there is still a lot of work to be done in many, many communities out there who still choose to educate their son over their daughter, to feed their son over their female child. I would like these funds to go specifically towards the education to stop that from happening.

The final one is the advent or the return of the knowledge of the feminine. Thousands of years ago, the feminine was the prime energy of the time. The world used to base its entire process on the cycles of a woman, which is equivalent to the cycles of the moon and nature. This is something that is slowly making its way back into the world thanks to work done by doctors such as Dr Azra and Seren Bertrand, authors of *Womb Awakening*. They are bringing back essential information such as the purpose of Shakti, the purpose of Mary Magdalene, and it gives women a chance to connect with the essence of femininity in a world that has lost the importance of natural cycles and rhythms of the human body and the earth.

JP: What is your message to people who are extremely affluent and wealthy?

Varin: It's interesting that we are all so unique when it comes to what we want to do in life. I believe there is a code sitting in each one of us that gives us these answers. I would highly suggest that the amazingly affluent people ask themselves what is the meaning of this moment that they are in. What are you receiving from it? Do you feel in your gut that you got what you came here for—that this life is amazing; its enjoyment, its joy, its dance, everything that you are going through every day—do you feel that high?

JP: Growing up in affluent places like the UK and Singapore, were you attached to materialist possession?

Varin: At one point, when I was getting divorced, I had all this money in my bank—I just gave £10,000 away. It really shifted me to think that happiness doesn't come from having a man in your life or having a job in your life. It came from knowing how you felt. It's a feeling; there is a drive that sits in everyone and so often, you don't know what you are supposed to do in life because you haven't focussed on that drive. What is that drive? What is it telling me? This is all energy and it's your soul trying to talk to you, but you don't understand it.

JP: What is your message to the millennials who are going to inherit a massive amount of wealth or are already incredibly affluent?

Varin: I would say get it out of your system. Do whatever you think it is you want to do—everything. You think you want to start a charity, you think you want to go to the most amazing holiday resorts in the world, create the best parties you can imagine, have your orgasm or your orgy—do everything and at the end of it, ask yourself how you are feeling? You will do all of it with that wealth but if you don't feel how you are supposed to have felt, when you set out to do all of that with your money, you didn't get to that point, then let's chat; because what I could do with your money might actually help you get that feeling which you are after.

JP: Any final words of wisdom?

Varin: There is one thing: that the journey of the soul is completely unrelated to, I think, any religions' purpose and I would really encourage people to start thinking outside of all boundaries when it comes to who they truly are.

Suzanne Toro
Spiritual Guide

JP: May I request you to introduce yourself.

Suzanne: I dropped in on the Hawaiian Islands in 1970. Currently, I assist others through birth, life, and death transitions, using ancient technologies with sound energy, and a dreaming practice, which gives me the ability to see beyond here, into the present moment and into the future and past. I use these gifts with people one-on-one and group settings; I work in medical clinics; help cancer patients, and people with eating disorders. I also help guide people that are here working in the world and trying to become a better version of themselves. I'm able to integrate all these skills to help guide them and help them build their dreams.

JP: What is your perspective on money today?

Suzanne: Currently, I use money in two ways. I feel like on a global level, money is our saber tooth tiger of today, meaning it can put people in fight or flight—if we don't have it, then our basic needs aren't met; everyone has the same basic needs—food, water, and shelter. Our relationship to currency, I feel is ready to shift. I see it, I sense it. Yet, there is this juxtaposition of controlling people with money.

There's a potential that everyone can shift and understand that money is just energy, something that's exchanged. That there is plenty of energy, there's no shortage of energy, there never will be. The construct of money has been placed on society—that idea that there is a shortage or surplus is nothing more than a construct that we hold in our mind. I don't like to say we can blame anyone for that—it's our own consciousness that creates a paradigm. Our locked perspective that there is a limited supply of something when nature really teaches us that it regenerates and there is the ability to be in harmony with that. I don't see money outside of nature, but I feel there are those two juxtapositions. We're kind of hopefully, moving to a place where we can be more regenerative with our currency, our energy exchange versus more of the all-or-nothing mentality or somewhere in between.

JP: You've come across plenty of friends and clients who are reasonably affluent. Can you describe your interactions and their perspective on money?

Suzanne: I've seen the full spectrum. I've seen people that hoard — they are affluent, wealthy influencers that hoard their money. They are carrying that fight or flight energy and they are not as generous with it. I think that's because of their internal relationship with it.

I've also seen people that have a lot of affluence and they are very generous and realise that they have this potential to keep regenerating, giving and it was their karma to come into that kind of wealth in this lifetime...to master what it means to have that wealth. That is really beautiful to witness.

Recently, I was made aware of a gentleman that has a high net worth. His goal is to die with nothing. He is funding every project that he can. Selecting and helping start a foundation to help out the generations to come, from his perspective, which I feel is a really valuable approach because who knows what happens after you get the chance to play in the world of wealth, what the next lifetime is going to be, and those who receive it on the other side know what to do with it.

JP: What do you think the affluent should do with all that money?

Suzanne: I think exchange it — move out of the mindset. I think years ago, I shared with you that there wouldn't be money. If we can move out of the mindset that there is a finite amount of money to control and move around and that that is what creates status and wealth, but wealth actually comes from within. I have been around enough indigenous people, people from impoverished communities, there is so much joy, and abundance coming from their heart and it's not about what's in their bank account.

For those that have wealth, they are really in this position to be the change agents on this planet, to switch our concept of what currency is and what it will be. In addition, the game is shifting. Higher states of consciousness are going to re-route how we know what our currency and value exchange is and if people are not working on their higher states of consciousness, they are going to find themselves attached to an old paradigm that will diminish. New things have already emerged, and they will continue to emerge. That's really deep spiritual practice and it's not something that you can just take from someone; you have to do the work.

So, for the future of money, I call it energy, what we should do with it is — we should practice exchanging it, practice generosity and really practice our inner work and work towards higher states of being, so that we understand the value of what comes out of doing that. It just keeps growing and growing—it's infinite. We spiral through space. There's no segregation in the way that we have gotten used to here on planet earth.

JP: Please expand a little bit more on the future of money itself.

Suzanne: Right now, the future of money itself is a construct. It's numbers, it's digits in bank accounts. It's not really real. That future within the system that we know is going to shift into something that is actually held here, and on an individual level and distributed out. Let's say, you have billions and billions of dollars in a digital bank account. That value is going to diminish because what's going to happen is as consciousness will increase those people who understand how to move energy will start to shift how we exchange things in our world. It will not be needed in the same way. We can build things; we can do things that can happen through moving of energy connected to people, places, and things. You can create masterpieces without exchanging a dime. Serendipity, mystery, and mystique can come through. For some people, that might sound like hogwash because they are attached to that old paradigm that they must have X amount to create this.

What I can share is, what I was taught at Hopi is that there is an alchemy that we have lost on this planet. You can take a single seed and put it in hard, hard earth. You don't need special soil; you don't need a hose; you don't need an irrigation system. All you need is a prayer and each seed that goes into that ground gets a prayer. Then the leader prays and has an altar and continues to pray and guess what? The rains come, the crops are bountiful, and he treats each one of those plants with deep care that all you see is this hard earth and these beautiful, bountiful plants and then they share every single aspect of that bounty with their community. They don't waste anything. In the modern age, we would say we need a tractor, we need special compost, we need all these things, but here one man can grow acres and acres of food that can feed his whole village just with a prayer.

JP: Can you tell us a little bit about Hopi?

Suzanne: Hopi is a tribe that is northeast of the Grand Canyon in northeastern Arizona. They have a history—they migrated several times and they chose this location so that they won't be bothered.

They are sovereign from the United States of America. Hopi is called Hopi Nation or Hopiland. There are 13 tribes that come from progressive to traditional, and they consider, like many tribes that they are at the galactic centre of the Universe. The things I have experienced out there are not tangible unless you are experiencing them yourself—very mysterious. The forces and the polarities, all exist right there. It seems to have a lot of people's interest from all over the world, meaning government leaders, people that want what they have. Again, I mentioned, we're not going to be able to take any of these practices from anyone. You have to do that work. You want to create that bounty; you have to do the work. There is no skipping ahead.

The one thing that they really hold on to is to take care of all people, that everyone is a human, to really be of service and care for your elders. It's a very yin and yang, feminine to masculine society. Women and men have specific roles but there is no push or pull like "I have to play the man role". There is an understanding that is part of how this planet was designed, for us to hold our roles, whether you are a biological female or a biological male, and that there is an alchemy that occurs when we do that. It's a very sacred society.

JP: Any advice for the Indian community with respect to money and affluence?

Suzanne: My recommendation would be to connect back to the spiritual roots. I know there are many deities there that still have a lot of power in my life, it's very mysterious and beautiful—one being Lakshmi, another is Ganesh. No matter what your belief system is, your practice is, there's something that India holds that is so loving and caring. Rather than those with affluence and wealth getting too caught up and becoming too much of a Western society—a pop-culture society, I would really, really encourage them to come back to those roots where there is importance placed on family, spiritual practice, taking care of your communities, and really understand that what we sow, we reap—cause and effect is very real and so with every action that we are taking in this present moment, know that you are paving the way into your future lives. To do that mindfully, don't get so caught up in things to have that bounty, be wise with it, and spread it forward.

Karishma Gill
Spiritual Awakening Teacher

JP: May I request you to introduce yourself.

Karishma: I am a spiritual awakening teacher and psychic channel. My mission is to guide people to navigate the awakening journey, fulfil their personal mission on earth, and transcend their earthly lessons.

JP: Can we just go back a little and talk about where you grew up, how you grew up?

Karishma: I was born and raised in Kuala Lumpur, Malaysia. I love this place. It's beautiful, it's vibrant, and this is where I grew up. I did my university in the States and I moved to the UK when I went on my soul-searching journey. Currently, I am residing in Malaysia.

JP: What was your perspective on money growing up? What did money mean to you?

Karishma: For me, it was more about what money represented to my parents. My reference to money was what my parents were telling us while growing up. We used to hear things about how you have to struggle to get the money. Money you have to earn though it is a struggle, which is a bit of paradox, but it was all about getting that money; like money has to be the biggest and most important thing that you have to work for, whether you sacrifice or whatever, you have to just work for it. That's what the message was growing up.

JP: How did you deal with it?

Karishma: I will be very frank. It was actually quite tough because I was not really taught about the concept of what money really was. As far as I was concerned, I was curious as to why we had to struggle for this money and why they struggle in the first place. Later on in my life, when I began my own spiritual journey, I realised that I have to start redefining what money was for me, instead of following what my parents were thinking about, what society wanted, how my ancestors dealt with it. If you were to ask me right now, I redefined money in my own terms, whereas, right now I feel it's an empowering, well-deserving, honest way of you exchanging your work, whatever it is in terms of this particular currency. It's an energy exchange and it needs to feel equal. Money is all about feeling. It has to feel equal for me.

JP: Did you go after money when you were young and then had a transition?

Karishma: Oh, absolutely. I failed miserably at it because it was all about going after something that I had no concept and clue of. It was like being a follower, you are just doing something blindly, but you don't know why you are doing it, until later on you realise that we are more conscious about what it is that you are going for and why is it important.

JP: You described what money means to you today. Do elaborate a little further?

Karishma: For me, money is an honest pay. What that means for me specifically is an equal energy exchange. For instance, if I were to exchange, let's say, intuitive reading for you, I ask for an honest pay and what an honest pay for me personally means is a well-deserving, empowering, honest and equal energy exchange with what I am giving you in terms of the intuitive reading. For me, it needs to feel like I have given something and I am receiving something of an equal value, if that makes sense.

JP: You are still young, going forward what is your perception of what you want to do with money?

Karishma: I feel now I would like to travel and see places that I love. See places that have meaning to me. I adore nature and I have huge compassion towards the safety of animals. I would also like to make it more accessible for people to gain spiritual knowledge.

JP: Can you elaborate some more?

Karishma: What I am playing with right now is to either have an online space where people can access courses or travel to places where people can attend my workshops. This way, I am able to share the knowledge to more people across the world. Still playing with some ideas.

JP: Do you have any advice for people who are incredibly wealthy and are trying to figure out what to do with their money?

Karishma: Do something that brings fulfilment and contentment in every way.

JP: As we wrap up, share with us your thoughts and insight about the concept of money.

Karishma: I personally feel that as we are moving forward as a conscious society there could be a time one day that we may not need this money after all. We may just come to a place in our lives where everything we ever need and desire comes to us naturally and easily. My true focus is abundance and the universe is abundant. From my experience, whenever I affirm that something I need and desire should come to me with ease, it usually does.

Gurus

Om Swami
Monk and Author

Nipun Mehta
Founder, ServiceSpace

Deepak Chopra, MD
Renowned Author, Lecturer, and Physician

Om Swami
Monk and Author

JP: I would like to get your perspective on money, especially from a spiritual basis.

Om Swami: If we look at chatur purushartha (dharma, arth, kama, moksha) these four are absolutely integral to individual and societal growth and evolution. If we neglect any of these, society will start to deteriorate. If you're depressed, you lose the desire to do anything, enjoy anything. Kama goes away when you are depressed. If I am ignorant, dharma goes away and if I am so caught up in the world in my selfish desires, moksha goes away. But money is a very powerful resource. Just like:

> 'Ek loha pooja mein rakhat, ek ghar badhik dharo,
> paras ke man juda nahi, dohe ko kanchan kaho'

A touchstone doesn't say I am not going to touch this knife because it's a knife used to slaughter an animal. Money in its own right is extremely important, it's vital, it's the life-force that affects society. To run welfare programs the government needs money; money is required to run an organisation, or a corporation, to pay people we need money. We have created this concept of money and today we are badly entangled in it. We cannot get away from it—it's too late. And from that perspective, as Lord Krishna says:

> 'adhiṣṭhānam' tathā kartā
> karaṇam' ca pṛthag-vidham
> vividhāś ca pṛthak ceṣṭā
> daivam' caivātra pañcamam'

That our approach, our mind-set, karnam our resources, our effort, and fifth is conditions: destiny, environment, climate, these all play a very important role in making anything happen. From that angle, money is a spiritual force and like any siddhi, you can either use it or abuse it, it's up to the individual.

JP: We pray to Goddess Laxmi; what is the prayer and what is the concept behind it?

Om Swami: If you look at any image of Goddess Laxmi, you will almost always see she is standing and praying, but when she is serving Lord Vishnu she is always sitting, always by his feet. This means that if money is our only goal, it will never prove to be enough. It will forever be moving—we may have a lot but like youth, it's running away because she is a beautiful woman who is going to have many suitors; but when she is joined with satvikta, which is what Vishnu represents—goodness, then money grows. The only way to grow anything in nature is to give it back. If I don't invest my money it will never grow. The same concept—praying to Goddess Laxmi that may you be blessed with goodness and may you be blessed with that wealth because if you have the competence—Vishnu represents competence, Vishnu represents that skill—then money is by your feet, otherwise you are constantly chasing it.

There is an old story in Vedic literature that sage Brighu was testing who is the kindest God. He went to Lord Brahma and tried to shake him out of his samadhi, but Brahma didn't wake-up. He went to Lord Shiva, but when he took his trident and poked Shiva with it, Shiva was furious and was looking ready to curse Brighu, so he ran. When he went to Vishnu, he tried to wake him up, he even hit him on his chest with his foot, "Wake up!" Goddess Laxmi was infuriated by this and cursed him, "I will never be there with Brahmins, they will forever be paupers." Brighu said, "You don't know my relationship with my Bhagwan, you came in between." Money clouds judgement. "You came in between therefore your curse will not hold any value. I will create such a scripture that you will first lay at a Brahmin's feet and then the scripture will open." Thus, he created Brighu Samhita, he created astrology. What I mean to say about money is that if you have something of value it comes, it must ensue, and we cannot pursue it. That is the secret of wealth creation. If I am doing something of value, money will come. I read somewhere that the amount of money you have in your bank is directly proportional to the degree of value you have added to society. Money is social debt because I have not created it. I may use the term wealth creation, but I have merely collected it and I have grown it.

There was this priest and he was announcing in a church and he said, "I have good news and bad news; what would you want to hear first?" They said, "Give us the good news, it's been a long time." He said, "The good news is we needed to raise $100,000 for the renovation of this church and it's done." Everybody applauded. Then he said, "And the bad news is that it's still in your pockets."

The money is already there, it just needs to come from where ever it is to make it happen.

JP: What is your advice and guidance to these affluent folks— the question that we are asking is, what should they do with all this money?

Om Swami: I think there comes a time when you get sick of growing money. How many cars can you have? What kind of restaurants can you dine in? What kind of places can you stay? Building wealth cannot be the purpose of your life. All these people who have money, somewhere they just need to take a short break, like Bill Gates takes a two week break every year. You need to take a short break and reflect on what really matters to you. The day you have an answer to what really matters to you, you will find a purpose in life. When you will find a purpose in life you will not find yourself just popping pills to take care of your depression, diabetes, cardio vascular health, blood pressure, hypertension—you will also find joy in living this life. Life then will not just be trying to stay busy because you have nothing else to do.

Somebody gave me this book, *Measure What Matters* by John Doerr, he is one of the top venture capitalists in the world. I have met some of the partners at KPCB, now it's only Kleiner Perkins in Silicon Valley. It talks about how it doesn't matter if you have too much money, or if you have very little. What matters is whether you have a purpose in life. It's been 10 years since 2010, when I renounced everything and marched out. I don't own a car, and the prime of my youth I have lived without owning a car, but I am getting by just fine. Sometimes, a devotee might give me a ride, otherwise I hire a taxi with air-conditioning if I can afford it, if I cannot I roll down the window and just travel in a small car. That contentment is the basis of our meaningful existence and that cannot come if I had no purpose in life.

JP: Millennials are going to inherit billions of dollars going forward. Any words of wisdom or advice you would give them?

Om Swami: Whenever anything has been created by human kind it's always going to be scarce. We have this knack of creating scarcity whenever we use anything from nature. We are so driven by economics that we are able to create demand and supply. It doesn't matter whether the wealth is in trillions or billions, if the use is not judicious it will deplete very quickly. Unless I find ways where I bring up the level of consciousness of the entire world, where I do something of value which benefits everybody—until I get to that level any amount of money I will burn very quickly. You perhaps know it better than anybody else, about start-ups that burn millions of dollars in months and there are start-ups that start with a $100,000 and grow it to millions and billions in months. It boils down to the use of money. Money—we can never say that we have enough money in the world. We also have enough problems in this world and this system of just handing out money to poor people has failed repeatedly, so that is not the way to go. When I say we need to raise collective consciousness, we must educate people because education alone will eliminate extremism. Exposure alone will give a new perspective to look at things. One thing grossly missing in school is moral education. We have nothing on communication, and we have nothing on self-awareness. Without these three things one is always relying on external things to make one happy.

The upcoming generation is constantly getting into bigger and better things—material things, thinking that will make them happy, but that is rarely the case. It's very important that from a young age they understand what human values are, so they learn to be humans, they learn the art of listening to their mind and talking to themselves, that self-dialogue is key; and third most importantly they learn non-violent, respectful, and loving communication.

We cannot train people for jobs that don't exist yet. We don't know what random event might totally change the course of the world, it could be nano-technology, it could be something that hasn't been perceived yet. Bitcoin came and took everybody by surprise and the world of mobile apps came, just changed the whole equation, the whole thing was moving on client server architecture at one time. People said, "Oh there will be no computing power needed on devices, everything will be served on the Web." And everything was moving there, and we were spending billions of dollars in organisations. I was heading huge programs when we were strategising our e-business and suddenly apps came, and everybody said, "No, we need powerful mobile devices; they are going to run locally and just communicate." Suddenly everything changed. The era of web browser is now almost antiquated. It's ancient. We don't know what random technology event might trigger a profound change. We cannot train people. I will teach you Java but 20 years from now, will you need Java? We don't know, but what we do know is that it doesn't matter where you work there will be people around. You will need to communicate with those people, you will need to inspire those people, you need to work in a team with those people, at home there will be people, at work there will be people, in restaurants there are people, wherever you go there will be people. If I can learn the art of inspiring people, making them feel important, and making them feel loved, my world will become a better place, and the world will become a better place.

Somewhere in our education system, somewhere in our usage of wealth, this must be factored in—how do we turn them into kinder people and more empathetic so that they think about something else. All these self-help books that say that you are special, you are great, everything you do is okay, don't worry—this is not taking us anywhere. In the 1960s and 70s there was the hippie culture; do whatever you like, don't listen to anybody, rebel and revolt and so on, and sleep with anybody you like, drink whatever you like, eat whatever you like. Has it led to happier people? That debauched way of living life, has it led to more happiness? Absolutely not.

Therefore, we must know that restraint in life is the bedrock of true fulfilment. If I don't practice any restraint, if I don't have any discipline in life then I won't have any freedom either. That's why very rich people are very often depressed because they can have anything they want and there is nothing left to do. The doing is what releases serotonin. I may get some dopamine if I just have a cup of coffee but it's the journey that becomes beautiful if I am doing something meaningful.

Nipun Mehta
Founder, ServiceSpace

JP: May I request you to introduce yourself.

Nipun: I'm the founder of ServiceSpace, which is an incubator of projects to encourage a culture of generosity. I was born in India, but grew up in Silicon Valley in California, at the epicentre of technological innovations. In so many ways, I had a typical immigrant journey—you work hard, you try to get through to a good college, and get a good job to make good money. In college, you are trying to get ahead and get a job and that whole cycle continued for me as well. I happened to be nestled in the time of the dot com boom and at some point, it just wasn't good enough that you were working at a really nice innovative company. You had to create your own start-up. That energy was in the air.

At that point, though, my journey took a slightly different turn. In my early 20s, I asked myself, what is it that is going to bring me the deepest satisfaction? Is it just going to be accumulation? Is it going to be about getting more and more and more and then making some good use of it at the tail end of my life? Alternatively, do I want this to be a very different process where I am growing along the way? What really resonated for me was this idea of generosity, service, and kindness. I realised that the more I gave, the happier I became. I would go to homeless shelters, I would go to hospice patients who are on their deathbeds, and it would totally inspire me. I had these deep insights about what life was about and I said, "I don't want to just wait till I'm 65 to retire and then do something meaningful. I want to do it now." For me, I found the greatest meaning in serving other people with no strings attached.

That's sort of how ServiceSpace started. A whole bunch of us got together for pizza one night and decided to go out and do something good. Out of that, four of us went to a homeless shelter and we ended up building a website for a homeless shelter. We came home, and we said, "Wow, that was pretty amazing. We should do it again." We did, and we just kept doing it again and again and again. We ended up building thousands of websites, leveraging tens of thousands of volunteers and that just became sort of a counterculture movement in Silicon Valley. I think for me the core insight was that giving is regenerative. The more I gave, the more I wanted to give and the more I had to give. It didn't deplete. It taught me the value of what deep connection to life looks like and how we can be nestled in that connection—not when we retire and/or when we have all our ducks lined up but here and now in this moment. We can actually have that connection with whatever life presents in front of us. That has been a big guiding light for me, and it's been a remarkable journey.

JP: Which university did you go to and what did you major in?

Nipun: I went to UC Berkeley and I did Computer Science and Philosophy.

JP: And then post graduation?

Nipun: Post-graduation? This is the Silicon Valley ☺. If you have a Bachelor's degree, that's already way too much education in the Bill Gates' world.

JP: I meant after graduation what did you do?

Nipun: I worked at Sun Microsystems, optimising C++ compilers as a software engineer. I did that for a few years and then I was doing some service projects on the side. At some point, what was below the radar came to the forefront. I quit my job. By my mid 20s, I was what I call a 'full-time volunteer'. I'm still a full-time volunteer, and I like to joke—so far so good.

JP: What was that inflection point? What was the epiphany that emboldened you to say that I think I'm not going to work in this mainstream rat race and I'm going to go do something else?

Nipun: The joy and connection I felt whenever I was in that state of giving was absolutely unparalleled. Even if it meant I'm giving something small to a stranger whom I'd never meet again, even if it wasn't sustained, even if I didn't know the impact of it, the fact that I was generating this intent of goodwill in my own heart was just very powerful. I felt that routinely—in some very big ways, and in some very small ways.

JP: What was your perspective on money growing up?

Nipun: I never knew if I had a lot or a little money, but I used to be mindful of my relationship. No matter how much I had, there always seemed like a greater target to catch along the horizon. Like a mirage. Yet, I was always respectful of it. I mean, you need it every time you go to the store. I always noticed this relentless pursuit of it in people around me. Everyone always sets the benchmark thinking once they have a certain amount, that's it! They will arrive and give up their greed. From what I saw, though, I never saw anyone actually get 'there'. For me, money had this elusive quality of triggering something unquenchable inside people.

For me, money was initially a tool for generosity. I was earning a fair amount of money, in the early days as a twenty-something; I wondered what I was going to do with all this money and so I started giving. As I gave, I thought it was fantastic that I could help people in these material ways. More than the impact even, what really motivated me was the giving process itself. I wanted to give even more. At some point, I had given away all the money that I could but didn't know what to do next. Do I earn more money to give away or can I give away in some other forms of capital? I asked myself what else I had to offer, and the answer was time, talent, and skills, so I started to give those. That felt really meaningful. But even then, after a while, it felt like I could only do so much. Only 24 hours in the day, right? Then, at some point, I realised that I just want to give of myself, and so that whole journey of deepening in generosity originated, initially with giving small amounts of money, and then I gave up the money part of the equation, but kept the giving part alive.

In that sense, money at that level became an instrument for learning generosity and for broadening into multiple forms of capital. We have this equation that wealth equals money, but money is one form of wealth. We actually have access to so many different forms of wealth. Listening is a form of wealth. Community is a form of wealth. Information, stories, and so on. There are infinite forms of wealth and I think that journey to go from 'money equals wealth' to 'multiple expression of wealth' has been my journey, but it started, in a way, with money.

JP: The original non-profit you formed was called CharityFocus. Can you take us through that journey of the early days?

Nipun: That's a great journey because that's how you and I got connected. We met at a hotel in Bangalore for one of those midnight conversations. It was a riveting conversation, I remember. ServiceSpace at that time was called CharityFocus. We used to build websites for non-profits and websites turned into different kind of web portals that we used to run, like Daily Good, which sends out a little bit of good news every day; and KarmaTube, which is like an inspirational version of YouTube where videos are combined with actions that people can take. We ran a lot of those kinds of portals.

Then we ran into ProPoor, which you had started, Jayesh. It was connecting thousands of different NGOs online. At that time, just getting access to content itself was a big deal. You had offices in various cities. Then you looked at ServiceSpace and you said, "Hey, you guys have these three rules—be volunteer-run, don't fundraise and focus on doing small acts. That sounds great but I actually see how it's so regenerative and so powerful." You ended up giving all of ProPoor to ServiceSpace at the time and we are still going. It was a remarkable journey at that point. Now, it has become more of an incubator. It's not just a web portal but also an incubator of so many different projects, and there's hundreds and thousands of members and millions of people visit our websites every month. With each interaction, with each sort of engagement, our hope is that we can really try to create a many-to-many network for compassionate actions. More people get connected to each other around a very different kind of narrative. That 'Greed is good' is one kind of narrative we heard from Gordon Gecko but maybe 'Generosity is better' is a different kind of narrative. We need to create those stories, we need to create the projects underneath to give it the foundation to sustain itself, and create a very different kind of culture, where relationships matter, and where we have a different sense of belonging and purpose to our existence.

JP: Can you give us some speeds and feeds of ServiceSpace, in terms of the number of volunteers, the budget, and the different kinds of activities that ServiceSpace is doing?

Nipun: ServiceSpace does a lot of activities online. We run many portals like Daily Good, KarmaTube, and Kind Spring that have online communities that distribute content. A lot of that content comes from all the community members themselves. It's a regenerative kind of feedback loop. Then we do a lot of stuff that's offline as well. We have weekly Awakin Circles in everyday homes. My parents have been hosting these circles for the last 21 years where you sit in silence for the first hour; second hour is a circle of sharing; and third hour is dinner. It's a beautiful thing that's now happening in over a 100 cities around the world.

Then we have different experiments like Karma Kitchen—a pop-up restaurant where you walk in and have a meal, but your bill reads zero because someone before you has paid for you and you get a chance to pay forward whatever you want for people after you. Most people think, "Oh my God, that can't work because people are selfish." It turns out that it can work if you create a strong enough context; people are wired to respond to generosity with greater generosity. That was an experiment we started in Berkeley and now it's been tried in more than 25 places around the world. There is all kinds of research on it—at UC Berkeley business school; the title for that seminal research paper was 'Paying More When Paying for Others'. Such experiments create a very different kind of narrative, and possibility.

One of my favourite projects is on KindSpring.org and it's the Smile Cards. You do a small act of kindness and leave a Smile Card behind, which tells the recipient that you don't know who did this kind act for you, but you don't need to just pay back—you can pay it forward. The card is a reminder that you can always pay it forward. I think just creating those kinds of ripples, when you have so many sets of ripples—it just makes you feel pretty satisfied.

Collectively, ServiceSpace is an ecosystem that encourages such acts of love. It's small in so many ways, but collectively, it adds up too. It depends on how you calibrate your lens.

JP: Tell us a little bit about the fundraising, about the number of full-time people, your office space, and your budget for such a big organisation.

Nipun: We don't do any fundraising and we haven't since the beginning. Our thinking behind that is that before we fundraise, we have to declare our expected impact—"Oh, if you give me this money, this is what I'm going to do with it, and these are the results you can expect." That whole process requires a subtle but significant form of coercion. For us, we figure that if we do acts of love, that will connect us by natural order; and those connections will create a web in which all kinds of wealth will circulate, and our job is to support the emergence of such a field.

We have a very tiny budget and it's partly because we don't need much more as we have volunteers. We have hundreds and thousands of members that are giving in so many different ways and there is just no shortage of that input of people wanting to give, if you know how to engage that kind of generosity.

JP: What is your personal perspective on money today and looking towards the future?

Nipun: My personal perspective on money is that we have designed it to bias towards accumulation. The more I leave in the bank, the more interest I get. I'm rewarded for gathering. At scale, what that does is depersonalises many of the interactions that we have. As soon as money comes in, it becomes a transaction and the cost of a transactional world is that we lose the dimensionality. Everything becomes quid pro quo.

The challenge facing us today is—how do we balance this idea of focussed efficiency with a relational resilience? My relationship to money is that it is good in its place but if it starts to take more of our mindshare, then it just encourages accumulation, which then encourages isolation borne of a me-versus-you zero-sum game. That leaves us feeling disconnected, which is what we're seeing in the world. We are disconnected not just with the systems but also socially and spiritually with our own selves. We have this big gaping void in our own selves. I feel that the technology of money needs to be balanced with technologies of relationships. As those get balanced, I think we have a field in which inner transformation can arise—that I feel, is the most sustainable way to create long-term change.

JP: Can you extend this philosophy into a little bit of wisdom and advice for the millennials who are going to inherit billions of dollars?

Nipun: If I were to talk to a millennial who says, "Look, I care to give. I want to make an impact in the world. I have all these resources. What should I do?" What I would say is, go, and solve a problem. Then see how you go upstream to solve a more fundamental problem. As you get closer to the root cause, you'll invariably realise that your inner ecology is bound up with the world that you are hoping to create. That insight changes everything.

I often say that we are not what we do, but who we become by what we do, so I would ask these millennials to pay attention to who they are becoming through the process of giving. There's a beautiful quote by Rachel Naomi Remen that says, "When you help, you see the world as weak. When you fix, you see the world as broken. But when you serve, you see the world as a co-creative whole."

That's the invitation—to go from helping, to fixing, to serving and seeing how the world outside of us and the world inside of us are constantly mirroring each other. If we lead with that, then no matter where we are contributing, that will have a really powerful unending ripple effect.

JP: And you discovered meditation along the way?

Nipun: I think meditation was at the very front and centre for me from the beginning. I typically spend 30 days a year meditating in complete silence and probably about 30–60 days a year in serving those who are meditating. If I didn't do that, I think I would have just become a 'human doing' instead of a 'human being' as the phrase goes.

What meditation has taught me is that every problem that you see on the outside is actually originating inside. Without meditation, that would just be an intellectual insight that feels a little overwhelming and you can almost discard it. However, as you go a little deeper inside, you start to realise that life is very intricately intertwined—your inner experience and your outer experience.

I sense that all sages have been pointing us to precisely this—go a little deeper inside. Get smart. See what is actually happening and then operate from that base of compassion. That will inevitably create very different designs and very different ripple effect on the outside and on the inside. For me, if I wasn't meditating regularly, I would've likely been serving for external impact and that would've left me burnt out by now. Instead, now I see practically everything as an opportunity to grow in service. It's beautiful and regenerative. The more I serve, the more I want to serve.

Deepak Chopra, MD

Renowned Author, Lecturer, and Physician

JP: May I request you to introduce yourself. We've got a large Indian diaspora all over the world that already knows you, however it would be great to have a bit of insight into your background, where you grew up, and where you went to school.

Deepak: I grew up in New Delhi. I went to school at St. Columbus. I did pre-med in Jabalpur, Madhya Pradesh. Then I went to medical school at the All India Institute of Medical Sciences (AIMS) in Delhi in 1964, graduated in 1969 and then moved to the US in 1970, and I have been here since then. My father was an army doctor. In the earlier years, before high school we travelled all over the country and went to several schools. Mostly I would say they were in a way convent schools run by Irish Christian missionaries and that's basically it. I came to the US in 1970 and I've been here since then. I have trained in internal medicine, endocrinology, neuroendocrinology, neuroscience and then I kind of branched off into what is today called Mind-Body Medicine integrated health and well-being, and now focussing on what is called The Hard Problem of Consciousness.

JP: What was your perspective on money while you were growing up?

Deepak: I never really thought much about it as I was growing up. We came from a comfortable middle-class, high middle-class family. My father was as I said a doctor as well as a cardiologist. We had a very comfortable life, and this is way before it was fashionable to be a millionaire or billionaire or all that. Money was never a concern, nor was it much in my thinking growing up.

JP: Fast forwarding to today, now that you have become a person of such huge influence worldwide with such a large audience, what is your perspective on money today?

Deepak: It's very interesting that you ask this, and your audience might be kind of surprised about this, but if I think about money that's a sign of poverty consciousness. If I know my net worth, then it is also a sign of poverty consciousness. I don't think about it.

I have no concern about it. I don't even read balance sheets, I let accountants do it. That's why they're there and I let money managers handle my income. I never check my bank account. I keep a credit card and $30,000 at my disposal and the rest is managed by others. That's what they're good at, and I like to focus on what I'm good at, which is creating content; you know I am on my ninetieth book right now. I'm focussed on that. I do a lot of public speaking.

Recently, with the help of hedge fund manager Paul Tudor Jones, I have helped create a non-profit called Just Capital, which now has its own ETF (Exchange-Traded Fund). It's about identifying businesses that are making a difference in the world and improving the quality of life for their workers, for their customers, of course for their investors and also for society at large. I have been teaching at two business schools, Columbia Business School and Kellogg Business School Northwestern University, and my course is called 'Just Capital and Cause Driven Marketing'. With this course, I am trying my best to change the current paradigm which says, you go to business school and the first thing you hear is that the purpose of a business is to improve stockholder value or nowadays stakeholder value; and my focus is that the business is to improve the quality of life on the planet and address big issues like social justice, economic justice, sustainability, conflict resolution, etc. I support these big causes and I encourage businesses to do the same. The December 2018 issue of *Forbes* magazine, the cover story is on Just Capital. You might want to look it up. It's becoming a very fast movement and I envisage that the Just Capital Index at some point will be more reliable than say Dow Jones or S&P because people are moving in this direction in any case. That's my relationship with money. I believe a lot of people who make money, make money to make more money and I think they never even get to enjoy it. You know, that's my attitude towards money.

JP: When and how was that inflection point as a doctor to become a healer of Mind-Body Health? How was that transition?

Deepak: Well it's not a total transition. You know they have a group practice in California. I have a license to practice medicine in both California and Massachusetts. I am also actually getting a license in New York now. I have advised physicians and group practitioners.

That transition was simply a result of my research into neuroscience and looking at brain chemistry, which is a long time before people had heard of words like serotonin, dopamine, and oxytocin, and all the neuro chemicals. I was seeing a connection between what was happening in people's consciousness, in their minds, in their emotional world, in their personal relationships, in their social interactions, in their lifestyle and how it affected their health and well-being.

I actually did not give up medicine at all. I only extended it from looking at the human body to looking at human emotions, human mind, human consciousness, social interactions, environment, nutrition, quality of life, sleep, stress management, meditation, exercise, yoga, breathing as very important ways to evoke the healing response in human biology. I think the mechanistic approach of current pharmaceutical and surgical interventions is very helpful in acute illness but when we look at chronic illness, 95 per cent have nothing to do with any mechanistic explanation, so only 5 per cent of disease-related gene mutations are fully penetrant which means they guarantee the disease. The remaining 95 per cent—even of genetic mutations that are associated with disease, chronic disease, whether it's cancer or autoimmune disease or premature aging or Alzheimer's or even susceptibility to infections—are all related to lifestyle. I'm focussing more on the 95 per cent than on the 5 per cent for which of course we have new technologies right now, like CRISPR (Clustered Regularly Interspaced Short Palindromic Repeats), which is going to be available soon, which is a way to cut and paste genes. Just the way that you can read a barcode on an item that you buy at the grocery store, it's now possible using molecular scissors to read the barcode of a gene and then delete the harmful gene and insert the beneficial gene, just like you would cut and paste an email. However, when you really look at it it's going to affect not more than 5 per cent of people. The remaining 95 per cent of disease related gene mutations are still lifestyle dependent.

I think we're shifting the way people think about disease, and what was alternative once upon a time is becoming mainstream and what is mainstream now is becoming alternative. That's a brief history over the last 40 years.

JP: There are so many wealthy people out there, as you mentioned, that are busy making money on their money, and then there are millennials who are going to inherit billions of dollars in the next decade or two. My request to you, as a Guru, who is followed by millions of people, what would your word of wisdom and advice be to these folks?

Deepak: My question would be, "Have you ever reflected on what makes you happy?" That's all. If money makes you happy, and making more money makes you happy and then making more and more money makes you happy then do it. But I have seen very few people who are happy only because they have money. By the time they become billionaires or trillionaires or whatever, even Jeff Bezos has a divorce and has to figure out the rest of his life.

By the time you've become a billionaire you might have rotten teeth and poor temper, impotence and heart disease. Is it worth it? Money is a great thing if you can do something worthwhile with it, including enjoy yourself with it, but I find these big people with lots of money are not enjoying life. I think somebody like a fisherman going on a fishing boat and earning enough money to sell his fish and take his family out, is probably more contented than a lot of people who took a vacation to go fishing at a fancy resort. Not that I think that's not worth doing.

I think the purpose of money should always be to create increased happiness for your friends, for your family, for your society at large. If that is not being done, then you are just a biological robot, following everybody else's direction and not even thinking about why you make money. Money is a human construct. We created it, there was no such thing. Humans created money and then they created Wall Street and then they created trading and they created money managers and they created colonialism, slavery, and empires all because of this construct, this human construct that we call money. Money is a means to an end, not an end in itself. People have to come to that stage on their own. Sometimes they do because they find that they are meaningless, or they have a poor relationship, or they lose a loved one or they themselves are diagnosed with terminal illness. We now know for sure that stress is the number one epidemic of our time and directly or indirectly, it's related to almost every chronic illness including addictive behaviour, which is rampant in Wall Street traders, and people that I deal with. I've recently been speaking at Goldman Sachs, Morgan Stanley, and JP Morgan and there's a desperate need in these organisations to reinvent themselves. Maybe they'll do it, maybe they won't, but you know each one has to make that decision on their own.

JP: And any final words for the millennials?

Deepak: I think the millennials, especially the ones who are inheriting all this money, should be grateful for it and do something wise with it to improve the world's life, improve your own life and make a difference in the world. Always ask yourself, "Why am I doing what I'm doing?" If you don't know what the underlying motivation is then you're basically behaving on conditioned reflexes and nerves, and you are not self-reflective human being.

The ultimate goal of all goals is to be happy and happiness is therefore the ultimate goal and it doesn't come only from money, it comes from meaningful relationships, comes from the ability to love and have compassion, and ultimately comes from meaning and purpose in your life. So, replace 'money' with the word 'meaning'.

Concluding Thoughts

Success is not only defined by how much money you make or have. Success is also defined by how well you utilise your money. If money just sits in the bank, it has limited value. There is no right or wrong way of spending or investing or giving away money.

Before I started these interviews, my bias was that you work hard to make money, then you work hard to make money-on-money, and then you die. After conducting over 50 interviews, I am humbled and sensitised. For some, making money is their lifeline, their passion. It is a way of life that keeps them excited, stimulated, engaged, and gives them a lot of satisfaction. For others, giving back thoughtfully and compassionately is their mission. The good news is, there isn't just one way to spend the money. However, for most of the affluent folks giving back is a way of life. Wealthy folks do enjoy spending their money and while material spending is so much fun, there are many who also enjoy experiential spending. As it turns out, travel at-will, and in style, continues to remain one of the top experiential spends. For example, immediately after a big exit entrepreneurs or retirement for senior executives, they all like to binge-travel.

The entrepreneurial start-up ecosystem is attracting a lot of attention especially in the tech and digital sector. This is of particular interest to most millennials. I would like to share my thoughts on angel investing and social impact investing, which are and will continue to be very important investment categories.

Angel investing

Angel investing in tech start-ups is on the rise. The start-up ecosystem is at an all-time high worldwide, especially in India. More young entrepreneurs are starting companies with innovative and disruptive ideas than ever before. Angel investing is an effective use of money because you invest mainly in young entrepreneurs who can potentially build successful companies. These companies would develop and distribute useful products and services, generate employment, and in many cases amass significant wealth for owners and their employees. Angel investing is a tricky and high-risk investment, however if the start-up succeeds it results in financial returns that are multiple times the initial investment. The successful entrepreneur would in turn support and mentor budding entrepreneurs and donate big chunks of their windfall to charities. This is a clear win-win strategy.

For those who are not familiar with angel investing, especially in technology start-ups, may want to consider joining angel networks. In India, the most popular network is the Indian Angel Network (IAN), which has well over 400 angel investors. The IAN has done very well as it takes advantage of the angel network for funding, deal flow and domain expertise. The Indus Entrepreneurs (TiE) also has an angel network. TiE charter members have a powerful worldwide network, most of whom are successful tech entrepreneurs. Many non-tech individuals have successfully co-invested alongside many experts in the network.

Angel investing is not for the faint-hearted. However, if you start by allocating a small percentage of your net worth to invest in a diversified portfolio of start-ups, it can be quite exciting and if it does well, very rewarding.

Social impact investing

Social impact investing is a relatively new asset class that is making a lot of headway. While it has been around for over 20 years, it has become a legitimate investment instrument only in the last 10 years.

There was a lot of confusion with the term social impact investing as to whether it is social impact or an investment. Earlier there were two distinctly separate uses of funds. One was to invest in equity, shares, or stocks of companies with a view to earn dividends and to generate profits from the appreciation of the shares. The second was to give grants or donate to non-profits with a view of making a social impact in the world. Social impact investing is a sort of fusion—you invest in the shares of a for-profit company that is making a social impact. While it has taken some time for the world to navigate through what may seem as a conflicting thesis—to make money and have social impact—in many parts of North America, South Asia, and Africa, social impact investing is gaining a lot of traction.

Individuals are investing in social enterprises as impact angel investors. Many impact funds are investing successfully in social enterprises. The economic returns from social impact investing are called 'double bottom line' as it is meant to return financial returns as well as social impact returns. The social impact returns can and are being measured, and quite a lot of progress is being made in fine-tuning the outcome measurement of social impact.

Among all the uses of wealth, social impact investing seems to be the most meaningful asset class. Individuals and family offices can choose the geography in which they want to invest; for example, I focus on India as it has more mature social enterprises and there are many urban and rural social causes that could benefit from impact investment. One can choose between many vertical sectors including education, health, sanitation, water, environment, waste management, women enterprise, fintech, and others. There is also a high amount of information and data readily available on social impact investing. There are angel networks worldwide that form groups that invest in social enterprises and get economies of scale. Moreover, there are many yearly informative conferences like Sankalp and SOCAP that discuss social impact investing topics and which are great networking platforms.

I feel strongly that wealthy individuals and families should consider making angel investing and social impact investing an integral part of their wealth portfolio, as an alternative investment asset class. While this is a high-risk investment, it is a good use of a portion of your money. You can also engage by becoming a mentor to some of the start-ups. Of course, if the start-up succeeds, you will get a different type of high.

Millennials

There may be some millennials who will inherit megabucks from their families and while away their time with an exorbitant lifestyle. However, I am hopeful though, that there will be many more millennials who will be thoughtful about how they will absorb and spend money with purpose. I am optimistic that they will change the world and impact our community in a very meaningful way.

There will be a shift in the way the millennials give back. It will certainly include philanthropy in the form of grants; however, many more millennials will take the growing social impact investing road, do good and be well. As a result, impact investing will flourish in the future. We will hopefully see many more millennial social entrepreneurs who will start and build for-profit businesses whose intent will be to make a social impact. The idea will be to invest not only wisely but also consciously in areas that will do good for the world and the under-privileged section of the society. My money is on the millennials!

Afterthoughts

Wealthy families build a solid safety net around them. Some families do use some of that money on material or experiential spending, however many live relatively simple lives and continue to accumulate more wealth. Most of the wealth then passes to the next generation.

Many wealthy individuals who grew up middle-class continue to lead a middle-class life, and many (like me) still have a middle-class value system. Even though they have financial independence, they do not indulge in any major material spend, like buying a Lamborghini or Bentley—other than maybe upgrading their home, occasionally buying a luxury car like a Mercedes and going on a 5-star Marriott hotel vacation to some exotic place in the world on Singapore Airlines' business class.

So, what do wealthy individuals and families do with all this money? Most are busy spending it on living well, travelling well, and some on shopping well. They have a nice home and many also have holiday homes. They spend significant time on carefully managing and investing their money, which is a source of joy for some. My own sense is that the next generation will probably spend more money enjoying their life compared to their parents.

Almost everyone wants to be altruistic and do good. For some wealth remains a status symbol. Philanthropy is based on the philosophy of either self-directed giving or helping someone else's non-profit. In doing this, most people have a well-researched view for choosing one or two vertical sectors like education, healthcare, or women empowerment. Microfinance and microlending have been around for some time now. In recent times, social impact funds as an investment vehicle are finding favour with many HNIs and family offices.

The other topic that we have not broached is the ethics of making money. This is a longer discussion, especially to figure out why some of the very wealthy people use seemingly not-so-ethical means to continue to amass incredible amounts of wealth. What is interesting is how some of them have a strong philosophy on giving. Either they don't believe that their money-making practices are unethical or, more likely, they are using philanthropy as a front to diffuse unethical practices with a view to gain fame and popularity.

Another mystery that is unresolved is why many of the wealthy folks continue to work so hard to make money-on-money. It is not a means to an end. There is no end game. There is no specific destination on how-much-is-enough or a specific target to achieve after which they will take their foot off the gas pedal. This seems baffling, and yet it is what it is.

In my opinion, the happiness quotient has three parts: wealth affluence, time affluence, and mind affluence. You need wealth to be happy, but that is only part of the equation. There is a myth that if you are wealthy you are automatically happy. Anybody who is affluent will confirm that money by itself and in itself is not the end all. Once wealth affluence is achieved, practicing time affluence becomes very important in life. Which requires introspection on contentment and deciding how much is enough.

Time is obviously a very important asset in our life. Time affluence means being able to do what you want to do, when you want to do it. At some point can we pause or slow-down the intensity of making money-on-money so as to enjoy the money we have made? To spend time effectively requires discipline, which includes the time to spend money! Happiness is doing things that you like to do the most. Somewhere there is an optimal balance between money, time, and happiness. Once you find that sweet spot, just keep repeating it.

Lastly, we have mind affluence—is your mind happy, is your mind at peace, is your mind calm, do you allow your mind to spend quality time on in-depth study of philosophy and consciousness; do you allow your mind to gracefully practice mindfulness and compassion? Do we focus our time and energy on spiritual ascent with the help of meditation, yoga, pranayama, chanting or focussing inwards?

If you are aware of how precious time and mind affluence is, then you will indeed think twice about "What shall we do with all this money?"

www.allthismoney.com

My Journey

I grew up in a humble middle-class home in Calcutta (now Kolkata). I never had enough money when I was at St. Lawrence High School in Calcutta. My uncle, Dr Jayant Parekh helped me with college tuition, boarding and lodging at the Maharaja Sayajirao University of Baroda. Train travel was a privilege. My first plane ride was at the age of 24. I dropped out of the Indian Institute of Management, Calcutta (IIM-C), after six months, when my brother Nilesh sent me a ticket to fly to the US. I borrowed the college tuition fees from a friend, Manjit Singh Kohli. I carried that unfair advantage of middle-class values throughout my life.

After graduating from the University of Texas at Austin, I continued to work for the university for a few years at the Center for Electromechanics. Then I moved to Houston with IBM. I got the opportunity to be part of IBM's Offshore Operations in Singapore under the able leadership of Dan Gupta and Venky Raman. We were a small group that was responsible for bringing IBM back to India. Today IBM arguably has more employees in India than in the US. I spent over 12 years at IBM, after which I started my journey of a serial entrepreneur, in Singapore. My first start-up was Frontier Technologies with Balwant Singh, who is a friend and partner till date.

The most exciting business journey was spent as co-founder of Sony Entertainment Television (SET); a network that is now a fully owned subsidiary of Sony Corporation. I continue my friendship with Raman Maroo, Kunal Dasgupta, Sudesh Iyer, and Sam Shergill of SET. It was Sam's visionary idea to start a cable and satellite TV channel.

After exiting from SET, I tried to retire but failed miserably. I became an angel investor and a social impact investor. I was invited by Vineet Rai to join the investment committee of three of Aavishkaar social impact venture capital funds. I am an advisory board member of Akhand Jyoti Eye Hospital, which is based in Mastichak, Bihar. Akhand Jyoti is a non-profit, which performs 65,000 cataract surgeries every year, 80 per cent of them for free. I was on the board of United Way International for six years; and on the investment committee of

SONG, a social impact fund with investment from Soros, Omidyar Network, and Google.

I also had the privilege of introducing Anurag Srivastava to Amit Anand, both of whom went on to start Jungle Ventures, a Pan-Asian tech venture capital fund. I was a general partner of Jungle Ventures in the first two funds, after which the founders recently promoted me to the role of a senior advisor, so now I am happily practicing time affluence.

My personal philosophy of giving is divided into three buckets. One bucket is for non-profits like Akhand Jyoti Eye Hospital and a few ad hoc contributions for calamities in India. The second bucket is for Milaap, which is a microlending platform in India, which lends small amounts of money to women entrepreneurs and under-privileged individuals, mainly women. The third and largest allocation is to invest in social impact companies and social impact funds.

Mona and I got married in Austin, Texas, and we have two children, Freya and Jesal. Freya married Vishal Ramchandani and they have an adorable daughter, Naomi. Freya and Vishal work in Bollywood and Jesal works for an Esports company. Mona and I live in Singapore.

17 October 2019
Singapore

Acknowledgements

Special thanks to:

- Patrick McGoldrick for reconnecting me to Mr Ratan Tata;

- Jennifer Santi and Dipika Chopra for reconnecting me to Dr Deepak Chopra;

- Vishal Vashisht for reconnecting me to Neeraj Arora;

- Deval Sanghvi and Megha Jain for reconnecting me to Rohini Nilekani;

- Vipul Shah and Nikhil Bardia for connecting me to Jasprit Bumrah;

- Ami Jobanputra for connecting me to Manubhai Chandaria;

- Manisha Gandhi for connecting me to Vijay Goradia;

- Professor Jagdish Sheth for connecting me to Professor Raj Sisodia;

- Raj Singh for connecting me to Satish Gupta;

- Rajeev Natarajan for connecting me to Syed Ali;

- Santosh Keni for connecting me to Raghuvinder Kataria and Anisha Kataria;

- Rajeev Srivastava for connecting me to Amit Chandra and Richa Dsouza;

- Satveer Singh Thakral for connecting me to Kamakshi Malhotra;

- Kamakshi Malhotra for connecting me to Rakesh Malhotra;

- Harish Shah for connecting me to Anushka Shah;

- Parijat Bose and Ritu Sarawgi Goel for the help with the transcription;

- Zafar Anjum, Swapnil Mishra, and Rajeev Natarajan for the initial discussions on this book;

- Harsha Bhatkal, Vinayak Gawande, Vijay Thakur, Anjali Sawant, and particularly editor Armaity Motafram at Popular Prakashan;

- Dipti Anand and Soma Mohanty Garg for reviewing the manuscript;

- Sheela Jaganathan for the hypnosis session for this book;

- Anil Shah for the cover design and the website www.allthismoney.com;

- Vimal Kothari for the photograph on the inside cover;

- To everyone in this book who agreed to be interviewed;

- And to you, for reading this book.